macromedia®
DREAMWEAVER® 4
FIREWORKS 4®
TRAINING FROM THE SOURCE

Patti Schulze

macromedia®
PRESS

Macromedia Dreamweaver 4 Fireworks 4 Studio: Training from the Source

 Published by Macromedia Press, in association with Peachpit Press, a division of Pearson Education.

Macromedia Press
1249 Eighth Street
Berkeley, CA 94710
510/524-2178
510/524-2221 (fax)
Find us on the World Wide Web at:
http://www.peachpit.com
http://www.macromedia.com

Notice of Liability

The information in this book and on the CD-ROM is distributed on an "as is" basis, without warranty. While every precaution has been taken in the preparation of the book and the CD-ROM, neither Macromedia, Inc., its licensors, nor Macromedia Press shall have any liability to any person or entity with respect to liability, loss, or damage caused or alleged to be caused directly or indirectly by the instructions contained in this book or by the computer software and hardware products described herein.

Trademarks

Macromedia is a registered trademark of Macromedia, Inc. Other product names mentioned within this publication may be trademarks or registered trademarks of other companies.

Printed and bound in the United States of America

ISBN 0-201-71162-1

9 8 7 6 5 4 3 2 1

CREDITS

Author
Patti Schulze

Editor
Wendy Sharp

Copyeditor
Judy Ziajka

Production Coordinator
Lisa Brazieal

Compositor
Patti Schulze

Indexer
James Minkin

Cover Design
Steven Soshea, Macromedia, Inc.

This edition is based upon materials developed by:
Digital Training & Designs, Inc.

Many thanks to everyone who helped me with this book: Joan Hilbert, Digital Training & Designs, who patiently read through many iterations of this book; all the staff at Digital Training & Designs who took over as I wrote this book; Mark Haynes, Karen Duban, and Julie Hallstrom, the technical reviewers from Macromedia; Allise Berger and Tiffany Beltis from Macromedia; and Diana Smedley from Macromedia who got me started.

This book is dedicated to my Mom, who is now painting rainbows.

table of contents

introduction

Macromedia Fireworks 4 is a powerful design and graphics editor, and Macromedia Dreamweaver is a robust visual Web page authoring tool. Used together, Fireworks and Dreamweaver are a powerful pair of Web design tools offering a complete Web development solution. The two programs offer integration features to aid your workflow as you design and optimize your graphics, build your HTML pages, and place the Web graphics on the page.

This Macromedia Training from the Source program introduces you to the major features of Fireworks 4 by guiding you step by step through the creation of several Web pages. The book's 11 lessons begin with the bitmap tools to edit an image and then take you though the steps of creating a logo for a fictitious company and designing Web pages. You then add rollover buttons and export your pages as HTML files. The last lesson covers the integration between Fireworks and Dreamweaver. This book is not intended to teach you Dreamweaver, but you will use Dreamweaver in Lesson 11 to see how Fireworks and Dreamweaver work together. For step-by-step instruction in Dreamweaver, see *Macromedia Dreamweaver 4: Training from the Source*, also published by Macromedia Press.

This roughly 16-hour curriculum includes these lesson topics:

Lesson 1: Bitmap Editing
Lesson 2: Working with Groups and Layers
Lesson 3: Using Vector Tools
Lesson 4: Text, Fills, and Live Effects
Lesson 5: Advanced Techniques
Lesson 6: Optimizing and Exporting
Lesson 7: Creating Animated GIF Images
Lesson 8: Creating Buttons
Lesson 9: Creating Image Maps and Slices
Lesson 10: Production Techniques
Lesson 11: Integrating with Dreamweaver

Each lesson begins with an overview of its contents and what you can expect to learn. Lessons are divided into focused, bite-size tasks to build your Fireworks skills. Each lesson builds on what you've learned in previous lessons.

SETTING UP THE LESSON FILES

You'll find all the files needed for these lessons on the accompanying CD. Copy the Lessons folder to your hard drive before you start the lessons.

As you work through the lessons, you will open files within the Lessons folder. If you are working on a Windows machine, the files you copy from the Lessons folder on the CD are locked. Within the Lessons folder is a DOS batch file (unlock_files.bat) that you can execute to unlock all of the files in the folder automatically. Double-click the batch file to begin the unlocking process. The locked files are a concern only in Lesson 11. If you do not unlock the files, you will get a warning message when you open them.

Folder names and file names are capitalized throughout this book for readability. Some Web servers do not support capital letters for file names. When you are building your images and HTML pages, it is a good idea to use lowercase for all your file names. That way, you are assured the file names are supported on any server.

AUTHORIZED TRAINING FOR MACROMEDIA

Each book in the Macromedia Training from the Source series is based upon curriculum originally developed for use by Macromedia's authorized trainers. The lesson plans were developed by some of Macromedia's most successful trainers and refined through long experience to meet students' needs. We believe that Macromedia Training from the Source courses offer the best available training for Macromedia programs.

The lessons in this book assume that you are a beginner with Fireworks but that you are familiar with the basic methods of giving commands on a Windows or Macintosh computer, such as choosing items from menus, opening and saving files, and so on. For more information on those tasks, see the documentation provided with your computer.

Finally, the instructions in the book also assume that you already have Fireworks 4 and Dreamweaver 4 installed on a Windows or Macintosh computer, and that your computer meets the system requirements listed on the System Requirements page.

THE TRAINING FROM THE SOURCE APPROACH AND ITS ELEMENTS

Throughout this book, you will encounter some special features:

Tips: These highlight shortcuts for performing common tasks or ways you can use your new Fireworks skills to solve common problems.

Power Tips: These highlight productivity shortcuts.

Notes: These provide background information about a feature or task.

Italic terms: Words in italic indicate the exact text or file name you need to enter in a dialog box or panel as you work through the steps in a lesson.

Menu commands and keyboard shortcuts: Alternative methods for executing commands. Menu commands are shown like this: Menu › Command › Subcommand. Keyboard shortcuts are shown like this: Ctrl+Z (Windows) or Command+Z (Macintosh). The + between the names of the keys means that you should press both keys simultaneously and both Windows and Macintosh commands will always be included.

WHAT YOU WILL LEARN

By the end of this book, you will be able to:

- Use the bitmap tools in Fireworks to edit an image
- Use the vector tools to draw shapes
- Combine simple shapes to create complex objects
- Add text effects, such as text on a path, to your pages
- Create buttons with rollovers and use effects for realistic-looking buttons
- Optimize and export your images
- Create animated GIF images
- Use batch processing to export a catalog of images
- Use Dreamweaver to add text to your exported HTML pages

Through the course of this book, you will learn Fireworks tools and techniques to create Web pages, like the one shown. You will export the graphics and create HTML pages you can edit in Dreamweaver.

MINIMUM SYSTEM REQUIREMENTS

Windows

- Windows 95, 98, ME, or 2000 Professional

- 64 MB available RAM

- 80 MB available disk space

- 166 MHz or faster Intel Pentium II processor (or equivalent)

- CD-ROM drive

- 256-color monitor with at least 800 x 600 pixel resolution

- For Windows NT 4 users: Service Pack 5 or later installed

- Version 4 or later of Netscape Navigator or Internet Explorer

Macintosh

- Mac OS 8.6 or 9.x

- QuickTime 3.0 or later

- 64 MB available RAM

- 80 MB available disk space

- G3 or later processor recommended

- CD-ROM drive

- 256-color monitor with at least 800 x 600 pixel resolution

- Version 4 or later of Netscape Navigator or Internet Explorer

bitmap editing

Macromedia Fireworks is both a bitmap editor and a vector drawing program. By combining these drawing methods into the same application, Fireworks gives you a very powerful and versatile set of tools.

Bitmaps are images that are composed of pixels. As with paint on a canvas, you can't just remove a mistake—you need to completely erase or "paint" over the mistake. Vector objects are images composed of mathematical lines and therefore can be moved and reshaped or even deleted with minimal effort.

Fireworks combines the look of bitmap images with the flexibility, control, and editability of vector graphics in a single environment. You can create soft, fuzzy drop shadows on objects and then change the shape of the object, and the drop shadow is re-created for you to match the new shape.

This graphic contains a bitmap image and a vector image. In this lesson you will make changes to the bitmap.

WHAT YOU WILL LEARN

In this lesson, you will:

- Learn the difference between bitmap and vector graphics
- Learn about the Fireworks interface
- Make selections in bitmap mode
- Edit bitmap images

APPROXIMATE TIME

This lesson takes approximately 1 hour to complete.

LESSON FILES

Media Files:

Lesson01\Color_wheel.png

Starting Files:

Lesson01\Flower_butterfly.png
Lesson01\Flowers.png
Lesson01\Biking.png

Completed Projects:

None

EXPLORING THE FIREWORKS TOOLS PANEL

Fireworks has a variety of tools you can choose by clicking the tool on the Tools panel or by using the shortcut key shown in the following figure. If a tool has a small black triangle in the bottom right corner, it is part of a group of tools; click and hold on the tool to access the pop-up tool group.

For example, click and hold the Pointer tool (top left on the Tools panel) to see the other tools in this area. If the Tools panel is not open, choose Window > Tools.

Fireworks has two modes for editing images: Vector mode and Bitmap mode. Vector mode is for creating vector images, and Bitmap mode is for editing bitmaps. Both modes share the same Tools panel, but some tools change based on the editing mode. For example, the Eraser tool looks like an eraser in Bitmap mode and a knife in Vector mode. The Rectangle tool in Vector mode creates a rectangle that can be resized and edited. In Bitmap mode, the same tool creates a bitmap rectangle that cannot be changed or resized while in this mode.

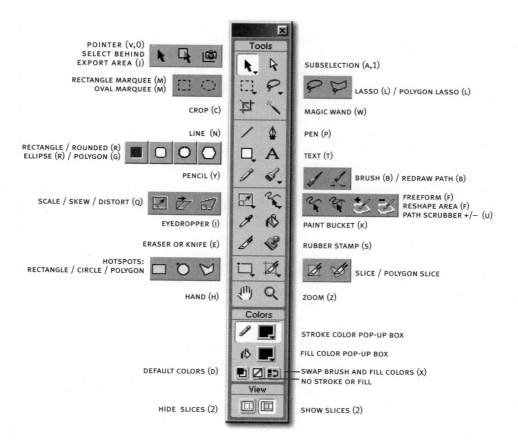

FLOATING AND TABBED PANELS

The panels used for making changes to images or objects "float" above the document, so they are always on top. Many of the panels are tabbed, with two or more panels combined. You can create your own arrangement by just dragging the tab away from the panel. To combine panels, drag the tab of one panel inside another panel. You'll see a black border appear, indicating that the addition is possible. To access a new panel, click its tab.

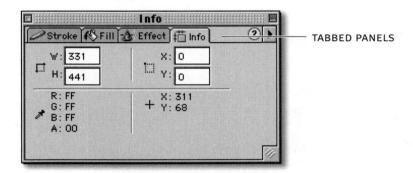

TABBED PANELS

As you work with the panels, you'll move them around or close them. To restore the panels to their original positions, choose Commands > Panel Layout Sets and choose from one of the listed screen sizes. A script runs that moves the panels based on the screen size you chose. This command is also very handy when you change your monitor—when you execute the command, the panels move to accommodate the new monitor.

EDITING BITMAP OBJECTS

Photographs or scanned art can be opened or imported into Fireworks. Fireworks recognizes the following bitmap file formats: Photoshop native files (PSD), TIFF, JPEG, GIF, BMP, PICT (Macintosh), PNG, and Targa. After you have opened or imported an image, you can make a variety of changes.

Before you can change pixels in a bitmap image, you must first select the area you want to affect. After you make a selection, you can edit only those pixels within the selection. Pixels outside the selection are protected from change. This exercise introduces you to the bitmap editing tools. You will learn to make selections, change colors in the image, and clone part of the image.

When editing bitmaps in Bitmap mode, you will be either editing pixel by pixel (with the Pencil, Pen, or Eraser tool) or editing a selection of pixels. Use the selection tools to select pixels either by their color value or by their location within an area. Only those pixels within the selection are affected by any changes you make.

1) Open the file Flower_butterfly.png file in the Lesson01 folder.

This file contains a bitmap image (the sunflower with the butterfly) and a vector image (the butterfly on the far right). The butterfly in the center of the flower is a bitmap. To change it, you need to select all the pixels that define the shape. To move the vector butterfly, you just need to select it with the Pointer tool. In this exercise, you will change the bitmap butterfly.

2) Select the Pointer tool from the Tools panel and double-click the image to switch to Bitmap mode.

You can also select a bitmap tool such as the Magic Wand tool or the Marquee tool, and click the image to switch to Bitmap mode. A striped border appears around the entire document to indicate that you are in Bitmap mode and editing pixels.

NOTE *When you are in Bitmap mode, any object you place on the canvas can't be moved or repositioned—you have permanently "painted" the object on the canvas.*

3) To exit Bitmap mode, click Exit Bitmap Mode (the red circle with a white X) located at the bottom of the document window.

NOTE *To exit Bitmap mode, you can also press the Esc key (Windows and Macintosh), Ctrl+Shift+E (Windows), Command+Shift+E (Macintosh), or Command+period (Macintosh only), or choose Modify > Exit Bitmap Mode.*

USING THE MAGIC WAND TOOL

With the Magic Wand tool, you can select neighboring pixels of the same or similar color. The level of similarity depends on the tolerance level you set in the Tool Options panel. The lowest level, zero, selects one color; you pick the exact color with the tip of the tool. The highest setting, 255, allows the greatest range of colors to be selected. For example, if the tolerance is set to 50 and the RGB value of the color selected is R = 100, G = 100, and B = 100, then colors from 50, 50, 50 to 150, 150, 150 are within the 50 tolerance level and thus are selected.

To understand this better, look at the many shades of blue in the sky in the bitmap image you have opened. The blue of the sky is dark at the top of the image and gradually lightens as it nears the horizon. If you used a low tolerance level, for example 10, then the number of blue pixels selected is limited to a small area around where you click with the tool. If you select the entire sky, you will need to continue to click to add pixels to the selection. If you use a large tolerance number, for example 255, then you will also select colors outside the blue color range.

The default tolerance level of 32 is generally a good starting point. Instead of increasing the tolerance level, try adding to the selection by holding Shift and clicking another color.

1) Select the Magic Wand tool on the Tools panel.

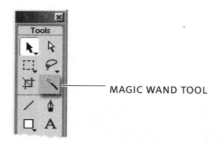

MAGIC WAND TOOL

2) Double-click the Magic Wand tool to access the Tool Options panel.

You can also click the tool icon (a wrench) at the bottom right of the document window. If the icon is not visible, resize your window, widening it until you see the row of icons.

3) Type a number in the Tolerance text box or use the slider to change the value.

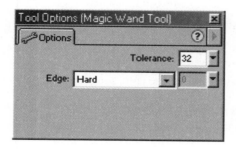

The tolerance level controls the number of pixels selected adjacent to the pixel you select with the tip of the Magic Wand tool. The lowest tolerance level, zero, selects only the exact pixel you select. Increasing the tolerance level increases the number of colors in your selection. Experiment with changing the tolerance level number to see the differences in the selected area.

For this exercise, start with a tolerance of *32*.

12

4) From the Edge pop-up menu, select Hard, Anti-Alias, or Feather.

The Edge menu controls the appearance of the edges of the selected pixels. For this exercise, use a hard edge for your selection.

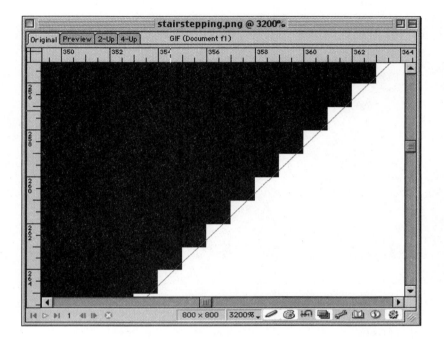

NOTE *You can change the appearance of the edge of the selection by picking Hard, Anti-Alias, or Feather from the Edge menu on the Tool Options panel. A hard edge on any shape that is not a horizontal or vertical edge creates a stair-step effect. This is the result of trying to create a curve or diagonal line from square pixels: it can't be done. Anti-aliasing makes the edges appear smooth by blending the foreground and background pixels on the edges. The lighter or darker pixels trick the eye into seeing a smooth edge. Feathering applies a blend between the edge color and the background color. If you choose Feather, set the amount of the blend with the Feather slider control. For other ways to modify your selection, see page 30.*

5) Click the area of the image you want to select.

Click the sky in the image. All neighboring pixels within the specified tolerance level are selected. You should now see the "marching ants" marquee around your selection.

SELECTED AREA

6) If you want, hold Shift and click outside the boundaries of your selection with the Magic Wand to add more pixels to your selection.

Continue to hold Shift and click in the sky area until all the sky area is selected. You'll need the selection for the next steps in this exercise, so don't take that coffee break yet.

TIP *To add to your selection based on color similarity, choose Modify > Marquee > Select Similar.*

ADJUSTING THE HUE AND SATURATION

Once you've selected the blue sky area, you can make changes to the color or look of the selected area. Any change you make will change only the selected area. For example, you can make subtle changes to the color of the sky by adjusting the hue and saturation.

Hue is the color of an object; saturation is the strength or purity of a color; lightness refers to the whiteness in the image. You can change the color and strength of an object, or in this case, of the selection, by adjusting the sliders in the dialog box.

1) Choose Xtras > Adjust Color > Hue/Saturation.

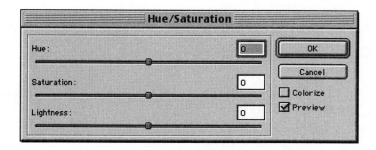

2) Select Preview to view your changes in the workspace.

As you make changes, the selected area will be updated automatically.

3) Drag the Hue slider until you get a color you want.

The values displayed in the text box as you drag the slider reflect the degree of rotation around the color wheel. A positive number rotates counterclockwise; a negative number rotates clockwise. Dragging the slider all the way to the left or right changes the hue to the color at 180 degrees from the original color.

If you are unfamiliar with the color wheel, open the Color_wheel.png file in the Lesson01 folder. Opposite (or 180 degrees) from blue in the color wheel is yellow. If you drag the Hue slider all the way to the left or right, the sky changes to yellow.

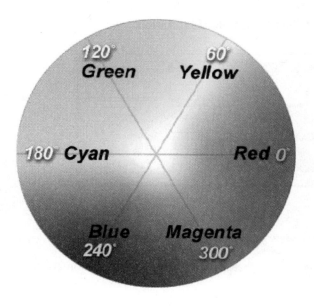

NOTE *If you change the color too much, the edges of the selection, especially around the flower, will look too harsh. Bitmap images are made up of pixels, which are square. Around the petals of the flower are pixels that are a color combination of the blue sky and yellow flower. These pixels trick your eye into seeing a smooth edge around the flower and are not in your selection because of their color. When you change the hue to magenta, for example, the color is far different from the blue, and those pixels stand out, resulting in a hard edge around the flower. Experiment with the slider until you get a darker blue or a violet-blue color.*

4) Drag the Saturation slider to change the intensity of the sky.

Dragging the slider all the way to the left changes the color to gray. Dragging the slider all the way to the right changes the intensity of the color to its brightest point.

5) Drag the Lightness slider to change the brightness level of the sky.

Drag the slider to the left to darken the overall color tone of the sky. At the far left end, the color turns to black. Drag the slider to the right to lighten the color. At the far right end, the color turns to white.

Adjust the sliders in the Hue/Saturation dialog box to your liking.

6) Click OK to close the Hue/Saturation dialog box.

If you want to hide the selection area to better view your changes, choose View > Hide Edges. To view the selection area, select the command again. If you are happy with the results of your changes, deselect the area by choosing Edit > Deselect.

TIP *If you want to save your selection before you deselect it, choose Modify > Marquee > Save Selection. To use the selection again, choose Modify > Marquee > Restore Selection. Fireworks only saves one selection.*

USING THE LASSO TOOL

The Lasso tool creates a freeform selection boundary around an area. Wherever you drag, you draw a selection outline. When you release the mouse button, the selection area closes automatically. To close the selection area yourself, return to the first point of the selection. As you come close to the beginning, the pointer displays a small square. To close the selection, release the mouse when you see the square.

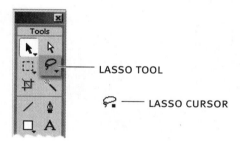

LASSO TOOL

LASSO CURSOR

The Polygon Lasso tool draws straight-line segments. This tool works differently than the Lasso tool; instead of dragging the tool to make the selection, click for your first point, release the mouse, move to a new location, and click again to define a line segment. Just as with the Lasso tool, you'll see a small square by the cursor when you are close to the beginning point. Click when you see the square to close the selection. You can also double-click to close the selection, even if you have not moved the cursor back to the beginning point.

As with the Magic Wand tool, you can control the edges of the selection you draw with the Lasso tool. Read about this in the note in the section "Using the Magic Wand Tool."

In the next exercise, you will select the butterfly in the center of the flower using the Lasso tool. To make it easier to see the edges of the butterfly, you will want to enlarge the view. You can use the Magnification pop-up menu at the bottom of the document window or the Zoom tool. The Zoom tool enlarges the image at the point where you click.

1) Select the Zoom tool and click the butterfly in the center of the flower.

The Zoom tool (also called the Magnify tool) lets you move in and out of your document to view it at different magnification levels. You'll sometimes want to use this tool to more easily see individual pixels in an image.

Each click you make with the Zoom tool further enlarges the view. To decrease the magnification of the view, hold Alt (Windows) or Option (Macintosh) as you click with the tool. The Zoom tool changes to a minus sign to indicate that you are decreasing the magnification of the view

You can also use the Magnification pop-up menu located at the bottom of the document window, or you can use keyboard shortcuts for zooming in and out. The keyboard shortcuts to zoom in are the same as in Macromedia FreeHand and Adobe Photoshop: Ctrl+Spacebar (Windows) or Command+Spacebar (Macintosh). To zoom out, use Ctrl+Alt+Spacebar (Windows) or Command+Option+Spacebar (Macintosh).

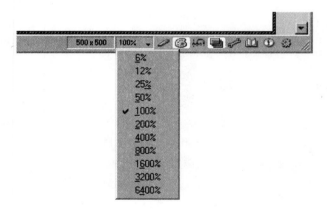

NOTE *In Windows, hold down the Spacebar first and then the Ctrl and Alt keys.*

POWER TIP *Double-click the Zoom tool on the Tools panel to return the view to 100 percent.*

2) Select the Lasso tool from the Tools panel and draw around the edges of the butterfly.

Don't worry if your line doesn't exactly match the edge of the butterfly or if you get a wavy line. Drawing with the mouse is equivalent to drawing with a brick in your hand, and it does take some practice to draw smooth outlines. In the next steps, you'll clean up the edges of the selection you make.

When you get close to the starting point, the cursor adds a small square to the tool. This indicates that you are about to close the selection. Release the mouse when you see the square. The "marching ants" selection marquee appears around the butterfly.

ADDING AND SUBTRACTING SELECTIONS

Holding Shift while you are selecting an area adds to the selection. Holding Alt (Windows) or Option (Macintosh) subtracts from the selection. You'll use these techniques to perfect your selection of the butterfly.

If a part of your selection marquee is outside the edges of the butterfly, you need to subtract that portion. If a part of your selection marquee is within the edges of the butterfly, you need to add to the selection.

After you select the butterfly, you will make a copy of it and place it on the flower.

1) Hold down Shift and move the lasso pointer within your selection.

A plus sign appears with the lasso pointer.

2) Drag the Lasso tool around the area you want to include in the selection and then release the mouse button.

The area is added to the selection. Continue this technique in all the areas that are within the edge of the butterfly.

CIRCLE TO ADD TO SELECTION   SELECTION

3) Hold down Alt (Windows) or Option (Macintosh).

A minus sign appears with the lasso pointer.

4) Drag the Lasso tool around the area you want to delete from the selection and then release the mouse button.

The area is deleted from the selection. Continue this technique in all the areas that are outside the edge of the butterfly.

COPYING THE SELECTION

There are several ways to make copies of your selection. You are probably familiar with the Copy and Paste commands on the Edit menu. You can use those commands, but there is a better method for controlling the placement of the copy.

1) Select the Pointer tool from the Tools panel, hold down Alt (Windows) or Option (Macintosh), and then drag the butterfly selection to a new location.

The pointer adds a plus sign, indicating that you are making a copy of the butterfly. Release the mouse when you are done. You can move the butterfly selection with the Pointer tool as long as the butterfly remains selected.

NOTE *If you are still zoomed in, you might want to return to 100 percent view to move the butterfly. You can use the Magnify pop-up menu or double-click the Zoom tool to return to 100 percent view.*

POWER TIP *You can copy the butterfly without switching to the Pointer tool. Hold down Ctrl (Windows) or Command (Macintosh) to display the temporary Pointer tool; then add the Alt (Windows) or Option (Macintosh) key. Now drag to make the copy.*

2) Choose Edit > Deselect to release the butterfly selection.

NOTE *Once you deselect the butterfly, it can no longer be moved on the page. You have permanently "painted" the butterfly on the image.*

3) Choose File > Save to save the file; then choose File > Close to close the file.

USING THE RUBBER STAMP TOOL

The Rubber Stamp tool works well for retouching an image or cloning a portion of an image. In this exercise, you will make a copy of a flower in an image.

When you use the Rubber Stamp tool, you are painting a pixel copy of some area of a bitmap image onto another area of the same bitmap object.

1) Open the Flowers.png file in the Lesson01 folder.

This file contains an image of a flower arrangement. You will clone a purple flower to add more flowers to the arrangement.

2) Select the Rubber Stamp tool on the Tools panel and then double-click the tool to access the Tool Options panel. Set the stamp size and edge softness of the cloned area on the Tool Options panel.

For this exercise, set the stamp size to 8 and drag the Edge Softness slider all the way to the top. If you decide that the stamp size is too large or small, you can adjust the size as you use the tool.

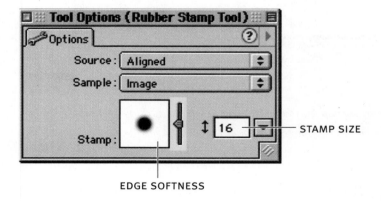

EDGE SOFTNESS

3) Move the pointer to the middle of the purple flower. Hold down Alt (Windows) or Option (Macintosh) and click the middle of the flower to designate the set point from where you will begin cloning the flower.

A circle appears to indicate your set point. The set point is the starting point of your copy. Remember using a compass in school to draw circles? At one end of a compass is a pencil; at the other end is a sharp point. You place the sharp end at a location on your paper and then drag the pencil around to draw the circle. The sharp end is the set point. The pencil is set at a fixed distance from the set point.

To use the Rubber Stamp tool, you designate the set point and then move the Rubber Stamp cursor to where you want the copy. The distance from the Rubber Stamp cursor and the set point remains constant, like the distance in the compass. As you move the Rubber Stamp cursor, it moves the set point, keeping the distance constant. The digital information from the set point is copied and painted in the new location.

SET POINT

RUBBER STAMP CURSOR

4) Move the Rubber Stamp pointer to another part of the image where you want to add a flower. Click and drag to paint the area with the flower.

The set point moves within the flower as you move the pointer. Watch the original flower to verify that you remain within the outlines of the flower. Continue to paint until you have a copy of the flower.

To clone another flower, repeat step 4.

The Tool Options panel provides other ways to control the behavior of the Rubber Stamp tool. Choose Aligned from the Source pop-up menu when you want to release the mouse without losing the relationship to your original cloned area. This option is useful when you want to copy a portion of the image to a new location. When you release the mouse button and click another portion of the image, the distance between the set point and where you click again remains the same. Again, think of the compass example. If you leave the distance fixed between the sharp end and the pencil, you can pick up and move the set point to draw in a new location.

Choose Fixed when you want to make multiple copies of the cloned area. When you release the mouse and move to a new location, the set point returns to the original position. Using the compass example again, after you complete one copy, you can increase or decrease the distance between the sharp end and the pencil, but you always begin your drawing at the same point.

The options in the Sample pop-up menu determine what portion of the document is to be cloned. If all you have in your document is a bitmap image, this setting doesn't apply. If you have vector objects along with the bitmap image, you can choose Image to clone only the pixels in the image, even if a vector object is on top of the bitmap. To copy the vector object as well as the bitmap image, choose Document.

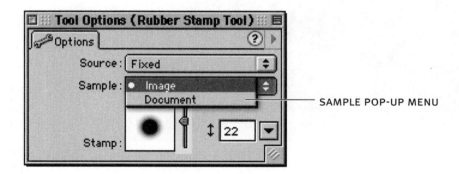

SAMPLE POP-UP MENU

USING THE ERASER TOOL

The Eraser tool is used in Bitmap mode to delete pixels or change their color. Double-click the Eraser tool to access the Tool Options panel if it is not already open.

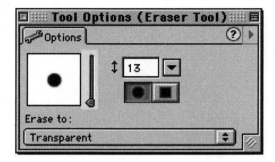

- Use the Edge Softness slider to change the softness of the edge of the Eraser tool.
- Use the Size slider or type a number to change the size of the Eraser tool.
- Use the Erase To pop-up menu to choose Transparent, Fill Color, Stroke Color, or Canvas Color.

If you use the Eraser tool with Erase To set to Canvas Color, you will, in effect, be painting with the color of the canvas. If you want to remove the visibility of pixels on a bitmap object, choose Transparent in the Erase To pop-up list. Note also that although the fill color and stroke color on the Tools panel may be set to None, the Eraser tool will still paint with the color last chosen for fill or stroke if you choose Fill Color or Stroke Color in the Erase To pop-up list on the Tool Options panel.

You can close the Flowers.png file. You do not need to save the file.

USING THE MARQUEE TOOLS

The Rectangle and Oval Marquee tools let you select specific shapes in an image. To control the size and proportions of the selections of the tool, use the Style pop-up menu on the Tool Options panel and choose Normal, Fixed Size, or Fixed Ratio. For Fixed Size, type the exact width and height in pixels for the selection. For Fixed Ratio, type the proportion of width to height before making the selection. You can also change the appearance of the edges of the selection. Read about this in the note in the section "Using the Magic Wand Tool."

MARQUEE TOOLS

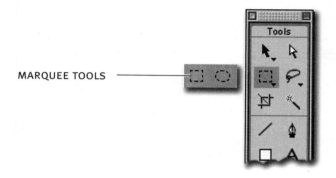

In the next exercise, you will select a portion of an image with the Oval Marquee tool.

1) Open the Biking.png file in the Lesson01 folder.

2) Select the Oval marquee tool on the Tools panel. Hold down Alt (Windows) or Option (Macintosh) to draw the selection from the center outward.

Click just to the right of the rider's left knee (forward knee), which is about the center of the bike and the rider, and then hold down Alt (Windows) or Option (Macintosh) and drag. The marquee selection is drawn from the center, where you clicked the image. Continue to drag until the oval selection surrounds the bike and rider. You'll use the selection in the next task.

CLICK TO THE RIGHT OF THE RIDER'S LEFT KNEE

To constrain your selection to a circle, add Shift as you drag. For this exercise, you want an oval shape, so you don't need to add Shift.

POWER TIP *When using modifier keys (Option, Alt, Shift) to constrain your selection, make sure you begin to drag with the selection tool before you press the additional keys.*

NOTE *If you want to change the shape or position of your selection, you might find it easier to deselect the selection and start over. Choose Edit > Deselect and make the selection again.*

MOVING A SELECTION

After you make a selection, you may want to use the same selection in another portion of the image. In Fireworks 4, instead of deselecting and then re-creating the selection, you can simply move the selection.

1) Create a selection with any of the selection tools.

You can use the oval selection of the biking image you created in the preceding task.

2) Move the pointer within the selection.

The cursor appears as a triangle pointer with a small rectangle below.

NOTE *Make sure you release any modifier keys you were holding to make the selection. In addition, don't switch to the Pointer tool to move your selection. The Pointer tool moves the image and the selection, not just the selection.*

3) Drag when you see the cursor to move the selection.

Dragging with the cursor pointer moves just the selection outline, not the pixels within the selection.

FEATHERING THE EDGES OF A SELECTION

With the bike and rider selected, you want to delete the background of the image. You also want a feathered (soft blur) edge to the selection instead of the default hard edge. First, you will feather the selection, and then you will delete the background.

1) Choose Modify › Marquee › Feather.

The Feather Selection dialog box opens. Change the feather amount to *25* and click OK. You won't yet see any change in the image.

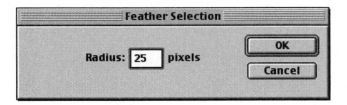

2) Choose Modify › Marquee › Select Inverse.

This selects all of the pixels that are not in the selection.

3) Press Delete.

The background is deleted, and you see a soft-feathered edge around the bike and rider.

4) Choose Modify > Marquee > Select Inverse again.

This restores the original selection.

ADDITIONAL SELECTION OPTIONS

You can also use menu commands to make or change your selections. These commands are found on the Edit menu or the Modify menu.

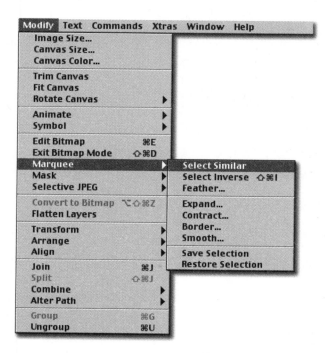

Select Similar: Within a single bitmap object, creates an additional selection around colors that are similar to colors in the existing selection. The Magic Wand tool (and, thereafter, Select Similar) can also select transparent pixels or the space outside of a bitmap object.

Select Inverse: Selects all pixels not in the current selection and deselects the currently selected pixels.

Feather: Feathers the edges of the selection.

Expand: Expands the selection by a set number of pixels.

Contract: Contracts the selection by a set number of pixels.

Border: Creates a selection outside the current selection using a set number of pixels. This selection can be filled with a color to create a border around the original selection.

Smooth: Smoothes the selection by a set number of pixels.

Save Selection: Remembers the current selection within the document.

Restore Selection: Restores the last-saved selection.

Select All: In Bitmap mode, selects all the pixels in a bitmap object on a selected layer. In Vector mode, selects all visible objects on all layers. If Single layer editing is on, Select All only selects objects on the current layer. Single layer editing is covered in Lesson 3.

Superselect: Selects an object's entire group when one object in the group has already been selected. Grouping, discussed in the next lesson, binds multiple objects together.

Subselect: Selects all of the objects individually within a group selected by the Pointer tool.

Deselect: Deletes the selection.

Crop Selected Bitmap: Creates a cropping box that fits the size of the selection. It also creates a cropping box around a bitmap object that has been selected by the Pointer tool. Double-click the box to crop the document.

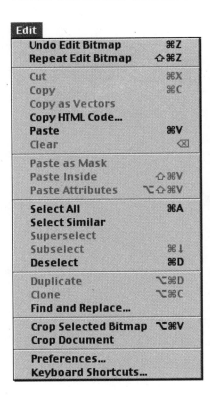

VIEWING THE GAMMA SETTING

When creating graphics for the Web, how do you make the color look good on all machines? This is a nearly impossible task. Monitors are usually not calibrated accurately, nor are they calibrated the same from one machine to another. To make matters worse, on different computer platforms, shades of colors appear differently.

The gamma setting on your computer affects the apparent brightness and contrast of the monitor display. The gamma setting for the Macintosh is lower than that on Windows machines. This makes images created on the Macintosh appear darker when viewed on a Windows PC. Knowing this, you have to compensate as you create your images. If you are designing on a Macintosh, create your images a little lighter; on a PC, create them a little darker.

To make your job easier, Fireworks 4 has a built-in function for viewing the gamma setting on the other platform. If you are using Windows, choose View > Macintosh Gamma. This lightens the image to simulate its display on a Macintosh. If you are using a Macintosh, choose View > Windows Gamma. This darkens the image to simulate its display on a PC.

If you are using Windows, choose View > Macintosh Gamma. If you are using a Macintosh, choose View > Windows Gamma. Look at the color difference when you choose this option.

WINDOWS GAMMA   MACINTOSH GAMMA

WHAT YOU HAVE LEARNED

In this lesson, you have:

- Used the Magic Wand tool to select pixels based on color [pages 11–14]

- Changed the hue, saturation, and lightness of a selected area [pages 15–17]

- Used the Lasso tool to draw a selection around an object and then added and deleted from the selection [pages 17–20]

- Copied a selection and then moved the selection [pages 21–22]

- Used the Rubber Stamp tool to clone an area of an image [pages 22–24]

- Selected an area with the Marquee tool and then feathered the edges [pages 26–30]

- Viewed the gamma setting of an image [page 32]

working with groups and layers

Layers and groups are powerful features that help you manage and organize objects on your page. You can create complex objects by combining simple shapes. Grouping the elements of the object together allows you to select and move them as one. You don't have to take the time to select each of the individual elements.

Layers are transparent planes where you can create and store objects. With layers, you can control the stacking order of objects on your page, quickly moving objects up or down if the stacking order changes. You can also lock and hide layers to make complex objects easier to manage.

This drawing was created using different layers, making it easier to manipulate and change. In this lesson, you will see how to add, delete, and move layers to make yourself more productive.

In this lesson, you will work with an existing document containing several layers and objects on the layers. You will add a new layer and move objects to different layers.

WHAT YOU WILL LEARN

In this lesson, you will:

- Group objects
- Explore the various tools for selecting objects
- Select points and paths in vector graphics
- Create and use layers
- Change the order of objects on a layer

APPROXIMATE TIME

This lesson takes approximately 1 hour to complete.

LESSON FILES

Media Files:
None

Starting Files:
Lesson02\Preserve.png
Lesson02\Preserve_text.png

Completed Projects:
None

GROUPING OBJECTS

Multiple objects are sometimes easier to work with if you tie them together as a unit. This is called grouping. When objects are grouped, they move together and can be manipulated as a single unit. Scaling and rotation control all objects in the group at the same time. You can also combine two groups or combine a group and an object. This is referred to as nested grouping.

1) Open the Preserve.png file in the Lesson02 folder.

This file contains several objects that create the image. Some of the objects are already grouped. You will group others to make the image easier to move.

2) Select the Pointer tool on the Tools panel and move the pointer over one of the objects. For example, move over the fire, but do not click the fire.

When you move over an object, four red handles appear around the object. If you don't see the red handles, choose Window > Tool Options to open the Options panel. Select Mouse Highlight on the panel. You might find this option distracting at first, but it does make it easy to determine what object you are pointing to before you actually select the object.

NOTE *If you move over a vector path, the entire path and points on the path highlights in red. You don't see four handles unless the path is grouped.*

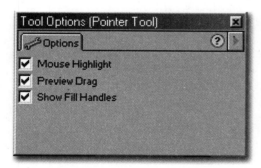

NOTE *If you click the beige rectangle at the bottom of the document, you won't see the red handles around the fire. Choose Edit > Deselect or click outside the image to deselect the rectangle.*

3) Select the text "Preserve Our Forests" and then hold down Shift and select the row of small black trees above the text.

Both objects display blue handles to indicate that they are selected.

When selecting two or more objects, you hold down Shift as you click each object. If you want to deselect an object, continue to hold down Shift and click the object again.

You can also use the selection rectangle to select multiple objects if they are isolated from other objects you don't want selected. Drag around the objects you want selected. A rectangle appears as you drag. All objects within or touched by the rectangle are selected when you release the mouse.

4) Choose Modify > Group.

The grouped object has four blue handles around it. If you move the group to a new location, the group now moves as one.

To ungroup the objects, you would choose Modify > Ungroup.

NOTE *In Windows, you can use the Group and Ungroup buttons on the Modify toolbar. Choose Window > Toolbars > Modify to access the Modify toolbar.*

GROUP
UNGROUP

5) Select the fire object.

The red handles change to blue, indicating that the object is selected. The fire is composed of many small objects that are grouped together.

6) Choose the Subselection tool on the Tools panel.

The Subselection tool is for selecting objects within a group or selecting points on a path. You could ungroup the object and then use the Pointer tool to select one of the objects in the group, but using the Subselection tool is easier. In addition, you don't have to select all of the objects to regroup them again.

SUBSELECTION TOOL

POWER TIP *Instead of switching from the Pointer tool to the Subselection tool, you can hold down Alt (Windows) or Option (Macintosh) as you click an object in the group.*

7) Click the yellow part of the fire and notice the blue line (the path) and the points on the path.

With a path selected, you can change the color of the fill or the shape of the path. A vector graphic is made up of two or more points that connect to form a path. You use the Pointer tool to select the path if it is not grouped. You use the Subselection tool to select the points on the path.

8) Click one of the points on the path.

The point turns a solid blue when selected. Once a point is selected, you can move it to change the shape of the path.

USING THE LAYERS PANEL

You can think of a layer as a transparent plane where you can create and place objects. Layers enable you to divide your artwork when building complex or composite images. Different portions of the image can be stored on different layers and selectively turned off or on so you can isolate just the portion you are working on. Layers can contain either vector or bitmap objects, or a combination of both.

The Layers panel in Fireworks is similar to Layers panels in other graphics programs such as Macromedia FreeHand and Adobe Photoshop, but it includes additional information.

When you create a new document, you get two layers by default: Layer 1 and the Web Layer. Layer 1 is where all of your objects and images will be placed initially. The Web Layer is where slices and hotspots are stored. We'll discuss these in a later lesson.

On each layer, you can place one object or multiple objects. If you place multiple objects on the same layer, each object is placed in the layer as an individual object within a stack of objects. New objects are initially placed on top of the stack. A thumbnail representation of the object is displayed to the left of the object name on the Layers panel. You can control the stacking order of each object in the stack using Modify > Arrange > Bring to Front, Modify > Arrange > Bring Forward, Modify > Arrange > Send to Back, and Modify > Arrange > Send Backward, or you can use the Layers panel to drag the object to a new position within the stack or move the object to a new layer.

Layers let you organize your drawings into distinct levels that can be edited as individual units or hidden from view when needed. The next exercise demonstrates how to use the Layers panel to add new layers, move objects between layers, and hide and lock layers.

1) Choose Window > Layers to display the Layers panel.

The Layers panel is grouped by default with the Frames and History panels. If the panel is already visible, click its tab to select it. The tab of the selected panel is a lighter gray.

Layers have already been defined for the Preserve.png file. You should see three layers: Web Layer, Title, and Background. The text and the row of trees above it are on the Title layer; the remaining objects are on the Background layer.

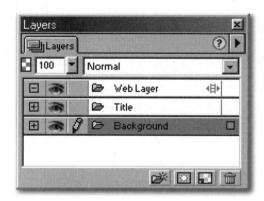

2) On the Layers panel, click the eye icon to the left of the Title layer to turn off the layer.

The title graphic disappears. If you have a complex drawing, it is sometimes helpful to display only the portions of the drawing that you are currently working on. This way, you don't accidentally delete or move another object that might be overlapping the object that you are modifying.

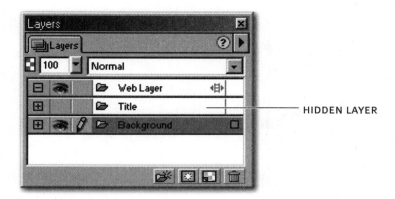

HIDDEN LAYER

Click the eye icon again to display the title graphic.

⊙ POWER TIP *Hold down Alt (Windows) or Option (Macintosh) as you click any Show/Hide button to make all layers visible.*

3) Click the Lock column to the left of the Background layer to lock the layer so its objects can't be moved or deleted.

A lock icon appears in the column. Locking a layer is helpful when you want to see all of the objects on the layer, but you don't want to accidentally move or delete any objects. Locking a layer also prevents you from adding new objects to that layer.

NOTE *If a layer is currently selected, the lock column displays a pencil. When you click the pencil, the lock column displays a lock. A blank lock column means the layer is not selected.*

Try to select the blue mountain. Because it is on the locked Background layer, you can't select it.

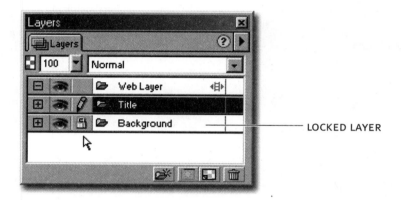

To unlock the layer, click the lock icon on the layer.

◎ POWER TIP *Hold down Alt (Windows) or Option (Macintosh) and click the Lock column to lock or unlock all layers at once.*

4) Click the plus (Windows) or triangle (Macintosh) on the Background layer to see all objects on the layer.

You'll see three objects on the layer: the fire group, the beige rectangle, and another group of the mountain and trees. Each object (or group) is in its own stack on the layer.

5) Drag the fire stack (labeled Fire Group) below the rectangle stack on the Layers panel.

As you drag the stack on the layer, you'll see a black line appear either above or below the other stacks. The stack you are dragging moves to the position of the black line when you release the mouse.

The order in which objects appear in the list determines the stacking order—top to bottom—on the canvas. The fire (represented by the top group) appears above the beige rectangle in the list. When you drag it below the rectangle, the fire disappears because it is hidden by the rectangle. Drag the fire stack back to the top to display it again.

The order in which objects appear on a stack depends on the order in which they were created. Just as in other graphics programs, the last object created is on top. You can also change the stacking order of individual objects by using the Arrange submenu (on the Modify menu). The stacking order on a layer is different from the order of the layers. An object can be at the top of the object list and still be underneath an object on a higher layer. Choose Modify > Arrange > Bring to Front to bring the object to the front, or choose Modify > Arrange > Send to Back to move the object to the back. Choose Modify > Arrange > Bring Forward to bring the object in front of another object on the same layer, or choose Modify > Arrange > Send Backward to move the object behind another object on the same layer. In Windows only, you can also use the Modify toolbar for these menu options.

6) Click the right arrow at the top right of the panel to access the Layers panel Options pop-up menu.

From this menu, you can add, duplicate, or delete layers as well as lock or hide layers.

7) Choose New Layer from the list.

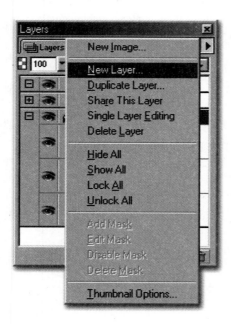

8) In the New Layer dialog box, type *Fire* for the name of the layer and then click OK.

NOTE   *You can also click the New Layer icon at the bottom of the panel. This creates a new layer with the default name Layer 1, Layer 2, and so on. You can easily change the name of the layer. Double-click the layer name on the Layers panel. In the Layer Name dialog box, type a new name. Do not check Share Across Frames. Press Enter (Windows) or Return (Macintosh) or click outside the Layer Name dialog box to close and save the new name.*

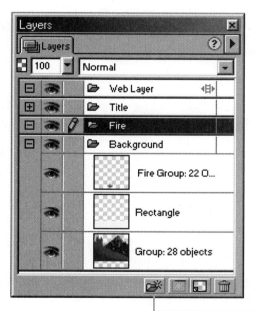

NEW LAYER

Now you want to move the fire object onto the Fire layer you just created. This way, you can then lock it or hide it if you need to modify other objects on the canvas.

9) Drag the Fire stack from the Background layer onto the Fire layer.

When you are over the Fire layer, a black line appears under the layer name to indicate the selected layer. Release the mouse when you see the black line under the Fire layer. The fire object is now on the Fire layer.

Since were only three objects on the Background layer, finding the fire object in the stack was relatively easy. Often, though, you will have too many objects in the stack to identify each object easily. The next step demonstrates another method for moving objects to another layer.

10) Use the Pointer tool to select the fire graphic on the page.

Notice the blue square (the selection indicator) in the far right column of the Layers panel. This indicates the layer position of the selected object. You can drag the blue square to another layer to move the object to the new layer.

11) Drag the blue square to the Background layer and then back to the Fire layer.

If you use this method, you don't need to open the layer to move an object to a new layer.

NOTE *Blue is the default highlight color. It can be changed by choosing Edit > Preferences and changing the highlight color on the General tab (Windows) or in the General category (Macintosh).*

USING SINGLE-LAYER EDITING

Single-layer editing, accessed from the Layers panel Options pop-up menu, makes only the currently selected layer accessible for editing. Objects on other layers cannot be selected. This is a little different from locking the layer and can be very handy when you are working with a complex image using many layers. When you lock a layer, you can't select, edit, or change any objects on that layer until you unlock the layer. With single-layer editing, you can edit only objects on the selected layer; the other layers act as if they were locked. To select objects on other layers, you need to select the layer on the Layers panel.

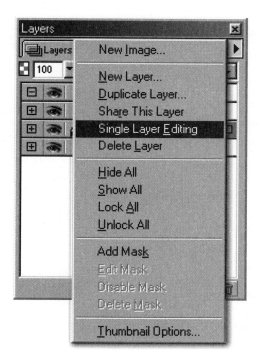

1) Click the right arrow at the top right of the panel to access the Layers panel Options pop-up menu; then choose Single Layer Editing.

A check mark (Windows) or a bullet (Macintosh) appears next to the command to indicate that it is selected. This works as a toggle. To remove the option, choose the command again from the Layers panel Options pop-up menu.

2) Make sure nothing is selected on the canvas and then select the Background layer on the Layers panel.

Choose Edit > Deselect or click outside the canvas area (but still within the document window) to deselect all objects on the page. Try to select the fire or the title graphic. With the Background layer selected on the Layers panel, you can't select any object on another layer.

3) Select the Title layer on the Layers panel.

Now try to select the mountain in the background or the fire. Again, they are not on the selected layer and so cannot be selected.

USING THE SELECT BEHIND TOOL

When you start creating complex graphics, you may find that a graphic consists of several objects stacked on top of each other. This sometimes makes it difficult to select an individual object that is behind or under other objects. The Select Behind tool makes it easy to select through other objects to reach one that is at the back.

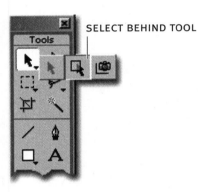

SELECT BEHIND TOOL

1) Open the Preserve_text.png file in the Lesson02 folder.

The file contains the "Preserve Our Forests" text with a gray color.

2) With the Pointer tool, drag the text to the Preserve.png document window.

As soon as the pointer touches the other document window, a plus sign is added to the cursor, indicating you are copying (not moving) the object. You could also copy and paste the object, but this method is faster.

3) Move the new text on top of the other text, but slightly offset to give a drop-shadow effect.

TIP *Use the arrow keys to nudge the top text for precise placement.*

The text is placed on the Title layer unless you selected another layer before dragging the object on the canvas. To select the text underneath, you'll use the Select Behind tool.

4) Click and hold the Pointer tool on the Tools panel to access the pop-up group that contains the Select Behind tool.

The Select Behind tool's cursor appears as a white pointer with a small arrow.

TIP *You can also press V or 0 (zero) to access the Select Behind tool.*

5) Click on the forest text with the Select Behind tool.

The first click selects the top object. Click as many times as necessary to select the object you want. Each click selects the next object in the stack. If you want to select all of the objects, hold down Shift as you click.

You can use the Select Behind tool, or you can use the object stack on the Layers panel, to select buried objects on the page. The layer stack provides you with a visual representation of all of the objects and may be easier to use.

NOTE *If no object is selected when you access the Select Behind tool, the top object is selected when you click. If an object is already selected, the next object in the stack is selected.*

6) You can close all the files.

WHAT YOU HAVE LEARNED

In this lesson, you have:

- Grouped and ungrouped objects [pages 36–37]
- Selected objects within a group [pages 38–39]
- Learned about the Layers panel [pages 39–46]
- Used the single-layer editing function [pages 47–48]
- Used the Select Behind tool [pages 48–50]

using vector tools

LESSON 3

Many objects can be created by drawing simple shapes and then editing them to create new shapes. In this lesson, you will create a compass logo that will be used in another lesson. You will learn methods to help you create a complex image from basic drawing tools.

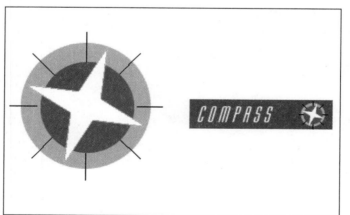

The compass is constructed from a series of basic vector shapes. You will see how in this lesson. The compass logo will use the compass you draw along with some imported text.

WHAT YOU WILL LEARN

In this lesson, you will:

- Use guides and grids for drawing

- Draw with the basic drawing tools: Rectangle, Ellipse, and Polygon

- Rotate an object

- Use the History panel to replay actions

- Use the Knife tool to cut objects

- Apply color and size to strokes

- Use the Info panel for precise positioning and sizing of objects

- Use the Eyedropper tool to select color

- Import graphics

APPROXIMATE TIME

This lesson takes approximately 2 hours to complete.

LESSON FILES

Media Files:

Lesson03\Compass_text.fh9

Lesson03\Site_colors.png

Starting Files:

None

Completed Projects:

Lesson03\Completed\Compass.png

Lesson03\Completed\Compass_logo.png

CREATING A NEW DOCUMENT

When you begin a new document, you need to set the canvas size and color and the image resolution.

1) Choose File > New to create a new empty document.

The New Document dialog box opens.

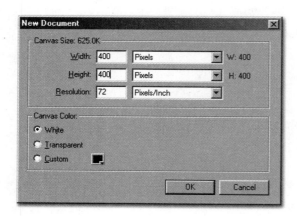

2) Set the canvas size, using pixels, inches, or centimeters. For this exercise, enter *400 Pixels* **for the width and** *400 Pixels* **for the height.**

You can alter the canvas size later by choosing Modify > Canvas Size or by using the Crop tool to crop the document or by choosing Modify > Trim Canvas to trim the empty edges of the canvas.

3) Define the resolution as either pixels per inch or pixels per centimeter. Choose a white canvas, a transparent canvas, or a custom color canvas. Then click OK.

Web graphics are saved at 72 pixels per inch (the default). The resolution of the entire document can be changed by choosing Modify > Image Size.

The canvas color is the background color of your document. You can change the canvas color later by choosing Modify > Canvas Color. For this exercise, use white as the background color.

NOTE *The color you choose as the canvas color is also the color of the background page when you export to HTML. If your canvas color is set to Transparent, then the transparent background will export as a white background.*

4) Save your file in the Lesson03 folder and name it *Compass.png*.

In Windows, the .png extension is added automatically to your file name. On the Macintosh, select Add Filename Extension in the Save dialog box to automatically add the .png extension. Once selected, this option becomes the default for all subsequent files you save. Although not needed for Macintosh computers, it is always a good idea to add the proper extension for all of your files, especially if you share files with Windows users.

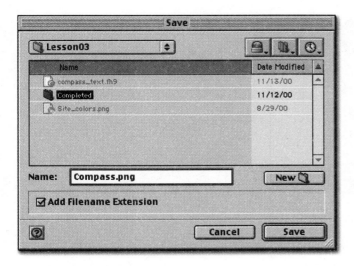

NOTE *The document window displays an asterisk when you make a change to the document to remind you to save your file.*

SETTING A GRID

To make it easier to precisely draw the compass, you'll use grid lines and rulers. The grid lines make it easier to size the circle, and the guides help you center the circle. Grid lines aren't saved when you export your images, nor do they print. They are there to help you place objects or control the layout.

1) Choose View > Grid > Edit Grid to edit the color and size of the grid.

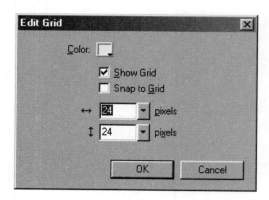

2) In the Edit Grid dialog box, enter _24_ pixels for both the width and height of the grid size. Click the color box to access the color palette. Use the Eyedropper pointer that appears and select a pale blue color from the color palette for the gird.

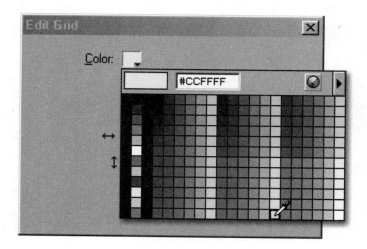

3) Select Show Grid and Snap to Grid in the dialog box. (Make sure the check boxes are checked.) Click OK.

With the Snap to Grid option enabled, you'll notice that objects on the canvas are pulled to the nearest grid line, similar to the way a metal object is drawn to a magnet. If you find that you don't like this feature, you can turn it off by choosing View > Grid > Snap to Grid.

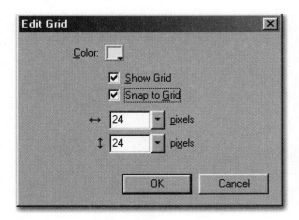

NOTE *A check appears next to Show Grid and Snap to Grid in the View > Grid menu when the options are on.*

DISPLAYING RULERS AND GUIDES

Guides are lines you can use to set the placement of objects on the canvas such as the alignment of buttons or the center point of an object. In this exercise, you'll use the guides to draw the two circles for the compass. The guides will mark the center point of each circle.

The page rulers must be visible for you to access the guides. If you don't see the page rulers, choose View > Rulers. A check next to the command indicates that the rulers are on. To hide the rulers, choose the command again to remove the check.

1) Drag from the white part of the top ruler to place a horizontal guide on top of a grid line on the page. Center this line between the top and bottom edges of the the canvas.

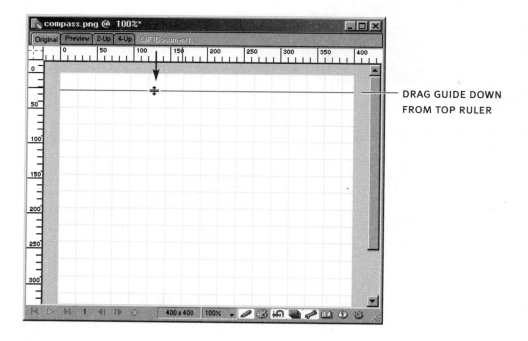

DRAG GUIDE DOWN
FROM TOP RULER

As you drag, you'll see a green line (the guide) move on the canvas. As you drag over a grid line, you'll feel the "pull" of the grid. You want the guide line over the center grid line. Release the mouse when you feel the guide snap to one of the grid lines.

2) Drag another guide from the white part of the left ruler to place a vertical guide on top of the center grid line on the page.

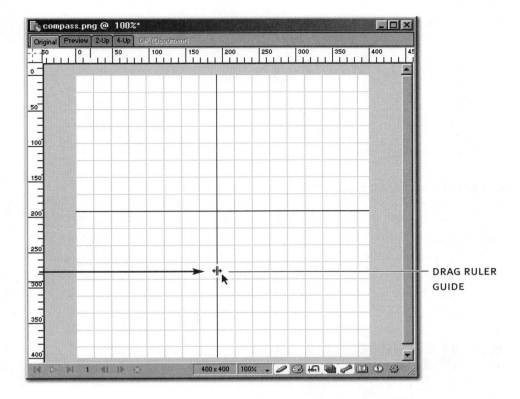

DRAG RULER GUIDE

3) Select the vertical guide by double-clicking it with the Pointer tool. In the Move Guide dialog box that opens, type *192*. Then click OK.

When you drag a guide from the rulers, you are visually placing the guide on the page. When you enter a value in the Move Guide dialog box, you are moving the guide to a set position (in pixels) on the canvas.

4) Repeat the process for the horizontal guide. Again, enter *192* in the Move Guide dialog box.

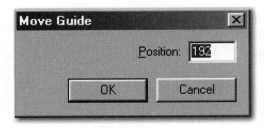

You can also move a guide by dragging it to a new location. When you move the mouse over a guide, the cursor changes to indicate that you have the guide and not another object. This works only if the guides are not locked.

 VERTICAL AND HORIZONTAL GUIDE CURSORS

To remove a guide from the canvas, just drag it out of the canvas area.

5) Choose View > Guides > Lock Guides.

You may want to lock the guides or rulers to avoid moving them inadvertently. You can also use the Guides dialog box to lock the guides. Choose View > Guides > Edit Guides to open the Guides dialog box. Here you can change the color of the guides, turn Snap to Guides on or off, lock the guides, and clear all the guides from the page. You can also change the color of slice guides (discussed in Lesson 9) and show or hide the slice guides.

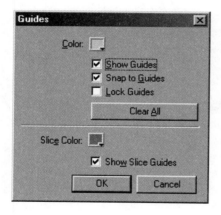

NOTE *Double-clicking a guide does not open the Move Guide dialog box if the guides are locked.*

DRAWING THE COMPASS

Now you are ready to begin drawing the compass using the Ellipse tool.

1) Choose the Ellipse tool on the Tools panel.

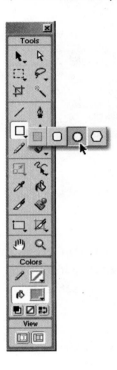

The ellipse you will draw needs to have a stroke and no fill. Strokes (the line around an object) and fills (the color or pattern within the object) are covered in more detail in Lesson 4. For now, you'll remove the fill and set the stroke to a thin line. The completed logo has a fill and no stroke, but it is easier to draw initially with a stroke. You will add a fill and remove the stroke at the end of the exercise.

2) Choose Window > Fill and choose None from the Fill category pop-up menu. Choose Window > Stroke and choose Pencil from the Stroke category pop-up menu. Click the color box on the panel. Use the Eyedropper to select black from the color palette.

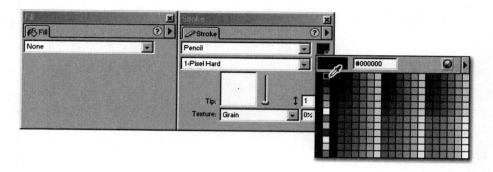

TIP *Changing the Stroke and Fill options before you draw on the canvas sets the defaults for subsequent objects you draw.*

3) Position the cursor where the guides cross. Hold down Alt (Windows) or Option (Macintosh) to draw a circle from the center; then, as you are dragging, add Shift to constrain the shape to a circle. Use the grid lines to create a circle that is three grid lines wide from the center point.

TIP *Release the mouse button before you release the modifier keys; otherwise you'll get an ellipse instead of a circle.*

NOTE *When you move over a guide, the Ellipse tool pointer turns red. The red color does not display on the Macintosh. Macintosh users: Try setting your preferences to use precise cursors to change the pointer to red when you are over a guide. Choose Edit > Preferences, then choose Editing from the Category pop-up menu, and then select Precise Cursors.*

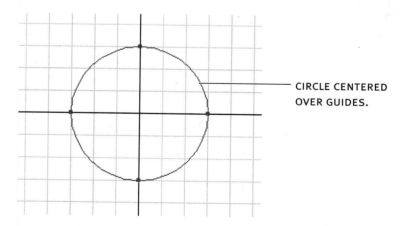

CIRCLE CENTERED
OVER GUIDES.

The next step is to draw tick marks for the compass. Tick marks are equally spaced around the compass. For this compass, you want eight tick marks. By doing a little math, you can determine that the tick marks will be 45 degrees apart: there are 360 degrees in a circle, and this value divided by the eight lines results in 45 degrees. You'll draw one line, copy it, rotate the copy, and then repeat the process for the remaining lines.

4) Select the Line tool on the Tools panel. Draw a vertical line that is longer than the circle.

Move the cursor above the circle about halfway between the grid lines, using the vertical guide to position the cursor. To draw a straight line, hold down Shift as you drag downward. Release the mouse when you are below the circle.

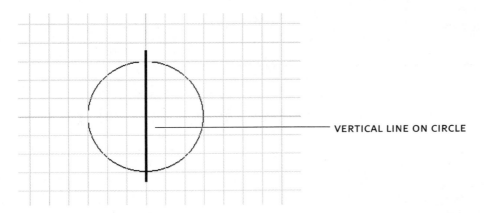

VERTICAL LINE ON CIRCLE

Before you drew the circle, you set the stroke to Pencil, with a black color. That default stroke is applied to the line you just drew.

5) Choose Edit > Clone to make an exact copy of the line.

The copy is placed directly on top of the line and is selected. Cloning a line is the same as choosing Copy and then Paste—it just saves you a step. It is important to realize that the clone of the object is on top of the copied object, even though you can't see it.

NOTE *After you draw the vertical line, the guide makes it difficult to select the line. You'll find that you select the guide instead of the line. You can lock or hide the guides to make this task easier. The guides should already be locked from a previous step, but you may want to hide the guides as well. Choose View > Guides > Show Guides to hide the guides.*

ROTATING AN OBJECT

The next step is to rotate the clone of the line for another tick mark.

1) With the cloned line still selected, choose Modify > Transform > Numeric Transform. In the Numeric Transform dialog box that appears, choose Rotate from the pop-up menu.

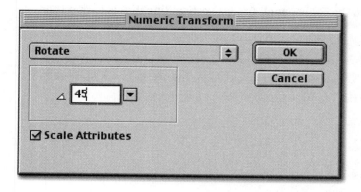

The numeric transform command rotates the object around its centerpoint. You can also rotate objects 90 or 180 degrees using the Modify > Transform submenu.

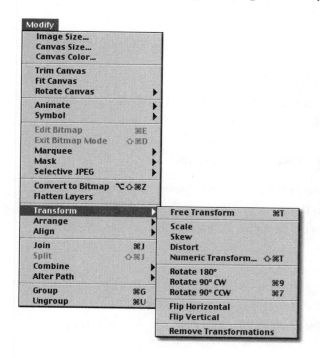

2) Type 45 in the Rotate text box and then click OK.

A positive number rotates the object clockwise; a negative number rotates the object counterclockwise. You need a total of four lines, each at a 45-degree angle from the last line. (The four lines when cut will give you the eight tick marks for the compass.) The lines cut the circle like a pie. You could repeat the steps of cloning and then rotating the clone, but there is an easier way to repeat the last steps you performed.

NOTE *The original line disappears, but it is only obscured by the guides. To verify that it is there, move the pointer over the line. The line appears in red. If you deselected Mouse Highlight on the Options panel, the red line is not visible.*

THE HISTORY PANEL

The History panel records each step you perform as you create objects on the canvas. Each time you use Edit > Undo, you are stepping back a step on the History panel. The History panel makes it easy to see your steps and undo multiple actions. You can also use the History panel to repeat a set of actions. For example, you've just performed two actions: you cloned a line and then you rotated the line. You will now use the History panel to repeat those two actions two more times to draw the remaining lines.

1) Choose Window > History to open the History panel.

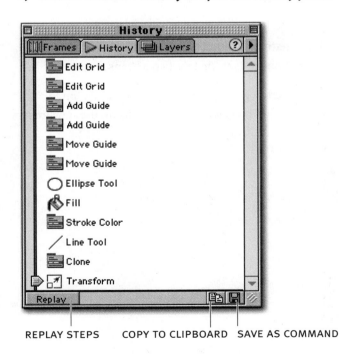

REPLAY STEPS   COPY TO CLIPBOARD   SAVE AS COMMAND

The History panel displays a list of all of your past actions. The number of actions saved is based on your preferences. The default number is 20. You can change this number by choosing Edit > Preferences. On the General tab, type a new number in the Undo Steps text box. You can enter any number between 0 and 100; however, a large number increases the RAM requirement for the application. Unless you have an enormous amount of free RAM, leave the default set to 20. That should be plenty for most of your work. If you do make a change to Undo Steps, you'll need to quit and then relaunch Fireworks to make the change take effect.

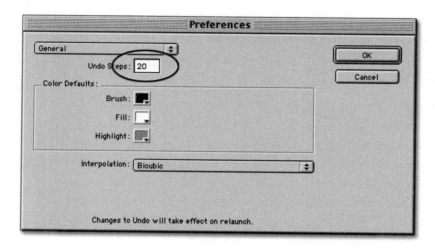

2) Scroll down to the bottom of the History list until you see the last two actions: Clone and Transform. Hold down Shift and select the last two actions.

These last two steps need to be repeated to get the other lines around the circle. Since the last rotated line is selected, when you clone and rotate again, the new line repeats the move around the circle.

3) Click Replay, located at the bottom left of the History panel. A new line is drawn at a 45-degree angle from the last line. Click Replay again to draw the last line.

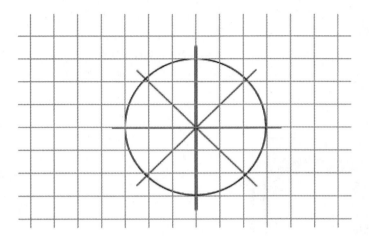

NOTE *The last line rotated needs to be selected, or Replay will not work.*

The History panel can replay steps, as you've just seen, and it can be used to step back through your actions, like a super undo function. To undo your steps with the History panel, just drag the slider on the left up; to redo the steps, drag the slider down. You can also save your steps for actions you will be performing again. For example, in the preceding step, you cloned and rotated the line. You used the Replay button twice to create the other lines. If you know that you will want to perform that same action again, you can save the steps as a command.

4) Hold down Shift and select the Clone and Transform actions on the History panel if they are not already selected. Click the diskette icon at the bottom of the History panel or use the Options pop-up menu on the panel and choose Save as Command. In the Save Command dialog box, type *Clone and Rotate*. Click OK.

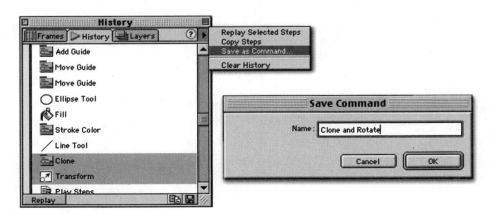

67

Those actions are now saved as a single command on the Commands menu for you to use again.

To see how the saved command works, draw another line off to the side of the compass you are drawing. Choose Commands > Clone and Rotate. (The command name you entered appears on the Commands menu.) The line is cloned and then rotated. Repeat the command several more times. You don't need those extra lines, so you can delete them for this exercise.

USING THE KNIFE TOOL

The Knife tool switches its appearance depending on the editing mode. If you are in Vector mode—editing vector objects—you will see the Knife tool. If you are in Bitmap mode—editing bitmap images—the tool switches to the Eraser tool. The Knife tool is used for cutting paths. The Eraser tool is used for erasing pixels.

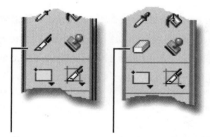

KNIFE TOOL (FOR VECTORS)   ERASER TOOL (FOR BITMAPS)

The finished logo has only tick marks (partial lines on the edges of the circle). The next step is to cut each line and remove the center portion. To cut a line, you use the Knife tool. To help you make the cuts, you will draw another circle, smaller than the first, and cut around the edges of the smaller circle (like a cookie cutter).

1) Choose the Ellipse tool and draw a smaller circle from the center out as you did before to create the first circle.

Use the guides you used for drawing the first circle as the center point for the smaller circle. This ensures that the smaller circle is centered within the larger circle. Use the grid lines to make this new circle two grid lines wide from the center point. (Remember to hold down the modifier keys—Alt or Option—to draw from the center out.)

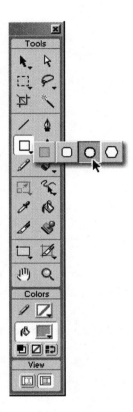

NOTE *A common mistake is choosing the Oval Marquee tool instead of the Ellipse tool. The Marquee tools are for selecting pixels in bitmaps. Here you are drawing vector objects. If you select the Marquee tool and click the canvas, you'll get an error message, and you will be switched to Bitmap mode. Click Exit Bitmap Mode (the red circle with the white "x") at the bottom of the document window to return to Vector mode.*

When you draw this circle, you get the stroke (Pencil) and fill (None) you set previously. If you don't, use the Fill and Stroke panels to set the circle to these options.

2) Select one of the lines with the Pointer tool and then select the Knife tool on the Tools panel.

The selected line appears blue, and you see the two end points on the line. Objects you draw with any vector tool are composed of paths. A path contains two or more points. The line you just drew is a path, with points at each end. The Knife tool is for cutting selected paths. If the path is not selected, the Knife tool won't work.

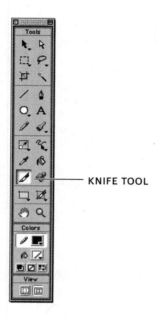

KNIFE TOOL

3) Drag the Knife cursor across the line, using the smaller circle to guide the placement of the cursor.

You don't have to drag a huge amount—just enough to cut through the line. When you release the mouse button, you'll see a point on the line. That is the cut you just made.

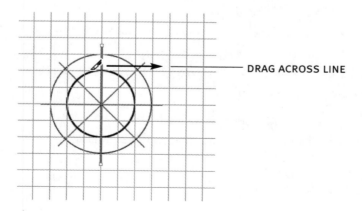

DRAG ACROSS LINE

4) Repeat the process at the other end of the line.

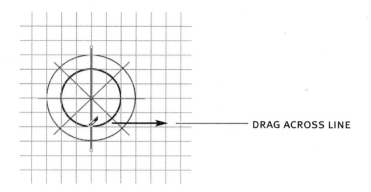

DRAG ACROSS LINE

5) Switch to the Pointer tool and click anywhere outside the circle to deselect the line. Select the center portion of the line between the two cuts; then press Delete to remove the line.

You just want the outside lines for the tick marks.

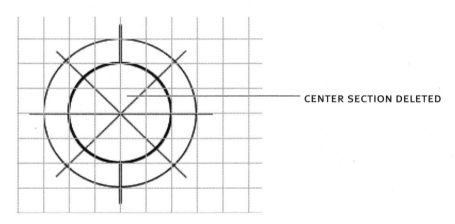

CENTER SECTION DELETED

6) Repeat from step 2 to cut and remove the center sections on the other lines.

> **TIP** *You have multiple items stacked on top of each other. Selecting the center portion of the line you just cut could be tricky. The Mouse Highlight option makes this task much easier. When you roll over objects, they appear in red. This makes it easy to see the center line before clicking to select it. If you don't see the red line, or if you've deselected the option, double-click the Pointer tool. Select Mouse Highlight on the Tool Options panel that appears.*

7) Save your work.

APPLYING FILL COLOR

When you draw objects on the canvas, the fill and stroke attributes last used are applied to the new object. You can use the Fill panel to change the fill type and color, or you can use the Fill color box pop-up window on the Tools panel to change the color of an object. For this next exercise, you will pick a fill color from a set of colors and apply the colors to the circles in the compass logo.

1) Open the Site_colors.png file in the Lesson03 folder.

This file contains the colors you will use for the circles and other objects you will draw in later lessons.

2) Resize and move the window so you can see both the compass logo you are working on and the color squares in this document.

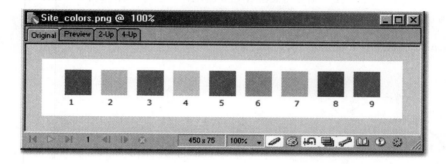

3) In your Compass.png file, select the outer circle in the compass.

The fill color for the selected object will be changed. For the outer circle, you want to use the second color square in the Site_colors.png file for the fill color.

4) Click the Fill color box pop-up window on the Tools panel and position the Eyedropper cursor over color 2 in the Site_colors.png file. Click this color to change the color of the selected circle.

The Eyedropper is used for selecting colors from the palette, but it also can be used for picking colors from an image on the canvas or from another document as you just did. This feature is very handy for ensuring that colors match from document to document.

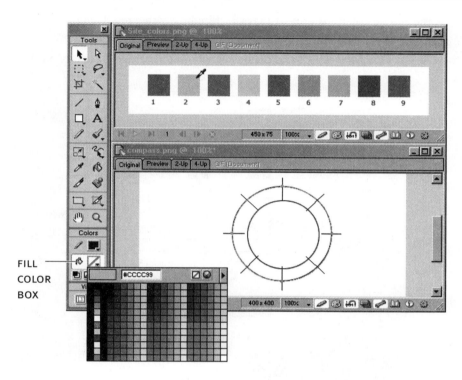

FILL
COLOR
BOX

5) Repeat step 4 to color the smaller inner circle in the compass using color 3 in the Site_colors.png file.

The circles still have the stroke you applied earlier to make them easier to work with. Now with the fill applied to the circles, the stroke is no longer needed. To add the stroke, you used the Stroke panel, and you could remove the stroke in the same manner. There is a another method you might prefer that accomplishes the same task.

6) Select both circles with the Pointer tool. Click the Stroke color box on the Tools panel.

In the top row of the color box palette, you see, from left to right, the selected color, the hexadecimal color value, a white square with a red diagonal line, and a color wheel.

7) Select the white square with the line to remove the stroke.

Notice that the Stroke color box now displays a white box with a red diagonal line, indicating that there is no stroke applied to the selected object. To apply a stroke again, you can just select the object and pick a color from the Stroke color box on the Tools panel.

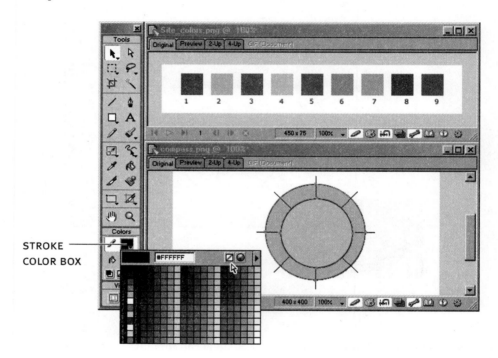

STROKE
COLOR BOX

NOTE *If you apply a stroke from the Stroke color box on the Tools panel, you get the default stroke applied to your object. To change the width or the stroke type, you need to use the Stroke panel.*

USING THE POLYGON TOOL

The last step in completing the compass logo is to draw a four-pointed star on top of the inner circle. Using the polygon tool makes this task a snap.

1) Choose the Polygon tool on the Tools panel.

With the Polygon tool, you can draw any equilateral polygon, from a triangle to a 360-sided polygon. With the star option on the Polygon tool, you can draw stars with 3 to 360 points and a full range of point angles.

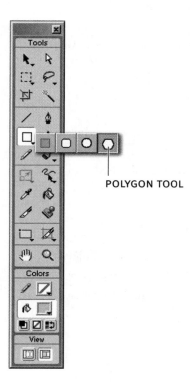

POLYGON TOOL

2) Double-click the tool to open the Tool Options panel. Select Star from the Shape pop-up menu. Type *4* in the Sides text box and *26* in the Angle text box.

If your guides are not visible, turn them on again by choosing View > Guides > Show Guides.

3) Click and drag from the center point of the guides to draw the star. Rotate the star as you drag to position the points between the tick marks on the circle. Make the star larger than the smaller circle. Change the color of the star to white.

You can use the Fill color box on the Tools panel to change the color of the star.

You now have the completed compass for the logo. It is composed of many objects. To make sure all the objects stay together if you move them, you need to group them.

4) Select all of the objects in the compass by choosing Edit > Select All; then choose Modify > Group.

TRIMMING THE CANVAS

The final step is to make the document size smaller. You need to trim the excess white area of the canvas around the image to make the image size as small as possible. There is a cropping tool you can use, but the easiest method is to use the built-in trimming feature.

1) Choose Modify > Trim Canvas, and the work is done for you.

Fireworks makes the canvas as small as it can without cutting off any object. Fireworks knows the exact size and placement of all objects on the page, even if they are not visible. Soft edges such as drop shadows and glows are even accounted for and preserved on the canvas.

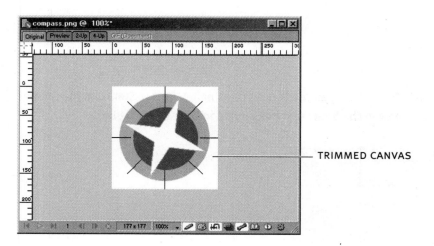

TRIMMED CANVAS

2) Save your file. You'll use this compass in later exercises.

You can close this file, but leave the Site_colors.png file open for the next exercise.

USING THE INFO PANEL

The Info panel provides you with the selected object's size and placement on the canvas. You can also change those values by typing the exact numbers you want on the panel. In addition, you can see the current pointer position and color values of the pixel under the pointer. These values are updated as you move the cursor.

1) Create a new document. Make the canvas size 400 x 400 and the color white. Save your file and name it *Compass_logo.png*.

You are going to create a logo using the compass you just created.

2) Draw a rectangle on the page using the Rectangle tool. Change the color of the rectangle to color 1 in the Site_colors.png file. Draw the rectangle any size on the canvas.

In the next step, you'll use the Info panel to change the size of the rectangle.

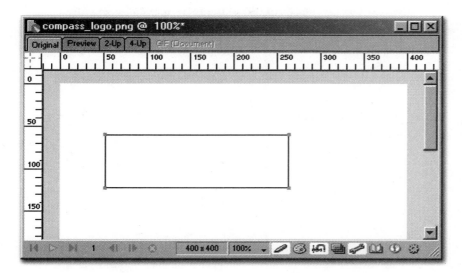

3) Choose Window > Info to display the Info panel.

The width (W) of the rectangle should be 165. The height (H) of the rectangle should be 35.

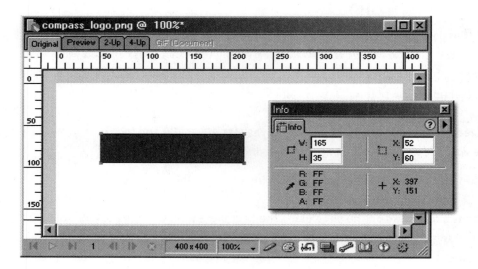

4) Type *165* in the text box for the width (W) of the rectangle and press Enter (Windows) or Return (Macintosh). Type *35* in the text box for the height (H) of the rectangle and press Enter (Windows) or Return (Macintosh).

This makes the rectangle the exact size you need for the logo.

TIP *You can use the Tab key to move to the next text box on the Info panel. Press Enter (Windows) or Return (Macintosh) to set the amounts and exit the panel.*

IMPORTING IMAGES

Macromedia Fireworks provides a wealth of tools for creating graphics, but you still may want to import graphics from other sources. For example, you may want to import a company logo created in Macromedia FreeHand or import a scanned image from Adobe Photoshop to combine with buttons you've created in Fireworks.

Fireworks can import these formats: PNG; GIF; JPEG; PICT; BMP; TIFF; xRes LRG; ASCII; RTF; Adobe Photoshop 3, 4, 5, and 6; Adobe Illustrator 7; Macromedia FreeHand 7, 8, and 9; and uncompressed CorelDRAW 7.

To finish the compass logo, you need to add the compass you just completed and some text. The text was created in Macromedia FreeHand and converted into a graphic for you to use.

1) Choose File > Import and navigate to the Compass.png file you created earlier. Select that file and click Open.

The cursor changes to a corner angle.

2) Position the Import cursor on the canvas where you want the upper left corner of the compass to appear. Click to place the object at its default size.

To scale the object, you drag it. The compass you created needs to be smaller. You can drag with the import cursor to scale it, or you can scale it after you import. For this exercise it is easier to scale after you import the compass.

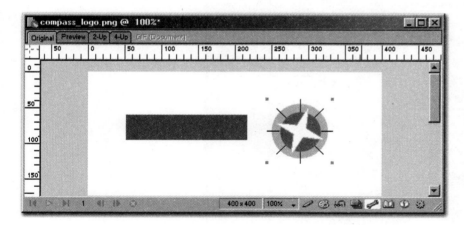

3) Move the compass on top of the rectangle. To make the compass smaller, hold down Shift and drag a corner handle.

Because you grouped the compass, all of the objects in the compass scale together as you drag a corner handle.

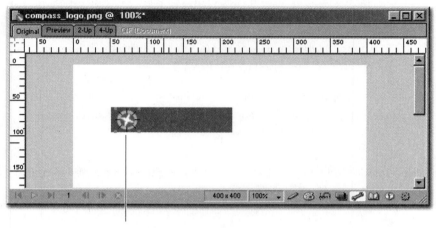

COMPASS ON RECTANGLE

4) Choose File > Import and navigate to the Compass_text.fh9 file located in the Lesson03 folder. Select that file and click Open.

In the Vector File Options dialog box, you define specific settings.

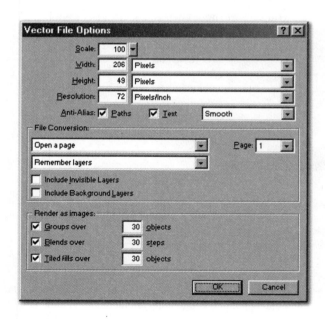

- **Scale**: Specify the scale percentage for the imported file.

- **Width and Height**: Specify in pixels the width and height of the imported file.

- **Resolution**: Specify the resolution of the imported file.

- **Anti-Alias**: Set a soft edge around imported objects.

- **File Conversion**: Specify how multipage documents are handled when imported.

  Open a Page: Import only the specified page.

  Open Pages as Frames: Import all the pages from the document and place each on a separate frame in Fireworks.

  Remember Layers: Maintain the layer structure of the imported file.

  Ignore Layers: Delete the layer structure of the imported file. All objects are placed on the currently selected layer.

  Convert Layers to Frames: Place each layer of the imported document in a separate frame in Fireworks.

  Include Invisible Layers: Import objects on layers that have been turned off. Otherwise, invisible layers are ignored.

  Include Background Layers: Import objects from the document's Background layer. Otherwise, the Background layer is ignored.

- **Render as Images**: Rasterize (convert to bitmap) complex groups, blends, or tiled fills and place them as a single image object in a Fireworks document. Enter a number in the text box to determine how many objects a group, blend, or tiled fill can contain before it is rasterized during import.

NOTE *Vector file options do not apply when you paste or drag an object from another application.*

5) Click OK to select the default vector options.

You don't need to make any changes for this project.

6) Click to place the graphic on the page. Move the text to the left side of the rectangle and scale (hold down Shift and drag a corner handle) to fit within your rectangle. To finish, trim the canvas and save the file.

WHAT YOU HAVE LEARNED

In this lesson, you have:

- Used grids and guides for placing objects [pages 56–60]

- Drawn basic shapes [pages 61–63]

- Rotated an object numerically [pages 64–65]

- Used the History panel and saved a command for steps you want to repeat [pages 65–68]

- Used the Knife tool to cut a path [pages 68–71]

- Used the Polygon tool to draw a star [pages 75–76]

- Trimmed the canvas [page 76]

- Used the Info panel to size an object [pages 77–78]

- Imported images [pages 79–82]

text, fills, and live effects

You can use Fireworks to create buttons or graphic elements for your Web pages, but you can also design and export an entire page for use on the Web. If you want to add text to the page, the resulting HTML document can be opened and edited in Dreamweaver. You'll do that in a later lesson. In this lesson, you will use Fireworks to create an entire Web page.

If you want to review the final result of this project, open the Adventure.png file in the Completed folder within the Lesson04 folder.

In this lesson you will create this Web page from scratch. You use the compass and compass logo you created earlier, create the buttons, and learn to mask images within a shape.

WHAT YOU WILL LEARN

In this lesson, you will:

- Add text and special effects to your document

- Fill objects with color, patterns, and textures

- Build a custom color palette

- Add a mask to isolate a portion of an image

APPROXIMATE TIME

This lesson takes approximately 2 hours to complete.

LESSON FILES

Media Files:

Lesson04\Images\climber.png

Lesson04\Images\diver.png

Lesson04\Images\kayak.png

Lesson04\Images\mountain_biker.png

Lesson04\Swatches\Site_colors.gif

Lesson04\Swatches\Site_colors.png

Lesson04\Text\Welcome.txt

Starting Files:

None

Completed Projects:

Lesson04\Completed\Adventure.png

ADDING TEXT

Fireworks is a very powerful graphics program for creating Web and interactive images. No matter how creative and informative your images are, though, you will still want to provide labels for your buttons or text for your banner ads. Fireworks provides many features for applying and formatting text in your images.

Text in a Fireworks document saved in the original PNG file format is always editable. However, after you export the image as a GIF or JPEG file, the text becomes part of the bitmap image and cannot be changed. Thus, you should always keep the original Fireworks file (the PNG file) along with the exported images in case the text needs to be changed.

1) Create a new document with a size of 640 x 480 pixels and a white canvas. Save your file and name it *Adventure.png*.

You will create a Web page for the fictitious adventure travel company Compass Adventure Tours. The page size (640 x 480) is the size of a 13-inch monitor.

In the early days of the Web, most users had 13-inch monitors. The price of monitors has dropped greatly, and now more users have 17-inch monitors. Today, most Web designers build their pages based on the larger 17-inch size: 800 x 600 pixels. You'll be using the smaller size in all these exercises, however. When designing your Web pages, you need to determine the smallest screen size of your users and design the pages accordingly.

2) Import the compass and compass logo you created in Lesson 3.

If you no longer have those files, you can use the Compass_logo.png and Compass.png files from the Completed folder in the Lesson03 folder. If the objects in the logo and compass are not grouped, choose Modify > Group after you import each one to make them easier to manage.

3) **Move the logo to the top left of the canvas and the compass to the top right. You may need to scale the compass. Be sure the objects are grouped; then hold down Shift and drag a corner handle to make the compass smaller.**

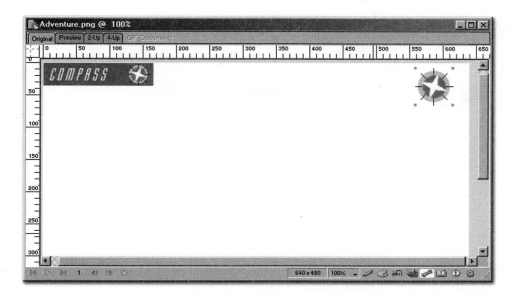

4) **Choose the Text tool from the Tools panel. Click where you want the text to start, or click and drag to draw a text box of the desired size.**

When you release the mouse, the Text Editor window opens.

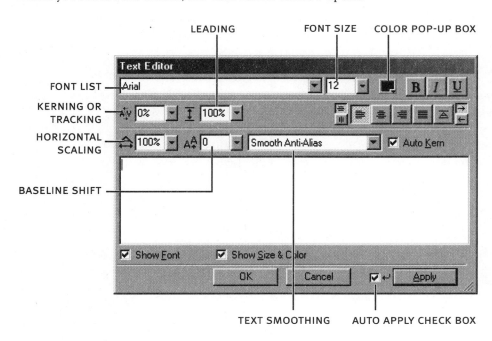

TEXT, FILLS, AND LIVE EFFECTS

5) In the Text Editor, type *Adventure Travel*.

Within the Text Editor window, you have all the formatting controls for your text. If you want to see the formatted text displayed in the Text Editor window, select Show Font and Show Size & Color. If you want to see the text you type constantly updated in the document window, select the Auto-Apply check box (to the left of the Apply button). Clicking Apply updates the document window if you don't select Auto-Apply.

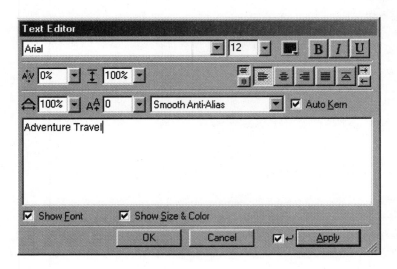

⊙ **POWER TIP** *If you click and drag with the Text tool, you can draw the text box the exact size you need. Any text you type in the Text Editor wraps within the text box. If you just click with the Text tool on the canvas, the text box expands horizontally based on the amount of text. You then need to resize the box with the Pointer tool.*

6) Format the text. Change the font to Impact (or Arial Black if Impact is not on your machine). Change the point size to 32. Change the fill color of the selected text to black. Click OK to close the Text Editor.

Formatting text in Fireworks is similar to formatting text in a word processor. If the text you want to format is not selected in the Text Editor, drag to select all or portions of the text.

Use the Font pop-up list to change the font. Use the Size slider (or type a number) to change the point size. Use the Fill color box pop-up window to change the color of the selected text.

7) Add the text *the latest in* **to your page. Format it as Times, 24 points. Then switch to the Pointer tool and move the text above the Adventure Travel text block.**

NOTE *You can position the text block on the page even while you are in the Text Editor. The cursor displays a Hand tool when you move outside the Text Editor window.*

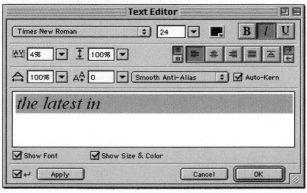

If you feel your text "pull" as you try to place it, you might still have Snap to Grid on from the preceding lesson. Turn it off if you find it distracting (choose View > Grid > Snap to Grid).

From the Text menu, you can make basic changes to the formatting of the text without accessing the Text Editor. These commands are handy when you want to change all of the text within the text box at once. If you want to make changes to a single word within the text, you will still need to use the Text Editor.

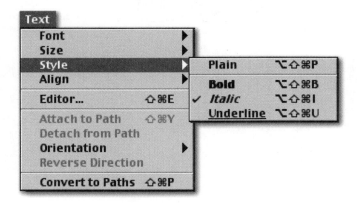

FORMATTING TEXT

Using the following text editing options, experiment with the text you just created.

1) Double-click the text—*the latest in*—with the Pointer tool to open the Text Editor window. Highlight the text you want to change. Use the Horizontal Scale slider to change the selected text.

You can alter text by using a technique called horizontal scaling. This changes the width of the text without changing the height, as if you were stretching the text on a rubber band. Be careful not to overdo the stretching; you are electronically distorting the text without regard to its original design.

The values are expressed as percentages. Values less than 100 percent condense the text; values greater than 100 percent expand the text.

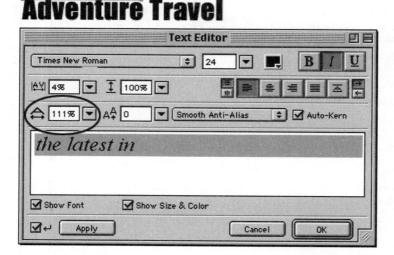

2) Use the Baseline Shift slider to change the selected text.

Baseline shift raises or lowers the text relative to the baseline (the invisible line the text sits on). You would use this option for formatting text such as H_2O, where you want the "2" to be lower than the letters. Normally, you would not format all of your text with a baseline shift, since it is just as easy to move the text on the canvas.

A positive number raises the text above the baseline; a negative number lowers the text below the baseline.

NOTE *Formatting, such as baseline shift, remains as the default in the Text Editor. The next time you add text, Fireworks remembers the last settings and applies them to your text. If your text appears to be outside the text box, you probably left baseline shift on. While this doesn't harm your text—it will export just fine—it is distracting as you design your page.*

3) Select all of the text in the Text Editor. Drag the Kerning slider to adjust the spacing between the letters.

Range kerning (also referred to as tracking in other programs) controls the amount of space between the selected letters. Negative values decrease the space; positive values increase the space. You can select all of the text or portions of the text and apply this formatting.

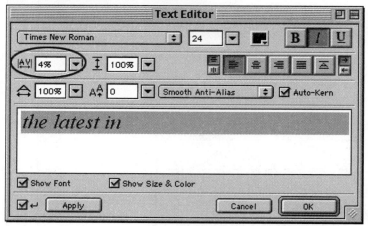

TIP *This formatting control can make it easier to read smaller text on the screen.*

Kerning is the amount of space between two letters. The same slider controls this formatting. If the cursor is between two letters, you are kerning; if you have two or more letters selected, you are applying range kerning. As with range kerning, negative values decrease the space; positive values increase the space.

NOTE *The Text Editor window does not show the effects of kerning and tracking.*

APPLYING FILLS AND COLORS

Next, you will draw a simple navigation button. In a later lesson, you will use the Button Editor to make fully working buttons. For now, you will create the design and pick the colors for the button.

When you create Web graphics, it is important to use Web-safe colors. Web-safe colors are colors that are displayed correctly in different browsers and on different computer systems. You can choose from 216 Web-safe colors. As long as you pick colors from this cross-platform palette, you are ensured of predictable results as users access your pages. The colors in your images will resemble your original design as much as possible.

There are several ways to pick colors in Fireworks. You can use the color boxes on the Tools panel as you did in the previous lesson. You can use the preset color palettes that Fireworks provides by using the Swatches panel. Or you can use your own color mix by creating it with the Color Mixer and then storing your color on the Swatches panel.

1) Draw a rectangle on the canvas.

There will be five navigation buttons across the page, so make sure that your button is not too large.

2) Use the Info panel to make the rectangle _115_ pixels wide and _25_ pixels high.

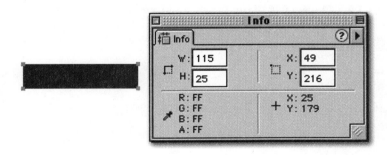

Next, you will pick a color for the button.

3) Choose Window > Swatches to access the Swatches panel.

If a check mark appears next to Swatches in the Window menu, the panel is open.

When you create your graphics, you generally will choose your colors from one color palette. This prevents colors on your page from shifting when you move from page to page or when your page is viewed on different computer platforms. You can also use palettes to ensure that all colors on your pages adhere to a particular color scheme. The Swatches panel holds the colors either from a set of preset swatches or from swatches you create or modify.

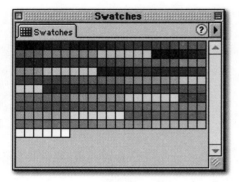

4) Click the right arrow at the top of the panel to access the Swatches options pop-up menu. Choose a palette from one of the preset palettes.

The preset palettes to choose from are Color Cubes, Continuous Tone, Windows System, Macintosh System, and Grayscale. Color Cubes is the default palette, displaying the Web-safe colors in groups of related colors. Continuous Tone displays the same Web-safe colors, but they flow from one color to another. The Windows

System and Macintosh System colors limit the colors to those found in each system. You would use those colors only if you are designing Web pages where all the users were on one system. The Grayscale palette limits the colors to grayscale.

5) With the rectangle selected, choose a color from the Swatches panel.

The rectangle changes to that color. The Swatches panel works well if you want your color choices always visible, but there are other ways to apply colors to selected objects. All the color boxes (on the Tools panel, Fills panel, Stroke panel, and Edit Gradient panel) contain the same Options pop-up menu for selected palettes.

6) Select the Fill color box on the Tools panel and click the right arrow to open the Options pop-up menu.

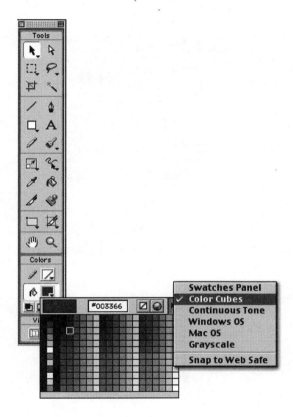

7) Choose a color palette from one of the options.

The color palette you choose now appears in the Stroke color box, the color boxes on the Stroke and Fill panels, and the color box in the Text Editor.

NOTE *If an object is selected when you pick a color, its stroke or fill (depending on the color box selected) changes to the color you pick. Any new object you draw uses that new color.*

8) Select the Stroke color box on the Tools panel and choose a stroke color.

If you add a stroke to an object by choosing a color from the Stroke color box on the Tools panel, the stroke style added is a 1-pixel soft pencil. If you change the color of an existing stroke using the Stroke color box on the Tools panel, only the color is changed. Look at the Stroke panel to see the stroke style of the object.

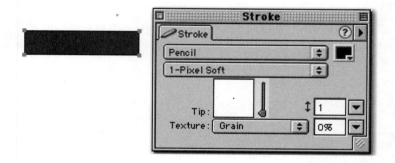

9) Select the Polygon tool to add the triangle on the button. Double-click the tool to access the Tool Options panel. Select Polygon from the Shape pop-up menu and type 3 for the number of sides.

Now draw the triangle.

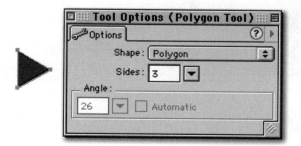

10) Draw the triangle off to one side of the rectangle, making it larger than would fit within the rectangle. Rotate as you drag, releasing the mouse when the left side of the triangle is vertical. Change the color of the triangle to a contrasting color from that of the rectangle.

> **TIP** *It is easier to see when the left edge of a triangle is vertical when you draw a larger triangle; you can later scale it smaller.*

11) Select the Scale tool on the Tools panel.

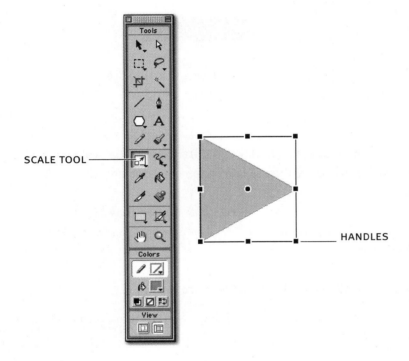

SCALE TOOL

HANDLES

Handles appear around the triangle.

The Scale tool can be used both to scale and rotate an object. Move the pointer close to (but not touching) one of the corner handles. The cursor changes to a circular arrow, indicating that you are in rotating mode.

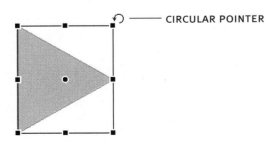

CIRCULAR POINTER

Move the pointer on top of one of the handles. The cursor changes to a double-ended arrow, indicating that you are in scale mode.

12) Using the Scale cursor, drag the corner handle, moving it in toward the center. Release the mouse when the triangle is small enough to fit inside your rectangle.

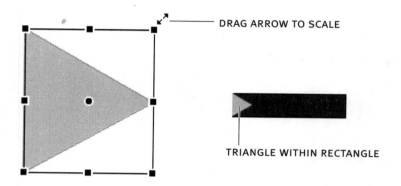

DRAG ARROW TO SCALE

TRIANGLE WITHIN RECTANGLE

13) Press Enter (Windows) or Return (Macintosh) to release the Scale tool and change the triangle size. Move the triangle on top of the rectangle.

NOTE *When you use the Scale tool, you do not have to hold down Shift to proportionally scale an object. If you scale a grouped object without the Scale tool, you must hold down Shift for proportional scaling.*

14) Select the Text tool and add the text *Adventure Tours*.

Use two lines for the text, pressing Enter (Windows) or Return (Macintosh) after *Adventure* to separate the two words.

15) In the Text Editor, change the font to *Verdana*, the point size to *10*, and the color to white. The text also needs to be aligned at the right, so click Right Alignment.

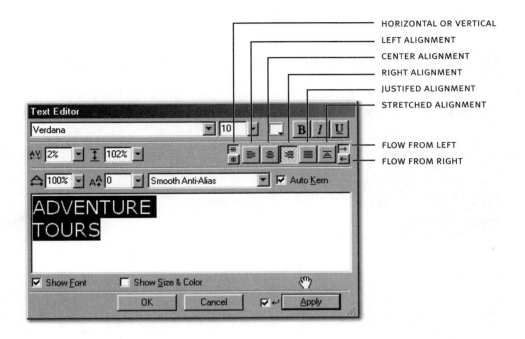

HORIZONTAL OR VERTICAL
LEFT ALIGNMENT
CENTER ALIGNMENT
RIGHT ALIGNMENT
JUSTIFED ALIGNMENT
STRETCHED ALIGNMENT

FLOW FROM LEFT
FLOW FROM RIGHT

16) While you are still in the Text Editor, move the text on the rectangle.

Since the text is so small, it may be difficult to read. Notice the soft edges around the text. That softness is caused by the anti-aliasing controls in the Text Editor. Anti-aliasing is a method of blurring the edges around vector objects so they appear smooth on the screen. On large-sized text, the smoothness enhances the appearance of the text. On smaller text, the anti-aliasing sometimes causes the text to blur together. You can control text anti-aliasing from the Anti-alias pop-up menu in the Text Editor.

17) If necessary, change the anti-aliasing setting to make your text easier to read. Then click OK.

Your choices here are No Anti-Alias, Crisp Anti-Alias, Strong Anti-Alias, and Smooth Anti-Alias. Experiment with each setting to determine the best choice.

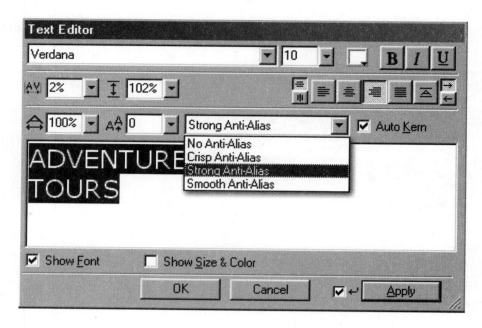

When you have text with two or more lines, you may need to adjust the spacing between the lines: the leading. The name leading (pronounced "ledding") comes from early hand typesetting days when lead blocks were placed between each row of the metal type. The size of the block of lead controlled the spacing between each line of type.

18) Drag the slider or type a value in the Leading text box.

Numbers less than 100 percent tighten the spacing between the lines; numbers greater than 100 percent increase the spacing between the lines.

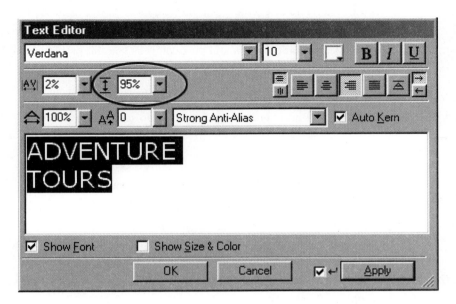

19) Select all of the objects in the button and group them. Save your file.

In a later task, you are going to duplicate this button for the other buttons. Grouping the button ensures that all the elements in the button stay together.

BUILDING CUSTOM PALETTES

In the last exercise, you explored the preset palettes on the the Swatches panel. You can also mix your own colors, and you can build a custom color palette to be used as you build the pages in your site. The Site_colors.png file you used earlier contained nine color chips. Say, for example, that you want to limit the colors in your site to those nine colors. You could leave that file open and pick colors as you did previously, but that method is a bit awkward, especially if you have a small monitor.

In this exercise, you will build a custom palette from the Site_colors.png file so the colors are always available as you build your pages. You will also see how to add new colors to that palette.

The Site_colors.png file you used to pick colors can be imported as a swatch. Then the colors you need will always be available. To create the swatch file, the Site_colors.png file was exported as a GIF file. All the colors (including the white canvas) are included in the GIF file. You will learn about exporting files in a later lesson. You can use any GIF image to create your own swatch files.

1) Click the right arrow on the Swatches panel to access the Swatches options pop-up menu. Choose Replace Swatches.

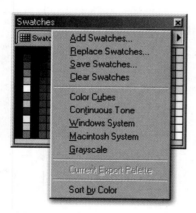

2) Select the Site_colors.gif file located in the Swatches folder within the Lesson04 folder and then click Open.

If you are on a Windows computer, you need to change the Files of Type setting to GIF.

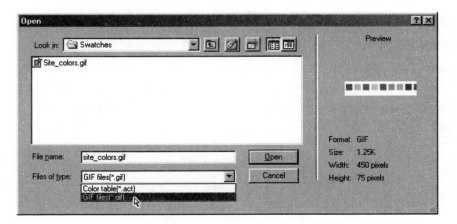

All the colors in your Swatches panel are replaced by the colors contained in that file. Your Swatches panel now displays 11 color chips—the 9 original colors, white from the canvas color, and transparent.

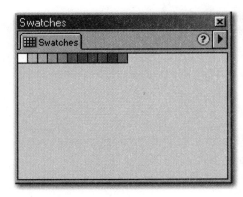

NOTE *You also have the option of adding, saving, or clearing the swatches. Add Swatches adds the new colors to an existing palette of colors, Replace Swatches replaces all the current swatches with new ones, Clear Swatches removes all of the current colors on the Swatches panel, and Save Swatches exports the current color palette. If you are working with a team, you can save your color palette and give it to the other team members. They can then use either Add Swatches or Replace Swatches to import your colors to their machines.*

The colors on the Swatches panel are now available within your Fireworks application and will remain available until you clear or replace them.

Notice that black did not appear as one of the colors. In the next step, you will add black to your custom Swatches palette.

3) Select black from the Fill color box on the Tools panel. Move the mouse over a noncolored (gray) area at the bottom of the Swatches panel.

The cursor changes to a paint bucket.

4) Click when you see the paint bucket to add the currently selected color (black) to the panel.

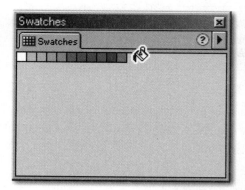

5) Choose a few more colors from the Fill color box and add them to the Swatches panel.

Now you will remove some colors.

6) Hold down Ctrl (Windows) or Command (Macintosh) and move the pointer over a color on the Swatches panel that you want to delete.

The cursor changes to a Scissors cursor.

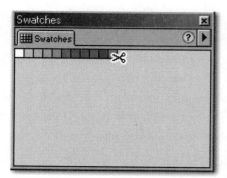

7) Click the color you want to delete.

TIP *If you find that the color chips on the Swatches panel are too small (especially when trying to delete one with the Scissors cursor), you can make them bigger by increasing the size of the panel. Drag the lower right corner of the panel to increase the size.*

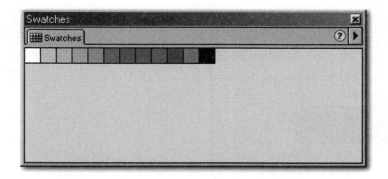

Once you have the Swatches panel to your liking, you can access it from any color box.

8) Click the Fill color box on the Tools panel and then click the right arrow to select the Options pop-up menu. Choose Swatches Panel from the list.

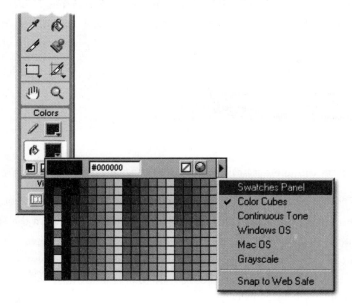

All the other color boxes will now display the colors from the Swatches palette. If you want to restore the color boxes to the preset colors, use the Options pop-up menu and choose a preset palette from the list.

ALIGNING OBJECTS

When you are creating buttons or other objects on your page, you may want to align the buttons or objects with each other. You can also distribute objects equally on the page.

1) Continuing in the same file as in the previous task, select the grouped button and choose Edit > Duplicate.

There are several ways to make a copy of an object. As you learn the different methods, you will find one method you prefer. In other lessons, you will learn production techniques that speed up the duplication of objects on your page.

2) Switch to the Pointer tool and move the new button to the right of the first button.

How can you confirm that the second button is placed vertically the same as the first button? You learned about the Info panel for controlling the width and height of an object. The Info panel also displays the X and Y values of the object. You can select each button and check the Y values to confirm that they are the same. You can also turn on Snap to Grid, aligning each button to a grid line, or you can pull down a ruler guide to the top of the first button and then move the second button to the guide. But wait; there is another method.

3) Using the Pointer tool, select both buttons and choose Modify > Align > Top.

Fireworks aligns objects on the left based on the leftmost object in the selected group, and it aligns objects on the right based on the rightmost object in the selected group. The topmost object controls Align Top, and the bottommost object controls Align Bottom. For Distribute Widths, Fireworks creates an equal amount of space between the objects, divided between the right edge of the leftmost and left edge of the rightmost objects. For Distribute Heights, Fireworks creates an equal amount of space between the objects, divided between the bottom edge of the highest and top edge of the lowest objects.

TIP *In Windows, you can also use alignment buttons located on the Modify toolbar. If this toolbar is not visible at the top of your application window, choose Window > Toolbars > Modify. This toolbar can float on the screen as an independent window, or you can manually attach it to the top or bottom of the application window by dropping it there.*

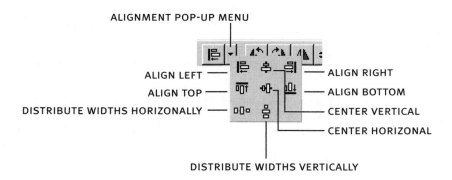

ALIGNMENT POP-UP MENU

ALIGN LEFT

ALIGN TOP

DISTRIBUTE WIDTHS HORIZONALLY

ALIGN RIGHT

ALIGN BOTTOM

CENTER VERTICAL

CENTER HORIZONAL

DISTRIBUTE WIDTHS VERTICALLY

ON YOUR OWN

Use what you've learned to create three more duplicates of the first button, for a total of five buttons. Align them all at the top and choose Modify > Align > Distribute Widths to distribute them horizontally (left to right). Move all of the buttons to the top of the page, below the Adventure Travel text. Change the text in the new buttons to *Featured Destinations*, *Adventure Gear*, *Travel Logs*, and *About Us*. Then save your file.

What is the easiest way to change the text in the grouped buttons? Remember the Subselection tool? It is for selecting one item in the group. With the Subselection tool, you can access just the text box in the group, double-click it, and then change the text in the Text Editor.

ADDING LIVE EFFECTS

Live Effects are pixel-based effects that apply to vector, bitmap, and text objects. Applying a Live Effect does not permanently change the original object—the object remains editable. If you make a change to the original object, the Live Effects change accordingly. For example, you can create a button with a bevel and a drop shadow. You can then change the color, the size, or the shape of the button, and the effects are reapplied to the new button. One or more effects can be added to an object. The effects can also be saved for use on other objects in the current document.

1) Select the triangles in the buttons. Select the Subselection tool and click the first triangle. Add Shift as you click the remaining triangles.

You are going to add a drop shadow to all of the buttons, and you want the same settings on each triangle.

2) Choose Window > Effect if the Effect panel is not already open. From the Effect menu list, choose Shadow and Glow and then choose Drop Shadow.

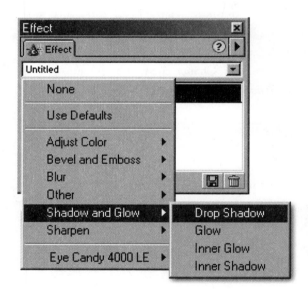

3) Change the settings to get the desired shadow effect.

Drag the Distance slider or type a number in the text box to control the distance of the shadow from the object. You can also control the opacity (darkness of the shadow), softness, color, and angle. Adjust the settings to your liking.

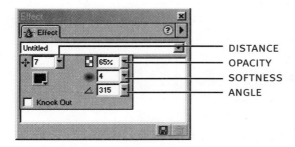

4) Click outside the Drop Shadow settings window to close it.

The Effect panel displays the first effect you have set for the object. You can apply multiple effects to an object by selecting other effects from the Effects list.

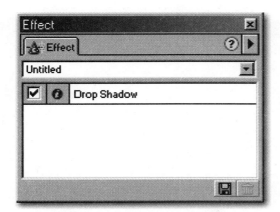

To change your effect, click the Info icon next to the effect you want to change or double-click the effect name in the list.

When multiple effects are applied to an object, the order of the effects in the Effect list can change the look of the image. Effects that change the interior of an object (such as Inner Bevel) should appear before effects that control the outer edge (such as Outer Bevel).

To reorder effects, select the effect name from the list and then drag either up or down. This procedure works like the procedure for changing the order of layers.

To delete an effect, select the effect on the Effect panel and then click the trash can at the bottom right of the panel. To remove (not delete) the effect, click the check box to the left of the effect in the list. Click the check box again to redisplay the effect.

If you find yourself using the same settings or combination of effects, you can save the set. Select the object with the effects you want to save. Use the right arrow at the top of the Effect panel to access the Options pop-up menu and then choose Save Effect As. Type a name in the dialog box and then click Save.

The name of your saved effect now appears in the Effect list. To apply a saved effect to another object, select the object and then choose the saved effect from the Effect list.

5) Save your file.

Your buttons now have drop shadows on the triangles.

WORKING WITH MASKS

Masking is the process of taking one object as a shape and using it (like a cookie cutter) to crop another object. To do this in Fireworks, one method is to use the Paste Inside command. You'll use another method in a later lesson. You can think of the mask as like a picture frame, except that only the area inside the frame is visible. You can move the object around within the frame to display just the area you want.

On the Web page you are building, you want to create circular buttons for each of the offered tours. Instead of text, you will use pictures of the activity. For example, for mountain biking tours, you will use an image of a person on a mountain bike. To create the circular button, you will draw a circle and then use Paste Inside to insert the image within the circle.

 biking

1) Import the mountain_biker.png file from the Images folder in the Lesson04 folder.

Place the image anywhere on the canvas. The image is too large, but you will scale it down later.

2) Select the Ellipse tool and draw a circle, holding down Shift as you draw.

The circle is the frame object for the image.

3) Use the Info panel to change both the width and height of the circle to 65 pixels. Use the Stroke panel to change the stroke to 1-Pixel Soft Pencil. Change the color of the stroke to a dark yellow and change the size to 2 pixels. On the Fill panel, set the fill of the circle to None.

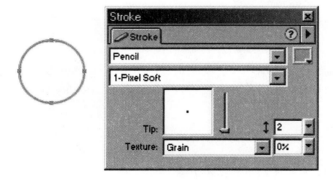

4) Move the circle on top of the mountain biker image.

You want the rider to appear in the circle, but the image is too large. The image needs to be scaled down. To scale the image, you can use the Scale tool, or you can drag one of the corner points with the Pointer tool. If you use the Pointer tool, you must hold down Shift as you drag to scale the image proportionally; with the Scale tool, you do not need to hold down Shift.

5) Slowly scale down the image until the rider fits within the circle.

Warning: When scaling bitmap images, you can usually scale the image smaller with good results; however, scaling images larger may degrade the quality of the image, resulting in a fuzzy image.

6) Choose Edit > Cut to copy the image to the Clipboard and delete it from the canvas. Select the circle and choose Edit > Paste Inside.

The image is pasted within the boundaries of the circle. The image is not cut in a circle shape; it is hidden except for the portions within the circle.

Select the image with the Pointer tool. You'll see the outline edges of the image outside the circle. There is also a small blue star within the circle: the move handle. If you don't like the placement of the image within the circle, you can drag the move handle to move the image within the mask.

If needed, you can split the image and the mask apart. Select the mask object with the Pointer tool. Choose Modify > Ungroup. The elements are now separated. To mask them again, repeat step 6.

ON YOUR OWN

Create three more circle buttons using the Paste Inside method you just learned. The images for the button are diver.png, climber.png, and kayak.png, all located in the Images folder within the Lesson04 folder. Place the final buttons vertically on the left side of the page. Add text descriptions to the right of the buttons. For example, add *biking* for the mountain biking image, *climbing* for the climbing image, *diving* for the diver image, and *kayaking* for the kayak image. Use the Alignment command to ensure that the descriptions all align on the left side.

ADDING TEXTURES AND PATTERNS

Your Web page is almost complete. You will add a rectangle that acts as a background for the descriptive text for the page. To make the rectangle more interesting, you'll add a texture. You can also experiment with patterns.

Textures are grayscale images that simulate a surface blended with the fill of the object. Adding a texture changes the intensity of the fill of an object. A texture of zero percent has no effect on the image. Increasing the texture value intensifies the effect on the fill. Textures can be applied to patterns, solids, gradient fills, and even strokes.

1) Draw a rectangle on the right side of the page.

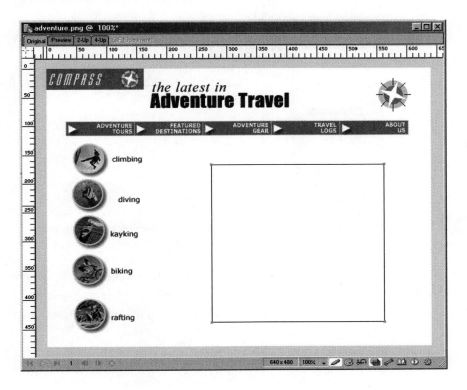

Don't worry about the size; you can resize the rectangle after you add the text.

2) Change the color of the rectangle to the pale yellow in your Swatches panel. Choose one of the textures from the Texture pop-up list in the Fill panel. Drag the Amount slider to 50 percent.

There are several options to choose from the list. Experiment with several and find one you like. For example, try Plaster or Grain. You can also experiment with the amount slider to vary the intensity of the texture. Remember that you will place text on top of this rectangle, so do not make the texture too distracting.

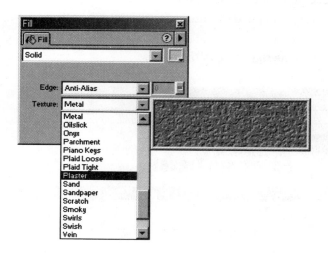

NOTE *Every fill has a texture applied to it. When the texture amount is set to zero percent, the texture is not visible.*

A pattern is a repeating image that fills an object. Patterns are used to create realistic fills, like wood or bricks, for your objects. You can use the default patterns provided with Fireworks or create your own. Patterns are simply bitmap files from artwork you've scanned or created on your own.

Instead of changing your rectangle, you will draw another one off to the side and experiment with adding patterns. After you finish experimenting with adding patterns, you can delete this rectangle as it is not needed for the final page.

3) Draw a new rectangle. Choose Pattern from the Fill category pop-up list. Choose a pattern from the list of pattern fills.

As you move through the list, a small preview of the pattern appears next to each name. When you select a pattern, a center point and two vector handles will appear within the rectangle. You can use these handles to control the appearance of the pattern. Move the handles in or out from the center point. You can also move the center point to change the look of the pattern. Move your pointer close to the center point where the handles meet. A circular cursor (like the rotate cursor) appears. When you see the cursor, you can drag to rotate the pattern. Note that this action rotates the pattern, not the rectangle.

4) Choose File > Import. Open the Welcome.txt file located in the Text folder within the Lesson04 folder.

Fireworks can import ASCII text for use in your document.

5) Click to place the text on the page. Use the Text Editor to format the text. Add bold to the Welcome to Compass line and increase the leading. Move the text on top of the rectangle.

You may need to change the width of the rectangle or the text box.

NOTE *ASCII (American Standard Code for Information Interchange) is text that can be read by Windows, Macintosh, and UNIX computer systems. When you save a document as Text Only, you are saving your file in ASCII format.*

6) Save your file.

You're done. You've just completed the design of your first Web page. The page is not ready for placing on your Web server, however; you still need to export it as an HTML document. You'll do that in a later lesson.

WHAT YOU HAVE LEARNED

In this lesson, you have:

- Created and formatted text [pages 86–92]
- Added color to objects [pages 93–96]
- Used the Scale tool [pages 97–98]
- Created a custom palette [pages 102–105]
- Aligned objects on the page [pages 106–107]
- Added Live Effects to objects [pages 108–110]
- Used Paste Inside to mask an image [pages 111–113]
- Added patterns and textures to an object [pages 115–116]
- Imported text [page 117]

advanced techniques

LESSON 5

In the previous lesson, you built a Web page using some of the basic drawing tools such as the Ellipse and Rectangle tools. In this lesson, you will use path operations, such as Punch and Union, to create more complex objects quickly and easily.

In addition, you will draw and modify a curved path and then add text that curves along the path. You will create another Web page for this lesson, importing some of the objects you created earlier.

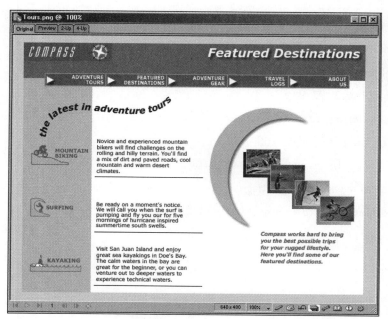

In this lesson, you will learn to create text on a path as you see in the latest in adventure tours text. You will also create the moon shape by combining two circles.

WHAT YOU WILL LEARN

In this lesson, you will:

- Use techniques for saving and duplicating your actions

- Create special effects for your objects

- Use the Repeat command

- Combine simple shapes into complex objects

- Create text on a path

- Mask an image

APPROXIMATE TIME

This lesson takes approximately 1 hour to complete.

LESSON FILES

Media Files:

Lesson05\Images\biking.gif

Lesson05\Images\climbing.gif

Lesson05\Images\rafting.gif

Lesson05\Images\fishing.gif

Lesson05\Images\Ballon.jpg

Lesson05\Images\diver.png

Lesson05\Text\Features.txt

Starting Files:

Lesson05\Tours_start.png

Lesson05\Travel_logs_start.png

Completed Projects:

Lesson05\Completed\Tours.png

Lesson05\Completed\Travel_logs.png

Lesson05\Completed\Buttons.png

DUPLICATING OBJECTS WITH THE REPEAT COMMAND

Many times you will find yourself creating copies of an object on a page. For example, if you are creating buttons, you might want them all to be the same size and color, with only the text label different. You also might want them aligned and offset the same amount from one another. Once you've created the first one, you can use Copy and Paste, Duplicate, or Clone, or you can hold down Alt (Windows) or Option (Macintosh) and drag to create the remaining buttons.

Although each of these methods results in another object, they all work differently. Using Copy and Paste or Clone puts the duplicate object directly on top of the first, and Duplicate offsets the copy down and to the right. You then have to move the copy to the new location and repeat the process for each new button you want. Then you have to use the alignment tools to make sure that the objects are properly aligned and spaced. When you hold down Alt (Windows) or Option (Macintosh) and drag, the new button is moved, but you guess the placement and still need to check the alignment and spacing. The Repeat command makes this process easier.

This exercise demonstrates how to use the Repeat command to repeat a duplicate-and-move process. The Duplicate command duplicates an object, offsetting the new object. This method lets you control the offsetting distance for each new object you create.

1) Open the Tours_start.png file in the Lesson05 folder. Choose File > Save As and save the new file as *Tours.png*.

This file contains some icons and text representing featured travel trips for the fictional Compass travel company.

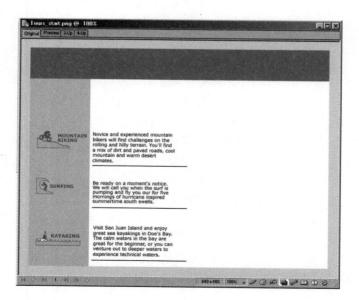

2) Draw a rectangle 65 x 49 pixels with a solid fill of any color and a stroke of None.

You want four rectangles diagonally offset from one another. There are several ways to make a copy of an object. For this exercise, you will use a method that not only makes a copy, but also duplicates the offset placement of the new rectangle.

NOTE *The example images display a fill of None to make it easier for you to see the shape. Your rectangle needs to be filled with a stroke of None.*

3) Select the Pointer tool and hold down Alt (Windows) or Option (Macintosh) as you drag the rectangle to create a copy of the rectangle. Move the copy down and to the right, overlapping the first rectangle.

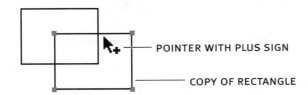

POINTER WITH PLUS SIGN

COPY OF RECTANGLE

As you drag, the cursor adds a plus sign, indicating that you are making a copy. You actually are performing two operations: you are making a copy, and you are moving the copy a set distance from the original. This method of making a copy is the only one that combines two events in one action.

4) Choose Edit > Repeat Duplicate.

Another rectangle is created for you and offset the same distance as the moved object.

5) Choose Edit > Repeat Duplicate again until you have four rectangles.

The Repeat command repeats the last action. Holding down Alt or Option and dragging to make a copy is one action that does two things: it both copies and moves an object. If you use the other copy methods, the Repeat command repeats only the last action, which is the move.

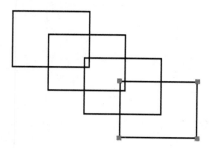

COMBINING SHAPES

A powerful feature in Fireworks is the set of path commands for automating path-drawing tasks that would be difficult, if not impossible, to accomplish manually. The commands, found on the Modify > Combine menu, help you create shapes you might not be able to create by hand. They also save you time, regardless of your drawing abilities.

Look at the stair-step shape formed by the outer edges of your four rectangles. The shape is a series of lines at right angles. You could draw that shape by hand, making sure that each line segment is equal, but it would take some time. You'll use one of the Combine commands to make that task a snap.

1) Select all of the rectangles by holding Shift and clicking with the Pointer tool.

You can also drag around the rectangles with the Pointer tool to select them all. As you drag, a selection rectangle appears. All objects within (or touching) the selection rectangle are selected.

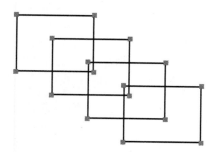

2) Choose Modify > Combine > Union.

The paths of the rectangles are converted to a single path, with overlapping areas merged into the common path's shape.

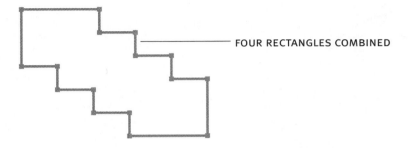

FOUR RECTANGLES COMBINED

3) Move the new shape off to one side.

You'll use this shape in another exercise.

Next you will use the Punch command. The command punches an object with the shape of another object. For this task, you want to draw a moon (or crescent) shape. To draw the curved shape of the moon, you'll draw two circles and use one to punch the other.

4) Draw a circle. Use the Info panel to change the size (width and height) of the circle to *250* pixels. Choose Edit > Duplicate to make a copy of the circle.

The duplicate circle is offset and placed on top of the first circle. This new circle will be the punch shape. You'll use it like a cookie cutter to cut out the other circle.

TIP *The Duplicate command is one way to create a new object. You could also hold down Alt (Windows) or Option (Macintosh) and drag to get a new circle.*

5) Drag the duplicate circle away from the first circle.

You'll start to see a crescent shape form between the circles. Drag just until you have a shape that looks like a crescent moon.

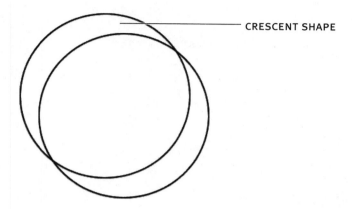

CRESCENT SHAPE

6) Select both circles with the Pointer tool and then choose Modify > Combine > Punch.

The duplicate circle is deleted, along with any part that overlaps the first circle, leaving a crescent moon shape.

7) Change the color of the moon to the yellow-orange color of the icons on the page.

With the moon selected, click the Fill color box on the Tools panel. Use the Eyedropper cursor and click the color (the yellow in the icons) you want to use for the fill.

The other two commands on the Combine menu are Intersect and Crop. You don't need them for this exercise, but you may want to experiment with them, to see what results you get. Draw two shapes, placing the last shape on top of the first. For example, draw a circle on a vertical rectangle. Select both shapes and choose Modify > Combine > Intersect. The area of the paths that is common to both objects is converted to a single path, and the nonoverlapping areas are removed.

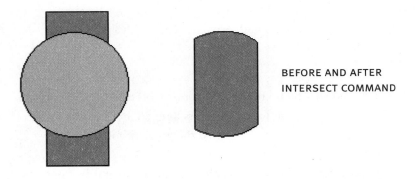

BEFORE AND AFTER
INTERSECT COMMAND

The Crop command is a bit more difficult to visualize. Draw two or more shapes with the Rectangle, Polygon, and Ellipse tools. On top of all the objects, position the object that you want to use as the cropping shape. Select all of the objects by holding down Shift and clicking each object with the Pointer tool. Choose Modify > Combine > Crop.

The bottom path is altered by the shape of the topmost path so that its area under the top path is removed. This could result in an altered simple path shape or a compound path, depending on the location and nature of the top path.

NOTE *Crop is the opposite of Punch. Whereas Punch removes the area inside of the top object, Crop removes the area outside of the top object.*

BEFORE AND AFTER
CROP COMMAND

As you design your Web pages, examine the shapes you want to draw. You may find that even the most complex shapes are just a combination of circles, lines, and rectangles. Those basic shapes are quickly and easily drawn in Fireworks. When you add the Combine commands to the basic drawing tools, you've made your job faster and easier.

Remove any extra objects you placed on your page from experimenting with the Combine commands. Keep the moon and the combined rectangles you created earlier. In the next exercise, you will fill the combined rectangle shape with a gradient.

CREATING GRADIENTS

Gradients are colors that gradually blend from one color to another to create a smooth color transition. A gradient must have at least two colors defined, but you can define as many colors as you want and change the angle that the gradient follows.

1) With the rectangle combined shape selected, choose one of the gradient options from the Fill Category pop-up list. The gradient options are at the bottom of the list, starting with Linear. For this exercise, choose Linear.

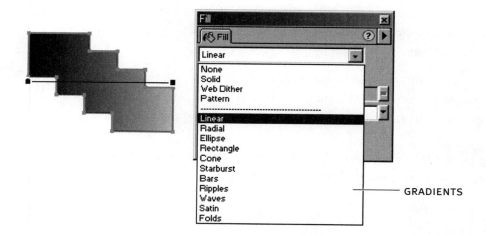

GRADIENTS

The fill of the shape changes to a gradient. The colors of the gradient are determined by the Stroke and Fill colors of the object. This object did not have a stroke, so the first color defaults to black. The color blends from left to right. You can edit the gradient to change the colors and the angle of the blend. Look at your rectangle. You'll see a horizontal line, with a circle handle on one end and a square handle on the other. The circle handle indicates the starting point of the gradient. (On a radial gradient, the circle represents the center of the gradient.) The square handle controls the width of the gradient.

126

2) Move the circle handle to the top left corner of the combined rectangle shape. Drag the square handle to the bottom right corner of the object.

The gradient now blends from the top left to the bottom right. Move the square handle away from the object. The colors of the gradient display more of the top color. Drag the square handle within the object. Now you see more of the bottom color. Drag the square handle, and you change the angle of the gradient. Similarly, you can move the circle handle in and out of the shape to change the amount and angle of the gradient.

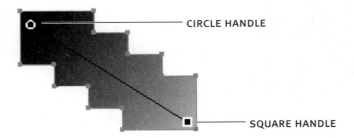

CIRCLE HANDLE

SQUARE HANDLE

3) Click Edit on the Fill panel to change the colors in the gradient.

The Fill panel opens to the editing area, displaying Gradient Color controls and a color ramp.

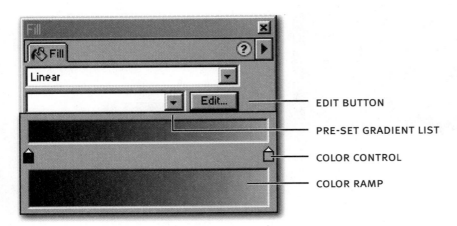

EDIT BUTTON

PRE-SET GRADIENT LIST

COLOR CONTROL

COLOR RAMP

You drag the Gradient Color control to change the amount of color in the gradient. The color ramp displays a preview of the final gradient. You click one of the color controls to change the color and then choose a color from the color palette. This is the same palette you see in all the color boxes. You can choose one of the color chips in the palette or use the Options pop-up list to switch to another color palette.

If you want more than two colors in your gradient, click the gray area under the first ramp. Click when the cursor adds a plus sign. Drag to move this new Gradient Color control, or click to change its color. To delete a Gradient Color control, drag it off the Fill panel.

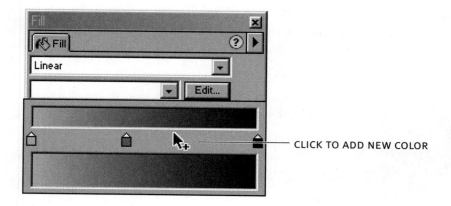

CLICK TO ADD NEW COLOR

4) For this exercise, change the left Gradient Color control to black and the right Gradient Color control to a light tan color.

The shape will be the backdrop for a series of images.

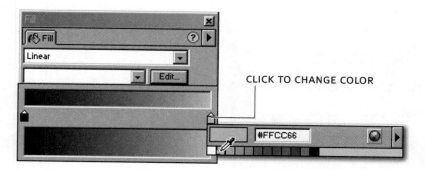

CLICK TO CHANGE COLOR

5) Import the four graphics biking.gif, climbing.gif, fishing.gif, and rafting.gif from the Images folder in the Lesson05 folder and arrange them on top of the combined shape.

6) Select all the images and the rectangle shape and group them. Then move the moon above and to the left of this group. Save your file.

ADDING TEXT ALONG A PATH

Text along a path is a popular graphic style, and it is easy to add in Fireworks. The text flows along the curve of the path and remains completely editable after it is attached to the path. The path can be a circle, a rectangle, or any freeform shape you create.

1) Create a new document with a size of 400 x 400 pixels and a white background.

You are going to add a curve to some text for your Web page, but you may want to practice on a new page. You can then copy and paste your text on a path in your Tours.png file.

2) Draw a curved line using the Pencil tool.

The curved line is the path the text will flow along. Drawing a curved line with the mouse is a bit awkward, and it takes some practice. Try moving the mouse faster to get a smoother line. If your curve is a little wobbly, the next steps will help you smooth it out.

There are points on the curvy line you just created. The points help determine the shape of the curve. If you have a lot of points, the line looks jaggy. (Drawing slowly with the Pencil tool creates a lot of points. The faster you draw, the fewer points are in your line.) The Freeform tool allows you to change the shape of a path without changing points on the line.

3) Select the Freeform tool on the Tools panel. Double-click the tool to access the Tool Options panel.

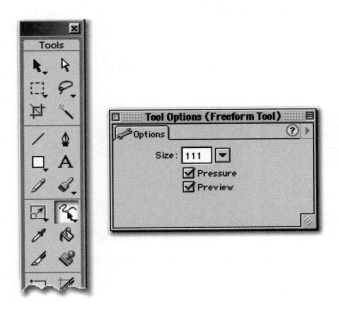

4) Click away from the line with the Freeform tool. (The line must be selected.)

A red circle appears. If the size of the circle is too large or too small, change it with the Size slider on the Tool Options panel. You want the size of the circle to match the curve of your line.

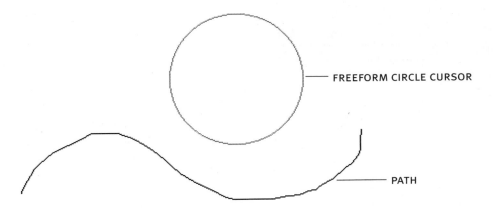

FREEFORM CIRCLE CURSOR

PATH

> **NOTE** *You can also use the left and right arrow keys or the 1 and 2 keys on the keyboard and on the numeric keypad to change the size of the circle as you move the cursor.*

5) Click away from the curve and hold down the mouse button as you gently push the red circle toward the curve. As you touch the curve with the red circle, you'll see the path change shape. When you get a smooth shape, release the mouse. Repeat this step for all the curves in the line.

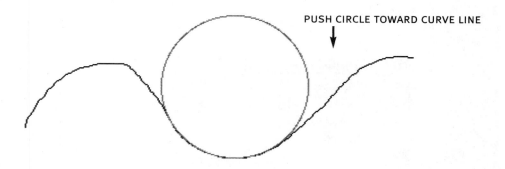

PUSH CIRCLE TOWARD CURVE LINE

Your path still may have a lot of points. You can remove some of those points to make the line even smoother.

6) Choose Modify > Alter Path > Simplify. Type *8* in the Amount box.

The line should be smoother. You can apply Simplify again if you want fewer points on the line.

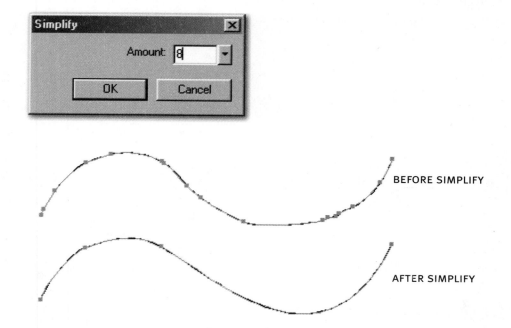

BEFORE SIMPLIFY

AFTER SIMPLIFY

7) Select the Text tool and type *the latest in adventure tours*.

This is the text you'll attach to the curve.

8) Change the font to Verdana, with italics. Change the size so the length of your text matches the length of your line; about 20-point type will do fine.

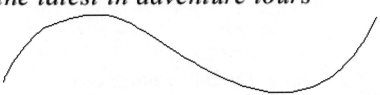

9) Select the text and the line with the Pointer tool. Choose Text > Attach to Path.

The baseline of the text attaches to the path. To change the text after it is attached to the path, double-click the text to access the Text Editor. If you want to detach the text from the path, choose Text > Detach from Path.

Several options control how the text flows on the path. First, the alignment of the text controls where the text is placed on the path. For a curved path, the placement on the path logically follows the alignment: left-aligned text starts at the beginning of the path; right-aligned text ends at the end of the path.

If your path is a circle, the text flow is a bit more confusing. A circle consists of four anchor points: top, bottom, left, and right. The path of the circle flows clockwise, with the beginning point located at 9 o'clock. Text is aligned on the circle based on the beginning anchor point.

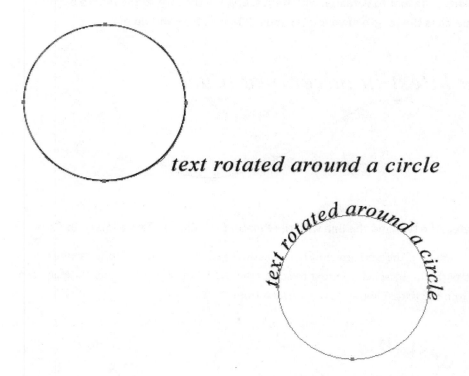

If you don't like the placement of the text on the path, you can make some adjustments. For example, if the path has a bump or sharp corner at the starting point, you might want to have the text start further along the line.

10) Select the path with the Pointer tool. Choose Window › Object to open the Object (Text on a Path) panel.

11) Type the offset value in the Text Offset text box to shift text on the path the specified number of pixels in the direction of the path.

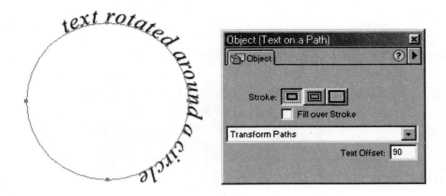

You might also want to experiment with the orientation of the text to the path. Choose Text > Orientation and choose Rotate Around Path, Vertical, Skew Vertical, or Skew Horizontal.

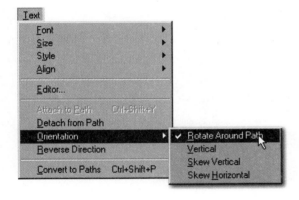

- Rotate Around Path is the default. Each letter is placed perpendicular to the path.

- Vertical positions each letter vertical to the page.

- Skew Vertical rotates the letters on the path, but skews them vertically.

- Skew Horizontal slants the letters horizontally based on the curve of the path.

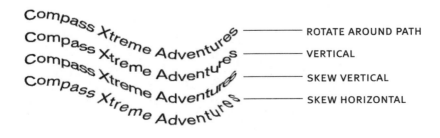

Once you have the text on the path set to your liking, you can copy it and then paste it into your Tours.png file, or you can just drag it to the Tours.png document window. This second method is the same as doing a copy-and-paste operation, but it is much faster, provided that you have a large enough desktop.

12) Place the path above the Mountain biking graphic on the left.

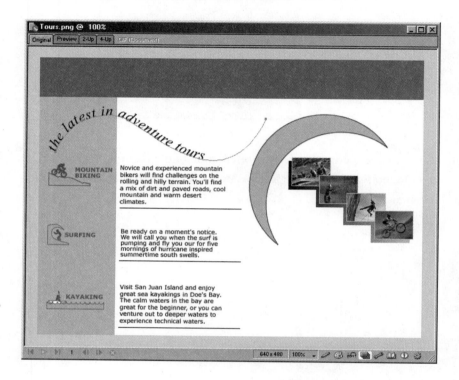

13) Save your file.

You are almost done. You'll make just a few more additions to complete the page.

14) Import the compass logo you created in Lesson 3 and the buttons you created in Lesson 4. Place the logo at the top left of the page. Group the logo if it is not already grouped.

If you no longer have the logo, you can use the Compass_logo.png file in the Completed folder within the Lesson03 folder.

15) Open the Adventure.png file you created in Lesson 4. Select all of the buttons, copy them, and then paste them into the Tours.png file. Move the buttons to the top of the page, onto the brown rectangle.

If you no longer have the file, you can open the Buttons.png file in the Completed folder within the Lesson05 folder.

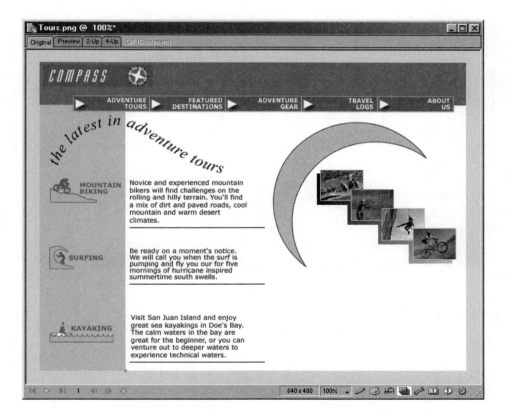

16) Type *Featured Destinations* and place the text at the top right of the page. Change the color of the text to white. Format the text as Verdana, 24 points, and add bold and italic. Add a drop shadow to the text and the moon. Import the Features.txt text from the Text folder in the Lesson05 folder and place it below the rectangle shape.

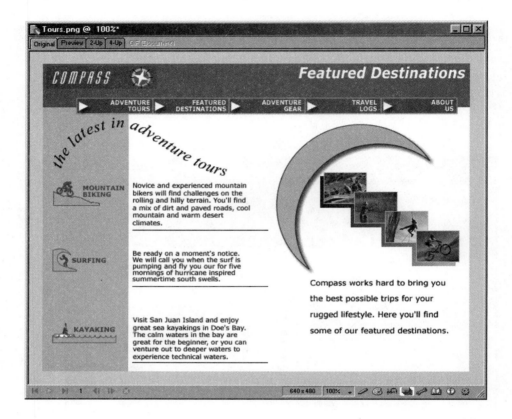

17) Save your file.

CONVERTING TEXT TO A PATH

When you use the Text tool, you create editable text. That means that you can change the font, size, and color of the text or change the text itself. There are occasions when you might want to work with the text as if it were a graphic element. To do that, you convert the text to a path. Converting text to a path changes the text outline to a graphic object; the text can no longer be edited as text. However, after converting, you can alter the look of the text shape by moving or reshaping the path.

Converting text to a path is also a way to provide type for a co-worker or friend, using a typeface the other person may not have. You can format the text and then convert the text to a path. Because the text is now a graphic, your co-worker can use the text; resizing, rotating, or changing the color, but your colleague cannot change the text itself.

1) Open the Travel_logs_start.png file in the Lesson05 folder. Choose File > Save As and save this new file as *Travel_logs.png*.

The file contains some starting images on the page. Travel Logs and Adventure Stories are text that was converted to paths. Double-click the text, as you would normally do to edit text. Because it is a graphic, the Text Editor does not open.

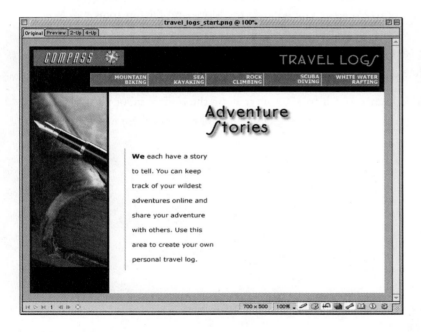

N O T E *The typeface for the type on the page is Eaglefeather. The Eaglefeather typeface family was designed by David Siegel and Carol Toriumi-Lawrence, adapted from a design by Frank Lloyd Wright and developed in cooperation with the Frank Lloyd Wright Foundation.*

2) Select the Text tool and type *Travel Logs*. Use a large font size such as 64 points.

You will change this text to a graphic and then alter the graphic.

3) Choose Text > Convert to Paths.

The text is converted to a graphic. The look of the text on the screen should not change, but four corner handles should appear. All of the converted characters are grouped together. If you want to work with individual characters, choose Modify > Ungroup to ungroup the paths. Then you can use the Subselection, Pen, or Freeform tool to modify the points in a letter to change its shape.

In the next exercise, you will use the text graphic and change its shape and orientation.

APPLYING TRANSFORMATIONS

Fireworks provides several commands and tools you can use to scale, rotate, distort, and skew an object, a group of objects, or a pixel selection area. These actions are referred to as transformations. You can use the transform tools on the Tools panel, or you can choose Modify > Transform and pick an option from the submenu. When you choose a tool or menu item, the selected item displays transform handles. Drag any transform handle to edit the object. You used the Scale and Rotate tools in a previous lesson; in this exercise, you will use the Skew and Distort tools.

1) Select your text graphic and choose the Skew tool or choose Modify > Transform > Skew.

Skewing an object transforms it by slanting it along the horizontal or vertical axis, or both axes. You can skew an object by dragging one of the transform handles, dragging inward or outward.

2) Place the cursor over any handle. Drag the handle to change the angles or side lengths of the object. Hold down Shift to constrain the skewing proportionally. Double-click the object or press Enter (Windows) or Return (Macintosh) to apply the transformation.

SKEW OUT

SKEW IN

3) With your text object still selected, choose the Distort tool or choose Modify > Transform > Distort.

The Distort tool allows you to change the proportions of the object by dragging any transform handle. Unlike with the Skew tool, you can control each handle individually.

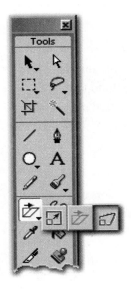

> **NOTE** *Although you are using the text you converted to paths, it is not necessary for applying transformations. You can transform normal text and keep it editable.*

4) Place the cursor over any handle. Drag the handle to change the shape of the object. Double-click the object or press Enter (Windows) or Return (Macintosh) to apply the transformation.

You can use your distorted text on your page, replacing the original Travel Logs text, or you can delete it. If you've made a lot of changes and want to start over, choose File > Revert. This command reverts your document to the last saved version. Leave the Travel_logs.png file open for the next exercise.

MASKING AN IMAGE

Masking is a method of using a shape and the fill of one object to control another object. A mask can be either a vector or a bitmap. In Lesson 4, you used Paste Inside to reveal a portion of an image within a circle. Paste Inside is a form of masking: the circle controls how much of the image is displayed.

Another form of masking uses the fill of an object, not just the outline of the object. Imagine a piece of white construction paper with a hole cut from the middle. Place the construction paper over a picture. As you move the picture behind the paper, only a part of the picture is visible through the hole. The construction paper is acting as a mask. The size and shape of the cutout area determine what part of the picture is visible.

The color of the hole controls the luminance (brightness) of the image. In the construction paper example, the cutout area is black, and all the colors of the picture are displayed. If you place a piece of frosted glass over the picture, you see fewer colors in the picture because the frosted glass filters out some of the colors.

If the color of the mask is black, you see all of the colors of the image beneath the mask. If the color of the mask is white, all of the image is hidden. Shades of gray show varying amounts of the image.

1) Choose Window > Layers to open the Layers panel. Select Layer 1 on the panel. Import the Balloon.jpg file from the Images folder in the Lesson05 folder. Draw a rectangle on top of the balloon image and color the rectangle black. Make the rectangle slightly smaller than the balloon.

The rectangle will be the mask for the image. Because you selected Layer 1 before inporting the file, it is placed on Layer 1.

BLACK RECTANGLE ON TOP OF IMAGE

2) With only the rectangle selected, choose Modify > Convert to Bitmap.

For this exercise, you want the mask (the rectangle) to be a bitmap so you can edit the pixels. The only visual change you will notice on the rectangle is a connecting blue line between the four handles on the four corners of the rectangle.

VECTOR RECTANGLE   BITMAP RECTANGLE

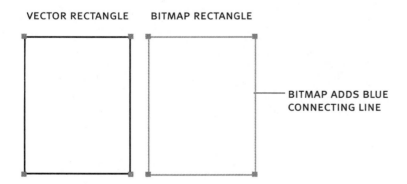

BITMAP ADDS BLUE
CONNECTING LINE

NOTE *A vector object can also be used as a mask, but in this exercise you will edit pixels, so you want the mask to be a bitmap.*

3) With the Pointer tool, select both the rectangle (now a bitmap object) and the balloon image. Choose Modify > Mask > Group as Mask.

The rectangle disappears, and you see a star—the move handle— in the middle of the balloon image. You can drag the move handle to move the image around in the mask. (You are moving the image within the mask, not the object itself. To move the image object, drag another part of the object.) After you create the bitmap mask, you can change the shape of the mask to give your image a special effect.

MOVE HANDLE

4) In the Layers panel, expand Layer 1 to see the Object stack.

On the Layers panel, the image and the mask appear together as a group. The icon of the mask is on the right.

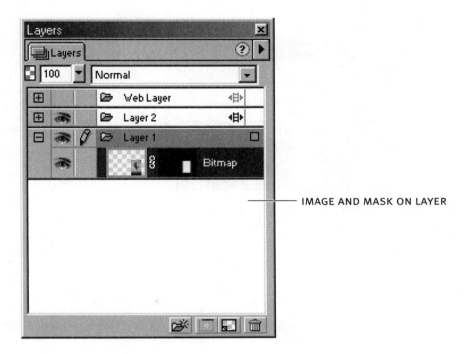

IMAGE AND MASK ON LAYER

NOTE *The image and the mask should be on Layer 1. If you did not select Layer 1 before importing the balloon, it may be on Layer 2. To move an object to a different layer, select the object and drag the blue square on the layer (the selection indicator) to the other layer.*

5) Click the bitmap mask icon in the Layers panel.

You want to edit the bitmap mask object. When you select the bitmap icon, a yellow border appears around the icon. You will also see the rope border around your document indicating you are in bitmap mode.

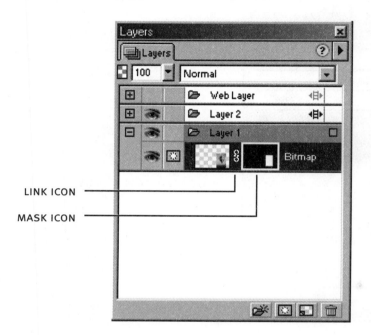

LINK ICON

MASK ICON

6) Select the Eraser tool from the Tools panel. Double-click the tool to open the Tool Options panel, or click the tool icon (a wrench) at the bottom of the document window. Choose the size of the eraser (try 8 for this example) and make sure Erase To is set to Fill Color. You can choose either the circle or square shape for the tool. Change the Fill color box on the Tools panel to black.

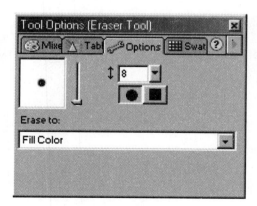

7) With the Eraser tool, draw around the outside edge of the picture to give a rough edge to the photo. Then exit Bitmap mode and switch to the Pointer tool.

Because the color of the eraser is black, you are adding pixels to the mask. The parts of the image not covered by the rectangle (the mask) are revealed. If you change the fill color to white, you delete pixels from the mask, thus hiding part of the image.

Notice that the layer also includes a link icon. The link icon ties the mask and the image together. If you click the link icon (the link icon disappears), the mask remains where it is if you move the image around the canvas. If the link icon is visible and you move the image, the mask moves with the image. You can still move the image without the mask by dragging the move handle within the mask.

8) Save your file. Then close it.

You're are finished with this file, so you can close it.

MASKING WITH VECTORS

Not only can you use a bitmap as a mask, you can also use a vector object as a mask. In the previous exercise, you converted the mask object to a bitmap so you could erase the edges. You could have left the object as a vector and used the vector tools to roughen the edges.

1) Create a new document with a size of 400 x 500 pixels and a white canvas.

You'll use this new document to experiment with using a vector as a mask. You don't need to save the file.

2) Import the diver.png file from the Images folder in the Lesson05 folder. With the Pencil tool, draw around the diver, creating a circle. Make the stroke of the line 2 points and the color black.

The circle can have wavy curves—it doesn't need to be a perfect circle.

NOTE *The figure shows a white line around the diver so it appears better in this book, but make your line black.*

CIRCLE AROUND DIVER

**3) Select both the diver image and the path with the Pointer tool. Choose Modify >
Mask > Group as Mask.**

The image disappears, and you see only the outline of the shape you drew. If you
look carefully, you'll see that the image is masked within the stroke of the path. You
want the shape of the path to be the mask, not the stroke.

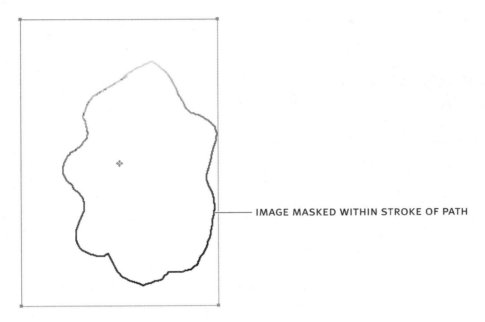

IMAGE MASKED WITHIN STROKE OF PATH

**4) Click the mask thumbnail on the Layers panel. A yellow border appears around
the thumbnail to indicate that it is selected. Choose Window > Object or click the
Object tab to view the Object panel; then select Path Outline.**

The image appears within the path outline, not just on the stroke of the path.

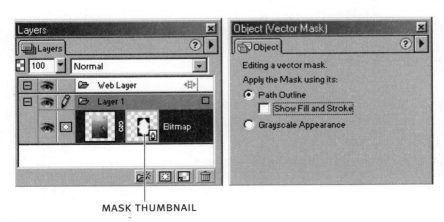

MASK THUMBNAIL

The mask is a vector path and can be modified like any other path. If you want to change the shape of the path, you can use any of the tools to move or modify the points on the path. You can also experiment with changing the stroke. Remember that you must select the mask thumbnail on the Layers panel before you can make any changes.

5) Check Show Fill and Stroke on the Object panel.

Now you see the black stroke around the diver.

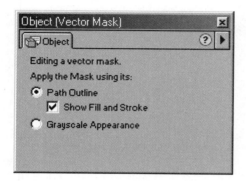

6) Make changes on the Stroke panel. For example, change the stroke category to Random and the stroke name to Fur.

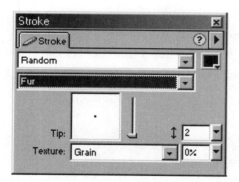

You can achieve another look for the mask by softening or feathering the edges of the fill. To see this effect, you need to remove the stroke you just applied.

7) Deselect Show Stroke and Fill on the Objects panel.

This removes the previous stroke.

8) Click the mask thumbnail to select the mask. Look on the Tools panel and make sure that both the stroke and the fill are set to black. Choose Modify > Alter Path > Feather Fill.

The edges of the image soften.

9) To adjust the amount of feathering, drag the Feather slider on the Fill panel.

WHAT YOU HAVE LEARNED

In this lesson, you have:

- Used the Repeat command to speed up duplication of objects [pages 120–122]
- Used Combine commands to combine simple shapes into complex objects [pages 122–125]
- Created and edited a gradient [pages 126–128]
- Used the Freeform tool to shape a line [pages 131–132]
- Added text on a path [pages 133–136]
- Changed text to a graphic (a path) [pages 139–140]
- Skewed and distorted an object [pages 140–142]
- Masked an image and then modified the mask [pages 142–150]

optimizing and exporting

LESSON 6

After you complete your artwork, you need to export it. Whether you are using your images on the Web or for multimedia presentations, Fireworks provides several methods for creating the best-quality images with the smallest file size possible. Fireworks exports the following formats: GIF, JPEG, PNG, TIFF, PICT (Macintosh), xRes LRG, and BMP.

Exporting your images is actually a two-step process. First, you set the optimizing parameters you want for your image on the Optimize panel, and then you export the image, saving it according to your optimization settings.

Creating small, high-quality images is one of Fireworks's strengths. In this lesson you will learn the proper way to optimize and then export your graphics for good-looking images on your Web page.

Fireworks's native file format is PNG. Although it is possible to use a PNG file in a Web page, this is not the best option. You should always keep a copy of your original PNG files along with the exported files you create. The PNG format retains your editable text and vector objects, making it easy to make changes. If you need to change an image, change the PNG file and then re-export it to get the graphic you place on your Web page.

WHAT YOU WILL LEARN

In this lesson, you will:

- Examine the various color palettes available for Fireworks
- Use the Export wizard
- Set the target export file size
- Use the Optimize panel
- Save export settings

APPROXIMATE TIME

This lesson takes approximately 1 hour to complete.

LESSON FILES

Media Files:

Lesson06\Banner.png

Lesson06\Palm_tree.png

Lesson06\Portrait.png

Lesson06\World.png

Lesson06\World_hard_edges.png

Starting Files:

None

Completed Projects:

None

USING THE EXPORT WIZARD

The Export wizard is a quick way to export your files. The wizard asks a series of questions and then suggests file types and optimization settings. You can also set a file size for the Export wizard to use as a target for the optimization. At the end of the question dialog boxes, the Export Preview dialog box opens with the optimization suggestions.

Ad banners are sprinkled throughout the Web. If you buy ad space on a Web site to place a banner, you are usually given a width and height size for your ad, along with a file size limit. The Export wizard is great for optimizing your ads; you just enter the maximum file size, and the wizard does the rest.

1) Open the Banner.png file in the Lesson06 folder.

This file is a sample banner that you will optimize and export.

2) Choose File > Export Wizard. Select the Target Export Size option and type *15* in the text box; then click Continue.

If you select Target Export File Size in the Export wizard, Fireworks attempts to optimize the file at that size by adjusting the quality of JPEG files, modifying the smoothing for JPEG files, changing the number of colors for GIF files, and changing dithering settings for GIF files. This feature is especially important when you want to create images or animated GIF files that don't exceed maximum file size limits for banner ads on commercial sites.

3) In the Choose Destination dialog box (also named Export Wizard), select The Web; then click Continue.

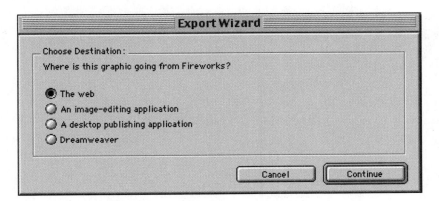

Your destination choice determines the file type for exporting your file. Selecting The Web or Dreamweaver results in a GIF or JPEG image. Selecting an image editing application or a desktop publishing application results in a TIFF image. After several seconds, the Analysis Results screen opens, displaying Fireworks's recommendations.

4) Click Exit to go to the Export Preview window.

The top right panel displays the image as a GIF file; the bottom right panel displays the image in JPEG format. Here you can use the settings Fireworks chose or make adjustment on your own.

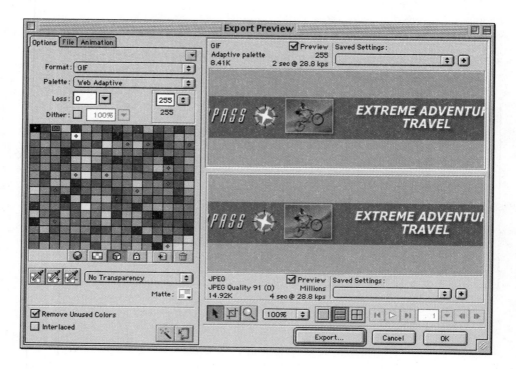

5) Click the top right panel and then the bottom right panel to display the settings the wizard chose for you.

Each panel displays the export format, the number of colors, the file size, and the estimated time needed to download the image. The download time is based on a 28.8 Kbps download speed. The speed option cannot be changed.

6) Click the panel you want to use and then click Export to export the image.

When choosing the export format, you need to look at the quality of the image within the preview window along with the file size. In this exercise, the GIF and JPEG images both look the same. The JPEG file size is 15K, whereas the GIF file size is 8K. Your choice here would be the GIF image.

7) In the Save As Type (Windows) or Save As (Macintosh) pop-up list, choose Images Only and navigate to the Lesson06 folder. Click Save to export and save your file.

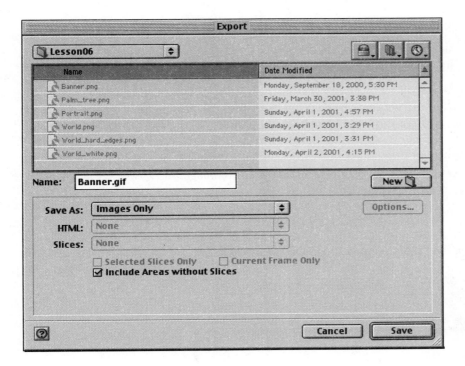

ON YOUR OWN

Use the same file (Banner.png) and repeat the Export Wizard command. This time, enter *8* for the target file size. Look at the difference between the GIF and JPEG images. The quality of the JPEG image diminishes at this lower file size.

NOTE *The Export wizard is an easy way to export your images, but you will want to use all the optimization controls covered later in this lesson for exporting the majority of your images.*

CHOOSING THE IMAGE FORMAT

The Export wizard does a good job of analyzing your images for you, but normally you will want to take control over the image optimization and export settings.

Picking the correct image format is crucial to the optimization process. The most popular file formats for Web graphics are GIF and JPEG. GIF images are generally used for line art and images with solid colors. GIF images can contain transparent areas and can be used for animation files. The disadvantage of GIF images is that they are restricted to 256 colors. JPEG is generally used for photographic images or images with gradients and more colors. JPEG files cannot be transparent or used in animations.

You use the Optimize panel to pick the formatting options for exporting the file. The choices you make in this exercise affect the entire image. In Lesson 9, you will apply these same settings to selected portions of a page to take more control of the optimization process.

1) Open the Palm_tree.png file in the Lesson06 folder.

2) Choose Window › Optimize to access the Optimize panel. Choose GIF from the Export File Format pop-up menu.

If you choose GIF as your export file format, you need to pick the color palette for the export. GIF files can be up to 256 colors (actually, only 216 colors; the other 40 colors are used by the operating system and the browser).

3) Choose Web 216 from the Indexed Palette pop-up menu.

The color palette is a group of colors used in the image. Fireworks contains 10 preset palettes for you to use.

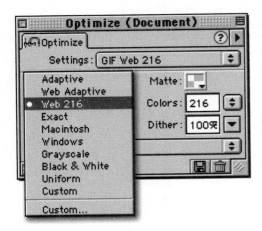

The following list describes the default palettes.

- **Adaptive**: Creates a custom palette containing the majority of the colors in the image, whether or not they are Web-safe colors.

- **WebSnap Adaptive (Windows) or Web Adaptive (Macintosh)**: Creates a bridge between the Web 216 palette and the Adaptive palette. Colors within a certain tolerance range are snapped to the closest Web-safe color.

- **Web 216**: Displays a palette of 216 colors that have a similar appearance on both Windows and Macintosh computers. This is sometimes referred to as a Web-safe or browser-safe palette because it generates the most similar results on different platforms and different browsers. Each color in the image is replaced with the closest Web-safe color.

- **Exact**: Contains the exact colors in the image when the image contains 256 colors or less.

- **Macintosh**: Contains 256 colors as defined by the Macintosh system colors.

- **Windows**: Contains 256 colors as defined by the Windows system colors.

- **Grayscale**: Displays a palette of 256 (or fewer) shades of gray. Using this palette converts your image to grayscale.

- **Black & White**: Displays a palette of only two colors: black and white.

- **Uniform**: Displays a mathematical palette based on RGB pixel values.

- **Custom**: Gives the user the option of importing another color palette saved from Fireworks or Adobe Photoshop.

4) Click the 4-Up tab at the top of the document window.

Fireworks 4 enables you to preview your images within the document window before exporting them. You can determine the export settings on the page as you create it and preview the results. You can also split the document window into two or four preview windows to view different settings. Fireworks also displays the file size and the approximate download times within each preview window.

While viewing in the Preview tab, you cannot make any changes to the image. The 2-Up tab divides the document into two preview windows; the 4-Up tab divides the document into four preview windows. In 2-Up and 4-Up modes, the first window displays the original image and can be edited. The other windows are previews only.

NOTE *You can display the original image (or no original image) in any of the preview windows in 2-Up and 4-Up preview modes. Select Original from the pop-up menu at the bottom of the preview window.*

5) Click anywhere within the bottom-right window to select it.

A black border appears around the selected window. The selected window reflects any changes you make on the Optimize panel.

6) On the Optimize panel, set the number of colors for the color palette in the Colors pop-up list. Choose 32 from the pop-up list.

Choosing a smaller number reduces the file size. Look at the top right panel and compare the file size and the number of colors. Depending on your image, your file size may be reduced significantly. With this image, the reduction amount is negligible.

Also look at the quality of the image after you reduce the number of colors. If you pick a number that is smaller than the actual number of colors in the image, some colors are lost. The pixels with the lost colors are converted to the closest remaining colors on the palette.

7) Reduce the Dither amount by dragging the slider on the Optimize panel to zero.

Dithering is a process of approximating colors not on the current palette. A dithered image often looks "noisy" or grainy; however, dithering can help smooth out the banding created by a gradient-like transition of colors. The higher the number, the more dithering that occurs and the larger the file size.

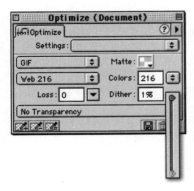

Look at the file size now that the dithering is removed. There is a noticeable difference in the file size.

Along with the file size, there is a noticeable difference in the image itself. There is a shift in the color of the water, because the original color was not a Web-safe color. When you use the Web 216 color palette, non-Web-safe colors are dithered to make them as close as possible to the original colors. When you remove the dithering, the colors are shifted to the nearest Web-safe colors.

163

8) With the bottom right panel selected, click the Original tab to return to the document window.

The settings you chose for the selected preview window are now applied to the document and will be used when you export the file.

9) Choose File > Export.

Fireworks uses your file name as the export file name.

10) Type a new name, if desired, in the File Name text box and navigate to the Lesson06 folder where you want to save the exported file. In the Save As Type pop-up list, select Images Only. Click Save.

The file is exported as a GIF file, using the settings you selected.

How do you determine whether a color is Web safe?

Colors for the Web are expressed in hexadecimal format—a base-16 numbering system. (Our normal numbering system is base 10.) In addition to the numbers from 0 to 9, the hexadecimal system uses the letters A, B, C, D, E, and F. Web-safe colors are limited to those colors whose hexadecimal values contain matched sets of numbers: 00, FF, CC, and so on, using only the values 0, 3, 6, 9, C, and F. If you see a color with the value CC 00 FF, then you know it's a Web-safe color. To view the color values, use the Info panel. Move the pointer over the middle blue section of water. Look at the Info panel. The color values are 1A 80 7E, indicating that the color is not Web safe.

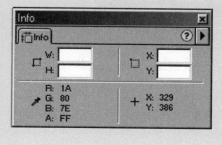

CREATING TRANSPARENCY

All artwork created on the computer is saved as a rectangle. In Fireworks, the shape of the canvas is always a rectangle. If you draw a circle on the canvas and export the circle, the resulting image shape is a rectangle. If you want your image to appear as a shape other than a rectangle on your Web page, you need to apply a transparent background. This enables you to have an image (a circle, for example) appear on a colored Web page background as if it were floating. You see just the circle and not the rectangle in which the circle appears. One way to create this illusion without using transparency is by drawing the image on the same colored background as the Web page, but this doesn't always give you the results you want (for example, if you are placing the image on a patterned background). Making the background transparent is the better choice.

1) Open the World.png file in the Lesson06 folder.

The file contains a globe image on a white background. If you export this image and place it on a Web page, you will get a rectangle image the size of the canvas. If your Web page has a background other than white, the rectangle around the globe will be clearly visible.

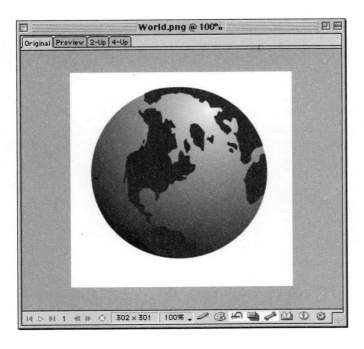

2) Click the Preview tab in the document window.

You need to be in preview mode to see the transparency.

3) Choose Index Transparency from the Transparency pop-up list on the Optimize panel.

The background of the image switches to a gray and white checked pattern to indicate the transparent area.

Index Transparency makes a best guess as to what color should be set as transparent. In this example, the white background is set to transparent. Any occurrence of the index color is set to transparent. If the globe image contained a white area, that area would become transparent.

The other option—Alpha Transparency—uses the outline around the images on the canvas as the shape of the transparency rather than just a color, to determine what part of the image is transparent. Any white area within the globe will not become transparent.

To test the transparency options, click the Original tab and draw a white rectangle on the globe. Click the Preview tab and look at the rectangle. Set the transparency to No Transparency and then Alpha. The white rectangle on the globe is transparent with Index Transparency and not with Alpha Transparency.

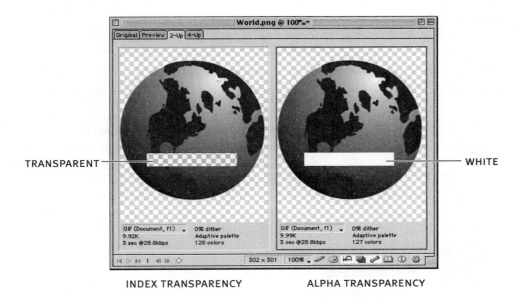

TRANSPARENT — INDEX TRANSPARENCY   ALPHA TRANSPARENCY — WHITE

Images such as the globe in this example display a light border (a halo) around the edges when you place them on a Web page with a dark background color. This is caused by the anti-aliased edge of the fill of all of the objects within the globe. Anti-aliasing adds lighter colors around the edges to trick your eye into seeing a smooth edge. When you pick transparency, the lighter colors remain, and the light border thus remains, too. To eliminate the border, you select all the individual objects in the globe and change the Edge setting on the Fill panel to Hard. (The edges in the World_hard_edges.png file in the Lesson06 folder have been changed to Hard; look at this image if you would like to see this effect.)

NOTE *If you are switching back and forth between Index and Alpha Transparency, make sure you reset the option by choosing No Transparency first, and then to either Index or Alpha Transparency.*

Switching the edges of an object to Hard makes the edges of some images rough looking and may not be acceptable. If you know the background color of your Web page, a better solution is to change the canvas color to the background color, leaving intact the anti-aliased edges of your objects. This way, the background color is used when the colors for the anti-aliasing are selected.

This method works well for images that appear on one page, but often you'll want to use an image on multiple pages with different background colors. The matte feature enables you to keep one master copy of the image and change the background color as you export the file. The matte color replaces the canvas color only in the exported image.

4) Click the Matte color well on the Optimize panel and choose the color from the color palette that matches the background of your page.

The anti-aliased edges use the matte color you chose to create the alternating colors around the edges of the globe. When the GIF image is placed on a Web page with the same color background as the matte color, the image blends smoothly on the page.

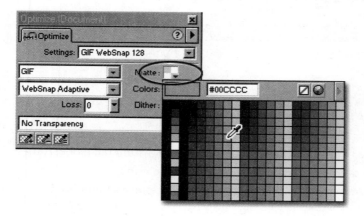

There are two more options to explore on the Optimize panel for GIF images: interlacing and loss compression.

5) Click the 4-Up tab to switch to preview mode. Select the top right window and then choose Interlaced from the Options pop-up menu on the Optimize panel.

Interlacing is a GIF file option for progressively displaying an image as it downloads. Although this option does not make the download time faster, it provides a visual cue to your visitors that something is happening. This option is especially helpful with large images: the user sees a portion of the image as it starts to download. You won't see any change in Fireworks with this option; it functions only in the browser.

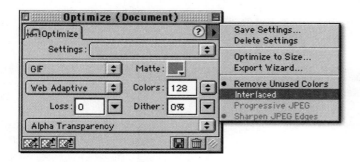

Interlacing adds to the file size, so you may not want to use this feature on all of your Web graphics. Examine the file sizes in the preview windows with and without interlacing applied. The file size is larger in the interlaced window.

6) Select the bottom left preview window. Drag the Loss slider to increase the Loss amount.

As you drag the slider to increase the Loss amount, watch the preview window. The file size decreases along with the some of the details in the image.

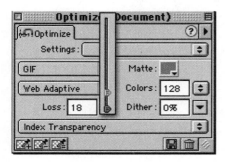

The Loss option makes your GIF image smaller by finding similar patterns of repeating pixels and making them identical. GIF images with identical patterns compress better than those with lots of different patterns.

169

Some images compress well with a Loss setting, although for some images, the file size actually may increase. You need to find the best balance between the file size and the quality of the exported image.

7) Choose File > Export. In the Save As Type pop-up list, select Images Only and then click Save.

Fireworks uses your file name and adds the GIF extension for the exported image name. You can change the file name of the GIF image, but it is a good idea to keep the original PNG file name the same as the exported file name. This way you can better manage your files.

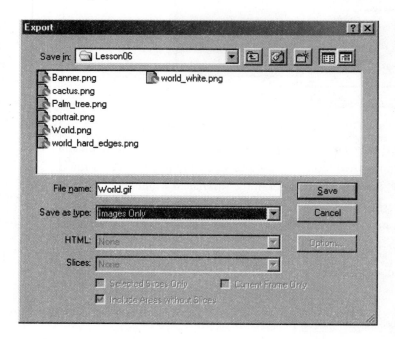

8) You can save and close the World.png file.

EXPORTING AS JPEG IMAGES

The GIF option exports 8-bit images, or a maximum of 256 colors, and works well for line art and images with solid colors. For photographs or any artwork with gradations or millions of colors, you'll want to export in JPEG format. JPEG is a lossy compression scheme, meaning that it looks at your image and removes information as part of its compression algorithm.

1) Open Portrait.png in the Lesson06 folder. Select JPEG from the Export File Format pop-up menu on the Optimize panel. Click the 4-Up tab to preview the image.

By increasing the compression level in a JPEG image, you reduce the quality. In this image, the quality is set to 80 percent.

2) Select the top right preview window and then drag the Quality slider on the Optimize panel to 60 percent.

Look at the image compared to those in the other preview windows. It appears softer, but still is an acceptable image. The file size is almost half that of the original.

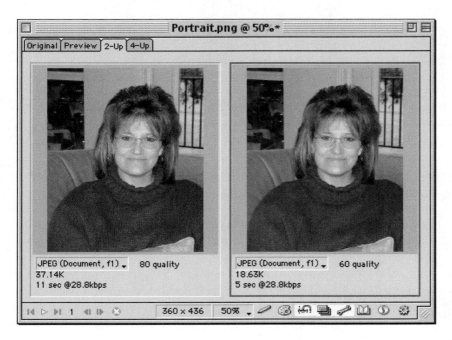

QUALITY:	80	QUALITY:	60
FILE SIZE:	37.14K	FILE SIZE:	18.63K
DOWNLOAD SPEED:	11 SEC	DOWNLOAD SPEED:	5 SEC

3) Select the bottom right preview panel and drag the Quality slider on the Optimize panel to 40 percent.

At this setting, the image displays compression artifacts—areas where you can see blocks of pixels. The file size savings does not justify the quality loss.

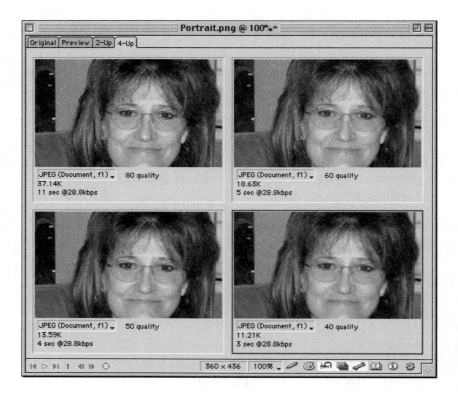

4) Select the bottom left preview panel. Move the Quality slider to 50 percent and change smoothing to 1 in the Smoothing pop-up menu.

The compression scheme in JPEG format sometimes leaves rough or blocky areas on the image. Smoothing is a method of blurring those rough edges so they are not as noticeable. The file size is reduced slightly with smoothing.

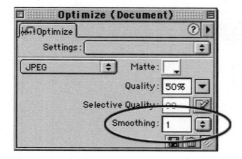

After you choose your export file format settings, you can save them for future export operations or for batch processing. All of the settings on the Optimize panel are saved.

5) Select the top right preview panel.

You want to save the optimization settings used on this panel. The settings on the selected preview panel are used when you export or save the settings.

6) Click the arrow at the top right of the Optimize panel to access the Options pop-up menu. Choose Save Settings.

The name of the saved settings now appears in the Settings pop-up list on the Optimize panel. This collection of settings remains for your use until you delete it. To use these settings in other images, choose the name of the settings from the Settings pop-up menu on the Optimize panel.

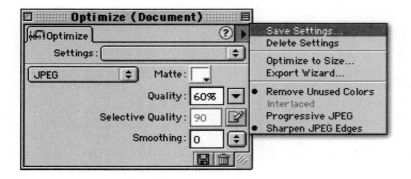

7) Type a name for your settings in the Preset Name text box. Click OK.

Your settings are available for you to use on all your images where you want the same optimize options. To use your saved settings, choose the name from the Settings pop-up menu on the Optimize panel.

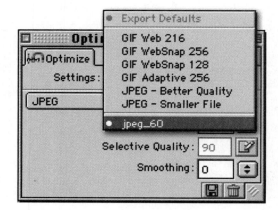

WHAT YOU HAVE LEARNED

In this lesson, you have:

- Used the Export wizard to quickly optimize a banner ad [pages 154–157]

- Used the Optimize panel to change the settings for exporting images as GIF files [pages 159–164]

- Set transparency and matte color for an image [pages 165–168]

- Used the Optimize panel to change the settings for exporting images as JPEG files [pages 171–172]

- Saved your export settings [pages 173–174]

creating animated gif images

LESSON 7

Animated GIF images use a variant of CompuServe's Graphics Interchange Format. In 1987 the specification was enhanced to enable GIF files to contain multiple images that play sequentially to provide flip-book-style animation. A 1989 amendment to the format added such controls as an optional delay between frames.

For all their advantages, animated GIF images aren't perfect. Because they are GIF files, they're limited to 256 colors. GIF files are far from ideal for photographic images, such as a time-lapse view of a sunset. They're best for animated banners, buttons, and line art.

You can stop a looping GIF animation with a browser's Stop button and start over by reloading the image, but you can't stop and resume playback where you left off. If you need VCR-like playback control, use a commercial animation program such as Macromedia Flash or Director.

Animated GIF images are silent movies; if you want to mix sound and animation, use Apple QuickTime movies or Macromedia Flash.

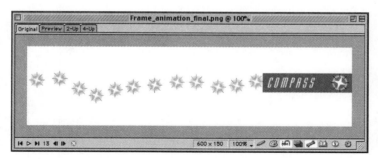

This image displays each frame in the animation you will create in this exercise. You will use the compass and the compass logo you created in an earlier lesson.

Despite its shortcomings, the animated GIF file is a good medium for simple Web animation—no plug-ins, no server tweaking, and relatively mild browser-compatibility headaches. GIF animation is a simple technology that came to lead the field because it's simple. In a Web world increasingly obsessed with bells and whistles, that's an important lesson.

WHAT YOU WILL LEARN

In this lesson, you will:

- Create GIF animations

- Use onion skinning

- Change the playback settings for an animated GIF image

- Use tweening to rotate an item

- Create symbols and use the symbol library

- Use an animation symbol

APPROXIMATE TIME

This lesson takes approximately 1 hour to complete.

LESSON FILES

Media Files:

Lesson07\Car.fh8

Lesson07\Symbols\Custom Symbols.png

Lesson07\Media\Compass.png

Lesson07\Media\Compass_logo.png

Starting Files:

Lesson07\Start\Frame_animation_start.png

Lesson07\Start\Car_animation_start.png

Completed Projects:

Lesson07\Completed\Frame_animation.png

Lesson07\Completed\Compass_animation.png

Lesson07\Completed\Car_animation.png

*Lesson07\Completed\
    Frame_animation_final.png*

CREATING AN ANIMATION

This exercise demonstrates basic frame-by-frame animation for creating an animated GIF image. You'll use the Compass.png file you created earlier and move the compass across the page. The method you'll use for this exercise demonstrates frame-by-frame animation. If you want to see the final animation, open the Frame_animation.png file in the Completed folder within the Lesson07 folder.

1) Create a new document. Make the canvas size 600 x 150 pixels and the color white. Save your file and name it *Frame_animation.png*. Import the Compass.png file you created in Lesson 3.

If you no longer have that file, you can use the Compass.png file in the Media folder within the Lesson07 folder. If the compass elements are not grouped, group them. Place the compass on the left side of the canvas and scale it smaller. You want the compass about one-half inch in size.

2) Make a copy of the grouped compass, holding down Alt (Windows) or Option (Macintosh) and dragging, and place the copy to the right of the original.

NOTE *The Alt or Option key is the keyboard shortcut for the Subselection tool. If you hold down the Alt or Option key first, the Pointer tool changes to the Subselection tool. Click and hold on the object with the Pointer tool first and then add the Alt or Option key to make a copy of the compass. Release the mouse before releasing the Alt or Option key.*

Continue to make new copies until you have 12 copies placed on the canvas. Move each compass in a path from left to right. Leave room at the far right edge of the canvas to place the compass logo you created in Lesson 3.

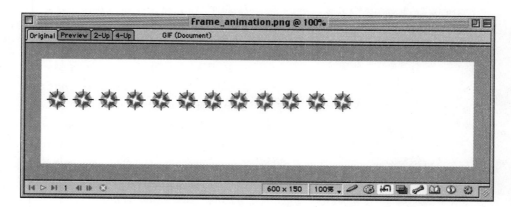

3) Select all the objects. Choose Window > Frames to open the Frames panel.

The Frames panel displays each frame of the animation. Perhaps you remember flip books from your childhood. As you flipped through each page, the cartoon images appeared to move. The Frames panel simulates the pages in a flip book. Each frame contains a different view of the animation. The next step copies the compass elements and places each one in a separate frame.

4) Click Distribute to Frames on the Frames panel or choose this option from the Options pop-up menu.

You should now have 12 frames displayed on the Frames panel. Placing the objects on the page before distributing them makes it easier to see the relation of each compass to the next compass in the animation.

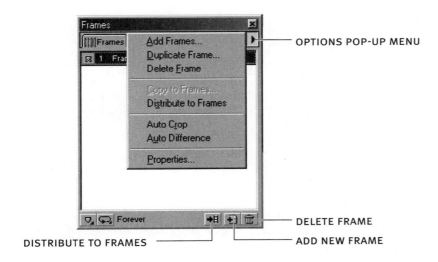

You can click each frame on the Frames panel to view successive frames of the animation.

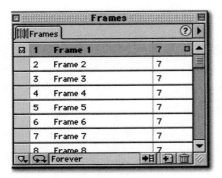

5) Click the Play/Stop VCR control button at the bottom of the document window to preview the animation.

The animation displays each compass object as the compass moves across the canvas. The animation loops, continuing to play, until you click the control button again. You'll change the speed of the animation later in this lesson.

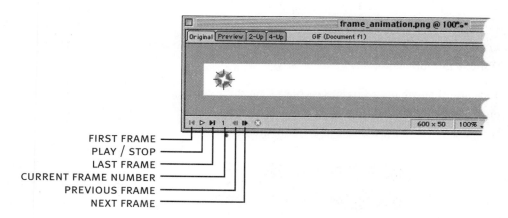

FIRST FRAME
PLAY / STOP
LAST FRAME
CURRENT FRAME NUMBER
PREVIOUS FRAME
NEXT FRAME

Next you will add a frame at the end of the animation and add the compass logo you created.

6) Click the right arrow at the top right of the Frames panel to access the Frames Options pop-up menu and choose Add Frames.

You need another frame to add the compass logo. Choose At the End in the Add Frames dialog box and add one frame at the end of your animation. Click OK.

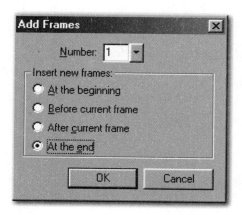

7) Choose the last frame (frame 13) on the Frames panel. Import the Lesson 3 Compass_logo.png file and place it on the page just to the right of the last compass.

If you no longer have the compass logo, you can use the Compass_logo.png file in the Media folder within the Lesson07 folder. Group the elements in the logo if they are not already grouped. You'll have to guess where to place the logo because you can't see the previous compass in this frame. You'll move each element on each frame in the next exercise.

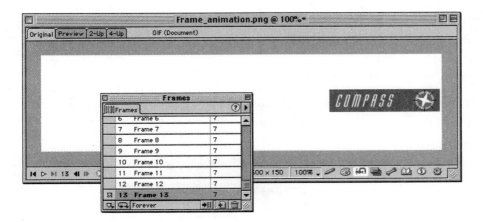

8) **Save your file.**

Keep this file open, as you will use it in the next exercise.

USING ONION SKINNING

Onion skinning is a traditional animation technique that enables you to see and manipulate objects before and after the current frame. When you are creating frame-by-frame animation, this helps you position objects in each frame without flipping back and forth between frames. When onion skinning is turned on, objects in frames before and after the current frame are dimmed so you can distinguish them from objects in the current frame.

1) Select frame 1 on the Frames panel.

You can turn on onion skinning for selected frames or for all of the frames. The onion skinning marker is located in the left column of the Frames panel.

ONION SKINNING COLUMN ———————

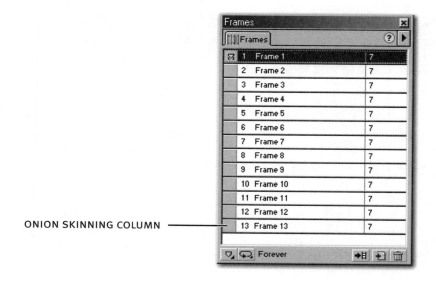

2) Click the left column of frame 13.

A vertical bar appears in the left column, indicating all of the visible frames.

ONION SKINNING
ON ALL FRAMES ——

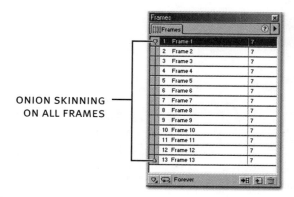

You can also control onion skinning from the Onion Skinning pop-up menu. Open it by clicking the button in the lower left corner of the Frames panel.

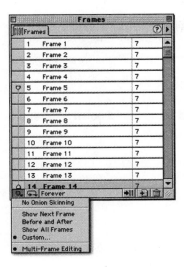

3) Choose Custom from the Onion Skinning pop-up menu to change the opacity of the frames before and after the current frame.

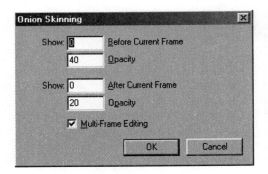

Onion skinning changes the opacity level of all frames other than the selected frame. You can use the Custom setting to change the opacity levels. Setting the opacity level to 0 hides the contents; setting the opacity level to 100 makes the contents appear as if they are in the current frame.

Choose Multi-Frame Editing to enable other frames to be selected and edited (even though they are dimmed).

With onion skinning on, you can now position your objects on the canvas so they appear to move from left to right.

NOTE *Onion skinning is turned off when you play the animation using the VCR controls.*

CONTROLLING PLAYBACK

Once you have the animation sequence working, you can change the playback speed by setting the frame delay. The frame delay determines the amount of time each frame is displayed. Frame delay is specified in hundredths of a second. For example, a setting of 100 displays the frame for a second, and a setting of 25 displays the frame for a quarter of a second. For the fastest animations, set the frame delay to zero.

1) Click Frame 1 on the Frames panel to select the first frame. Hold down Shift and click the last frame to select all of the frames in the animation.

You can change the frame delay for each frame individually or for all frames at once.

2) Click the right arrow at the top right of the Frames panel to access the Frames Options pop-up menu. Choose Properties from the list.

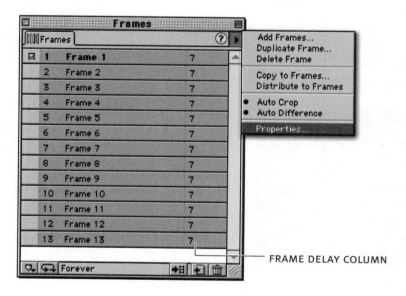

FRAME DELAY COLUMN

NOTE *You can also double-click the selected frame to display the properties for that frame. Double-click the frame delay column (the right column), not the frame name. You can rename each frame; double-clicking the name enables you to type a new name. If multiple frames are selected, double-click one frame delay column. The value you enter for the frame delay is applied to each of the selected frames.*

3) Type 5 in the Frame Delay box. Click outside of the Frame Delay settings window to close it.

The smaller the number, the faster the animation plays.

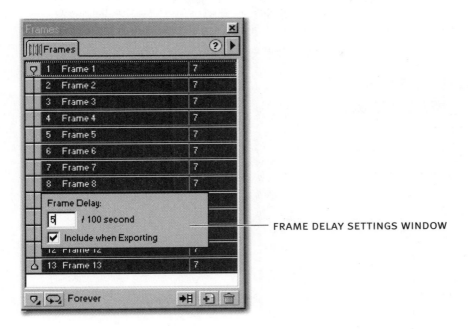

FRAME DELAY SETTINGS WINDOW

N O T E *You can set the delay separately for each frame by choosing the Frames Options menu with only one frame selected on the panel.*

4) Click the Play/Stop control button to view the speed of your animation.

Repeat step 3 with a different frame delay if the animation is too fast or too slow. Next you will set the looping control for your animation.

Looping makes the animation play over and over. Make sure that looping your animation is absolutely necessary before you change this setting. There is nothing more irritating on a Web page than an animated GIF image that loops for no apparent reason. Make sure that the last frame of your animation contains the final information you want to display and that you limit the number of loops.

185

5) Click the Looping button on the Frames panel if you want the animation to play more than once.

On the pop-up menu that opens, you can choose the number of times that you want the animation to loop. The number you choose does not include the first sequence of the animation; you'll actually see one more loop than the number you choose here. To remove the looping, choose No Looping.

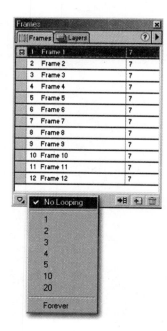

N O T E *When you play your animation with the Play/Stop control button, it continues to loop regardless of your loop setting.*

6) Save your file.

EXPORTING A GIF ANIMATION

Once you have your animation the way you want it, you need to export it as an animated GIF file. You want to make sure that the file size is as small as possible, just as you do for the other images on your page. The more frames and colors in your animation, the larger the file size.

1) Choose Window > Optimize to access the Optimize panel. Change the export file type to Animated GIF. Change the palette to WebSnap Adaptive (Windows) or Web Adaptive (Macintosh).

Make any changes to the number of colors or other options on the Optimize panel as you learned in Lesson 6. View the images on the Preview panel to make sure that your color choices appear the way you want.

2) When you are satisfied with the settings, choose File > Export to export the file. Select Images Only from the Save As options and then click Save.

USING THE EXPORT PREVIEW WITH ANIMATIONS

The default settings for animated GIF files will work for most of your animations. If you need to tweak the settings, use the Export Preview command. You can set any number of loops, change the frame disposal method, and even hide a frame from view. The disposal method specifies what happens to the previous frame after the current one is displayed. The disposal method works only with transparency, so if your frames aren't transparent, you don't have to worry about it.

This section is for your reference only. Your current animation does not need changing.

1) Choose File > Export Preview to access the Export Preview window. Choose Animated GIF from the Format pop-up menu.

The Export Preview window displays three tabs for setting export options: Options, File, and Animations. The Options tab displays the same information as the Optimize panel. You can make changes here or use the Optimize panel.

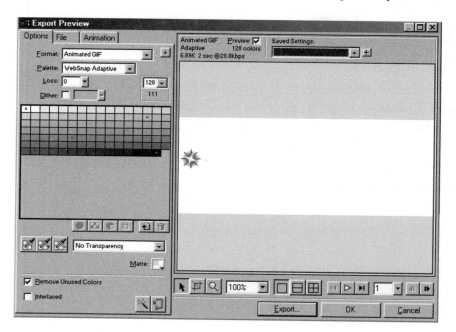

2) Click the Animation tab.

The Animation tab displays the frames in the animation, similar to the Frames panel, but with additional options.

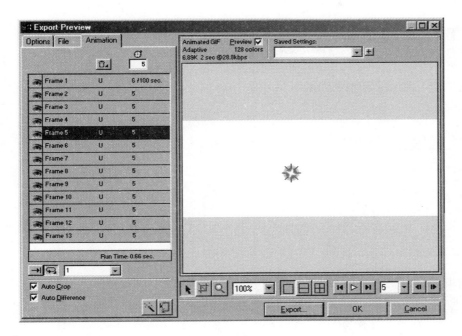

3) Select a frame on the Animation panel. Click the Disposal Method button (the trash can icon) and pick a method from the pop-up menu.

- **Unspecified**: No disposal method is specified. Fireworks automatically selects the disposal method for each frame. Choose Unspecified to create the smallest possible animated GIF file.

- **None**: The frame is not disposed of before the new frame is displayed. The next frame appears on top of the current frame. Choose None to add a smaller object to the existing frame.

- **Restore to Background**: This option erases the current frame's image and restores the area to the background color or pattern that appears in the Web browser. Choose Restore to Background when moving an object in a transparent animated GIF file.

- **Restore to Previous**: This option erases the current frame's image and restores that area to the previous frame's image. Choose Restore to Previous to animate objects across a background image.

189

Here are some guidelines: For full-frame animations, use Unspecified or None (frames overwrite each other). For frame optimization and transparency, use None (each new frame overlays the previous frame). To move frames within a larger frame, use Restore to Background to avoid multiple images.

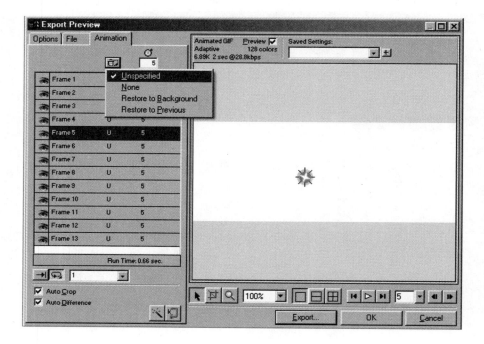

NOTE *You don't need to worry about the Disposal settings. Fireworks automatically selects the best method for your animation. Leave it set to Unspecified, the default.*

On the Animation tab, you can also turn off individual frames in the animation.

4) Select a frame on the Animation panel. Click Show/Hide Frame (the eye) next to each frame to turn that frame on or off.

If a frame is turned off, it is not visible when you preview the animation in Fireworks, and it will not be exported with the animation.

FRAME OFF ———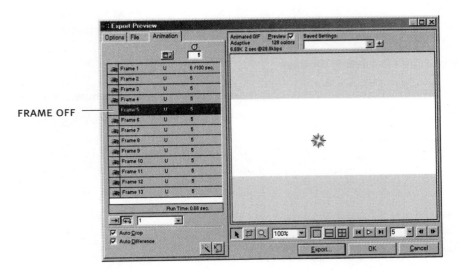

5) When your settings are complete and the preview of the animation is to your liking, click Export. Name your file and click Export. The .gif extension is added automatically. Choose Images Only from the Save As pop-up options and then click Save.

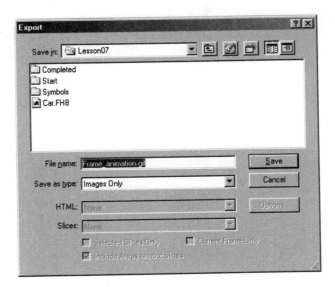

PREVIEWING IN THE BROWSER

Your animation is complete, and you have exported your file. You will want to view the animation in the browser to determine whether the speed is to your liking and whether the animation plays smoothly. You can open your browser and then open the animated GIF, but you can also access the browser while within Fireworks. This method is much easier and can be used for all of your pages, not only animations.

1) Choose File > Preview in Browser.

If a primary browser has been set up, you will see it listed in the submenu. You can then select the browser from the submenu.

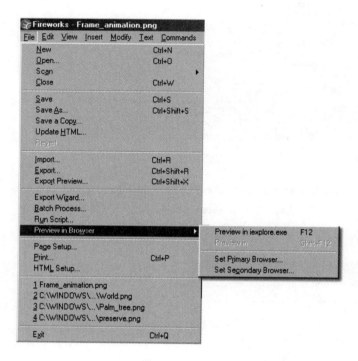

2) If you do not see a browser in the list, select Set Primary Browser from the submenu. In the Locate Browser dialog box, navigate to the location of the browser application you want to use as your main browser. Select the browser and then click Open.

After you set your browser, repeat step 1. If you want to set a secondary browser, repeat step 2, choosing Set Secondary Browser from the submenu.

Your animation plays within the browser window. Click Refresh in the browser to play the animation again. If you set looping to play forever, the animation continues to loop in the browser.

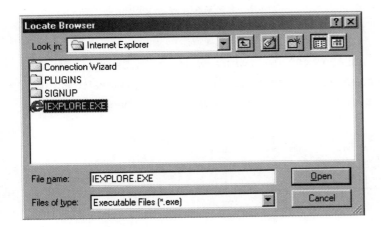

3) Save your file.

You can close this file.

APPLYING TWEENING

Tweening is the process of defining beginning and ending frames and then creating images in between to give the appearance that the first frame slowly changes to the last frame. This is similar to tweening in Macromedia Flash. You define the first image as a symbol, make a copy of the symbol, and then let Fireworks calculate (tween) the images in the middle.

In this exercise, you will use the compass you created earlier and animate the center star clockwise and then counterclockwise. This time, instead of having to create each frame as you did in the previous exercise, you will create the first and last frames and use tweening to create the steps in between. To see a final version, look at Compass_animation.png within the Completed folder.

1) Create a new document 400 x 400 pixels with a white canvas. Save your file and name it *Compass_animation.png*. Import the Compass.png file you created earlier. The compass consists of several objects. If you grouped your compass, ungroup it.

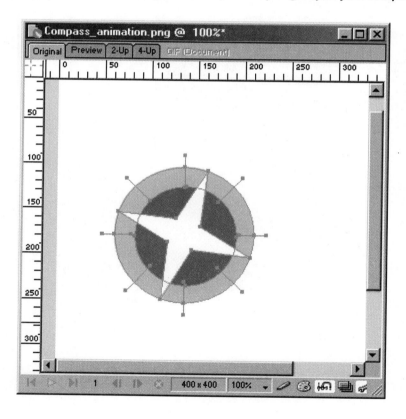

If you no longer have the Compass.png file, you can use the file in the Media folder within the Lesson07 folder.

2) Change the name of Layer 1 to *Background*.

To rename the layer, double-click the layer name on the Layers panel. Type the name and then press Enter (Windows) or Return (Macintosh) to set the name.

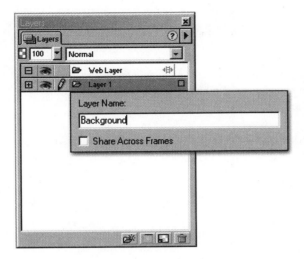

3) Add a new layer and name it *Star*.

For this animation, you want the star on its own layer to make it easier to animate.

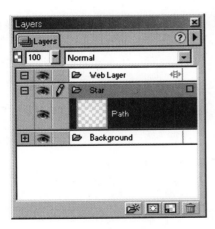

4) Move the star object within the compass to the Star layer. (The Star layer should be above the Background layer.)

Select the star object and then drag the blue square (the selection indicator) to the Star layer.

In this animation, only the star will animate. All of the other objects, now on the Background layer, remain static. The objects on the Background layer need to appear in each frame of the animation. Instead of pasting all of the objects into each frame, you will set the layer to be shared across every frame in the animation. After the layer is shared, you can modify the objects on the layer from any frame, and all of the frames will be updated. If you had pasted copies of the objects into each frame, you would instead have to modify each copy.

5) Double-click the Background layer to open the Layer Name dialog box. Select the Share Across Frames option.

Everything on this layer is automatically placed in any new frame you create in your animation.

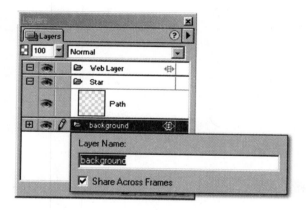

NOTE *If you have content in your frames and then check this option, Fireworks deletes all objects in the frames. You'll then need to re-create all of the frames. Fireworks does display a warning message before deleting your contents.*

TIP *You can easily see which layers have the Share Layer option selected. Look at the Background layer on the Layers panel. An icon is added to indicate this option.*

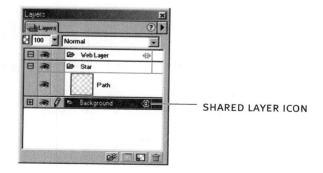

SHARED LAYER ICON

196

CREATING SYMBOLS

Symbols are objects or groups of objects that you use when you want to control multiple copies of objects. Usually symbols are used in animations to create different views of the same object in the animation. Copies of the symbol are referred to as instances. The advantage of using symbols over frame-by-frame animation is that the initial image—the symbol—controls the overall look of all of the other images. If you change something in the symbol (the color, size, or rotation, for example), the instances are changed as well. They are, in a sense, linked together. If you had created the animation frame by frame, you would need to make your changes in each frame.

To apply tweening to make the star animate, you first need to convert the star to a symbol.

1) Select the star object. Choose Insert > Convert to Symbol.

The Symbol Properties dialog box opens, where you can give your symbol a name and choose whether it is to be a graphic, animation, or button.

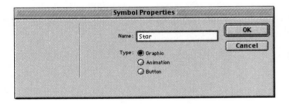

2) Type *Star* as the name, choose the Graphic option (the default), and then click OK.

The star on the canvas appears surrounded by a dashed square, indicating that it is a symbol.

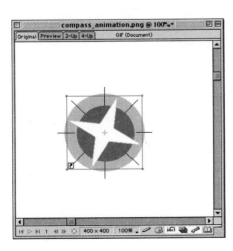

197

3) Make a copy of the star by choosing Edit > Clone.

The copy is placed directly on top of the original and is selected.

4) Choose Modify > Transform > Rotate 90° CW.

You won't see a change in the document window, but you now have two objects, with the top one rotated.

5) You need to select both stars. Choose the Select Behind tool from the Tools panel. (The Select Behind tool is the middle tool when you click and hold the Pointer tool.) Hold down Shift and click the star again.

Both stars should now be selected. To verify that you have two objects selected, check the Object panel. It should display "Object (2 Objects)" in the title bar.

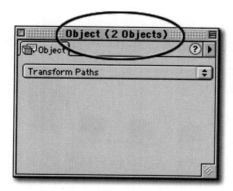

NOTE *Can you think of another way to easily select the two objects? Since you have the stars isolated on a separate layer, you could lock the Background layer and choose Edit > Select All, or you could choose Single Layer Editing on the Layers panel Options pop-up menu.*

6) With both objects selected, choose Modify > Symbol > Tween Instances. In the Tween Instances dialog box, enter 10 as the number of steps and select Distribute to Frames.

The original star is the beginning point, and the rotated clone of the star is the ending point. Tweening creates new instances (copies) of the star based on the number of steps you enter. Distribute to Frames places the copies in new frames. If you forget to check the Distribute to Frames option, all of the stars are placed in frame 1.

7) View the animation by clicking the Play/Stop button in the document window.

The star rotates clockwise. To make the star rotate back the other direction, you need to add more frames to the animation, beginning at the last frame.

8) Select the last frame on the Frames panel and then select the star on the canvas.

You are selecting the last instance (copy) of the star.

9) Repeat from step 3, but change the rotation to counterclockwise (Modify > Transform > Rotate 90° CCW) in step 4.

The star now rotates back and forth. Selecting the last frame in the animation added the new frames at the end of the clockwise rotation.

10) Save your file.

After you complete the animation, suppose you decide that you want to make a change to the star. For example, suppose you want to add a drop shadow to give the star some depth. Since the star appears in every frame, you may think that you have to change each occurrence; however, since the star is a symbol, you just have to change the symbol, and all instances of the star will be changed.

11) Double-click the star graphic on the canvas with the Pointer tool to open the Symbol editing window.

All of the tools are available for you to use in this window.

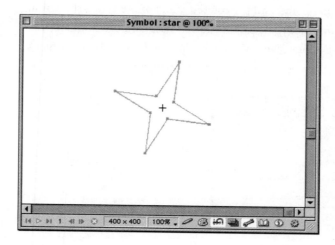

12) Add a drop shadow to the star.

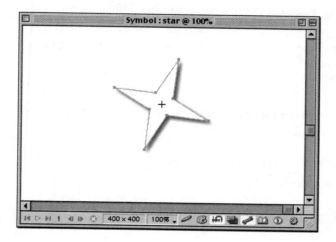

13) Click the close box or choose File > Close to close the Symbol window.

All of the stars in your animation are updated to reflect the change. If you want, you can speed up the rotation of the star on the Frames panel as you learned in the previous exercise.

14) Save and close your file.

USING ANIMATION SYMBOLS

If you want control over every object in each frame of your animation, you must create your animation using the frame-by-frame animation method as you did in the first exercise. The star you animated was created as a graphic symbol and then animated. If you only need to make an object move across the canvas, you can create an animation symbol that makes the task much easier. An animation symbol adds a bounding box and a motion path to the symbol that indicates the direction that the symbol moves. You can change a variety of features, from the animation speed to the opacity and rotation.

1) Create a new document 400 x 400 pixels with a white canvas. Save your file and name it *Car_animation.png*. Import the Car.fh8 file from the Lesson07 folder and group it. Move the car to the left side of the canvas, partly off the canvas.

2) With the car selected, choose Insert > Convert to Symbol. In the Symbol Properties dialog box that opens, type *Car* in the Name text box and select the Animation button. Click OK.

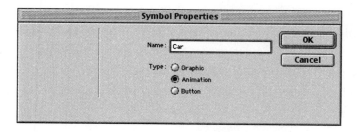

3) Change the number of frames to 10 in the Animate dialog box. Click OK.

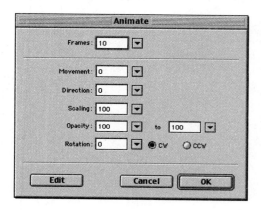

4) A message box opens alerting you that frames will be added to your document. Click OK to close the message box and add the frames.

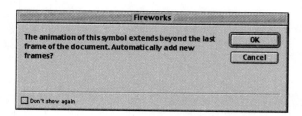

NOTE *This message box contains an option to not show this message again. You can check this option if you do not need the reminder. If you ever want to see the message again, choose Commands > Reset Warning Dialogs. This message, and any others you have opted not to view, will be restored.*

You'll now see the car surrounded by a dashed square, indicating that it is a symbol. You'll also see a red dot in the middle, indicating that it is an animation symbol.

NOTE *Since the car symbol is partly off the screen, the red dot may not be visible.*

5) Drag the red dot to the right, away from the car. A line appears with several dots.

The path of the line is the animation path of the car. The dots on the line indicate the number of frames and the location of the car at that frame.

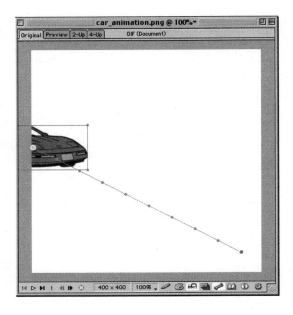

6) Click Play/Stop at the bottom of the document window to preview the animation.

The car moves along the animation path from left to right. You can change the speed of the animation on the Frames panel as you did in the previous exercise.

NOTE *You can change the number of frames, scaling, rotation, or opacity of the animation symbol as it moves along the motion path. Select the symbol and then change the settings on the Object panel.*

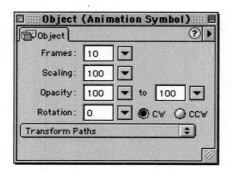

7) Save and close your file.

You will use this file in a later exercise.

MAKING AN OBJECT FADE IN

You can also use an animation symbol to make an object slowly fade in, changing from zero percent opacity to 100 percent. The next steps demonstrate this process. You'll use the Frame_animation.png file you created at the beginning of this lesson. If you no longer have this file, you can use the Frame_animation_start.png file located in the Start folder within the Lesson07 folder. In this animation, the compass moves across the screen, and then the compass logo appears. Instead of the logo just appearing on the page, you will have it slowly fade it. To see the final animation, open the Frame_animation_final.png file in the Completed folder within the Lesson07 folder.

1) Open your Frame_animation.png file. Select the logo in the the last frame.

The compass logo is in the last frame. If the objects in the logo are not grouped, then group them.

2) Choose Insert > Convert to Symbol. In the Symbol Properties dialog box, type
Logo **as the name, choose Animation as the symbol type, and then click OK. In the**
Animate dialog box, change the number of frames to 12. Change the left Opacity
setting to 0. Leave the right Opacity setting at 100. Click OK.

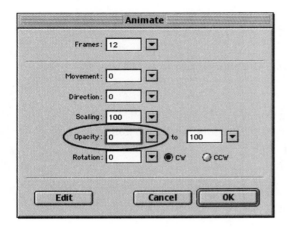

A warning box appears (see the preceding note) informing you that new frames are to
be added to your document.

3) Click OK to close the warning box. Click Play/Stop to preview the animation.

The compass animates across the canvas, and then the logo slowly fades in. If you
want to slow the animation, change the frame delay in the Frames panel as you did
in the previous exercise.

4) Save and close your file.

USING THE LIBRARY

The Library panel is a repository for the symbols and buttons you create. When you create a symbol, it is automatically placed in the library for you. The library is document specific; the items within the library are only those created in that document. You can, however, export library items and import them to other documents.

After you have an item in the library, it is an easy task to drag the item onto the canvas. Each time you drag another copy from the library onto the canvas, the item becomes an instance.

In the next exercise, you will use the Car_animation.png file you created earlier. If you no longer have that file, you can use the Car_animation_start.png file located in the Start folder within the Lesson07 folder.

1) Open your Car_animation.png file. Choose Window > Library to access the Library panel.

The name of the symbol (Car) appears in the Library list. Car is the name you entered when you converted the object to a symbol.

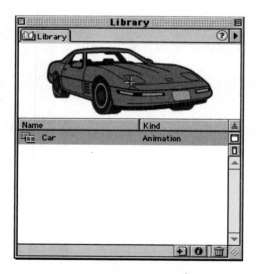

2) Double-click the car picture in the top pane of the Library panel.

The Symbol editing window opens.

NOTE *You can also just double-click the symbol on the canvas to open the Symbol editing window.*

3) Select the headlights of the car and change the color to yellow.

If the car is grouped, switch to the Subselection tool to select the headlights. Close the Symbol editing window.

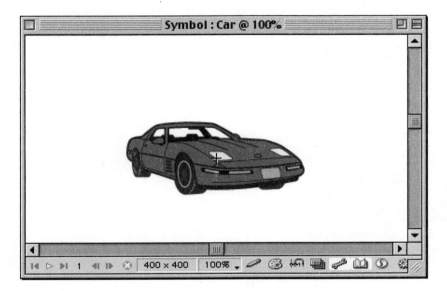

4) Play the animation.

Because the image was defined as a symbol, all instances of the car in each frame are updated to reflect the change.

EXPORTING LIBRARY ITEMS

Symbols appear only in the document where they were created. If you want to use a symbol in another document, you need to export the symbol and then import it into the other document. If you have symbols in a Fireworks PNG file, you can import symbols from that file. Choose Insert > Libraries > Other and select the Fireworks PNG file that contains the symbol.

1) Click the arrow at the top right of the Library panel to access the Options pop-up menu. Choose Export Symbols.

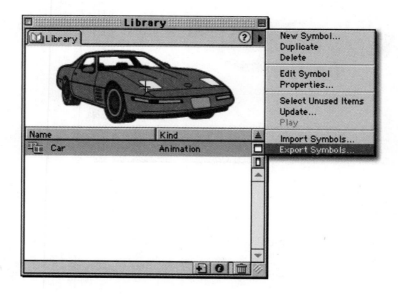

2) In the Export Symbols dialog box, choose the symbols to export.

If you have multiple symbols in the Library to export, hold down Ctrl (Windows) or
Command (Macintosh) and click to select noncontiguous symbols in the list. If you
want to export all of the symbols, click Select All.

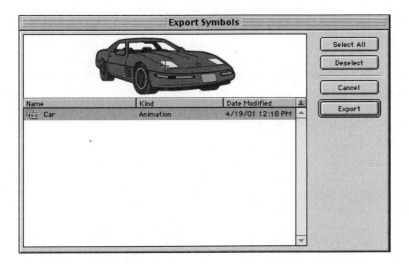

3) Click Export. Type a name for your exported symbols and click Save.

NOTE *If you save the library in the Fireworks 4/Configuration/Libraries folder, it will
appear on the Insert > Libraries menu.*

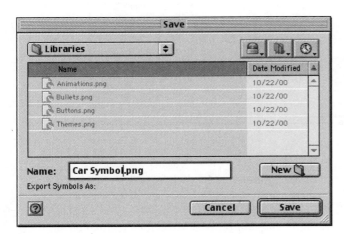

IMPORTING LIBRARY ITEMS

Once you've exported your symbols, they become available to share with co-workers or use in other documents. In the next steps, you will import an exported symbol library.

1) Create a new document 400 x 400 pixels with a white canvas.

You do not need to save this file.

2) Click the arrow at the top right of the Library panel to access the Options pop-up menu. Choose Import Symbols.

In the Open dialog box that appears, locate the Custom Symbols.png file in the Symbols folder within the Lesson07 folder. This file contains some symbols that you can place on your page.

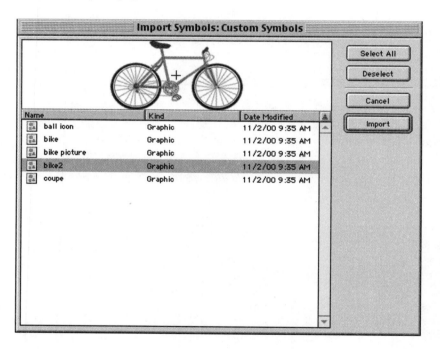

3) Click Select All to import all of the symbols; then click Import.

The symbols are now placed in the library for the current document. To use one of the symbols, drag it from the Library panel onto the canvas. You can drag either the name from the list or the picture of the symbol from the top of the panel.

WHAT YOU HAVE LEARNED

In this lesson, you have:

- Created a frame-by-frame animation [pages 178–181]

- Used onion skinning to position objects in an animation [pages 182–183]

- Controlled playback timing [pages 184–185]

- Exported an animation [pages 187–191]

- Previewed an animation in the browser [pages 192–193]

- Created a symbol and used tweening to create an animation [pages 194–200]

- Created an animation symbol with a motion path [pages 201–204]

- Created an animation symbol to fade in an object [pages 204–205]

- Exported and imported symbol libraries [pages 206–210]

creating buttons

As you design your Web site, you may want to create buttons to add interest and interactivity to your pages. The buttons you make can be simple rectangles with the name of the link or 3D buttons that react to the mouse by changing color, glowing, or taking on the look of a mechanical button that has been pressed down.

In Fireworks, you can create a variety of buttons, complete with all the JavaScript and HTML that make them work. You can create simple buttons, and you can use the Button Editor; you can even create your own custom buttons that you can save to use again.

A rollover button is an image that changes appearance when the user moves the pointer over it or clicks it. There are four common rollover states, although you can choose to use only two or three states. Each state reflects the user's interaction with the button: when the user moves the mouse pointer over the image, when the user moves the mouse pointer away from the image, when the user clicks the image, and

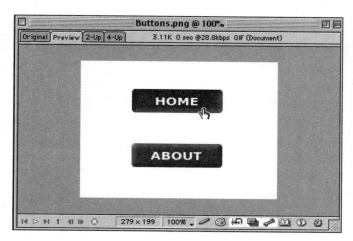

In this lesson you will learn the quick and easy way to create rollover buttons using the Button Editor.

when the user holds down the mouse button with the pointer positioned over the image. First you create each of the different looks of the image; then Fireworks creates the HTML and JavaScript needed to make the rollover work in your browser. Fireworks uses frames to store the individual images for the different states of the rollover. The Up state image goes in frame 1, the Over state image goes in frame 2, the Down state image goes in frame 3, and the OverWhileDown state image goes in frame 4.

WHAT YOU WILL LEARN

In this lesson, you will:

- Use the Button Editor to create buttons

- Turn graphics into buttons

- Add effects to create realistic-looking buttons

- Use the Link wizard to add links to your buttons

APPROXIMATE TIME

This lesson takes approximately 1 hour to complete.

LESSON FILES

Media Files:

Lesson08\about.htm

Lesson08\home.htm

Starting Files:

Lesson08\Start\Adventure.png

Completed Projects:

Lesson08\Completed\Buttons.png

Lesson08\Completed\Adventure.png

USING THE BUTTON EDITOR

The Button Editor steps you through the process of creating all states of a button and adding the links and HTML to make everything work. Most of the time, you'll want to use this editor, but you can still create buttons manually if you prefer. When you use the Button Editor, the button is added to the library. This makes adding other buttons of the same type a snap—you just drag the new button onto the canvas.

Most often, you'll create simple rollovers for your buttons. A simple rollover switches to a new image when the user rolls the pointer over the button and then switches back as the user rolls the pointer off of the image. A simple rollover requires only two graphics, making downloading fast. The next exercise shows you how to create a simple rollover button using the Button Editor.

1) Create a new document 400 x 400 pixels with a white canvas. Save your file in the Lesson08 folder and name it *Buttons.png*. Choose Insert > New Button to access the Button Editor.

The Button Editor is a separate window where you design your button. All of the tools and panels are available just as they are in the standard document window.

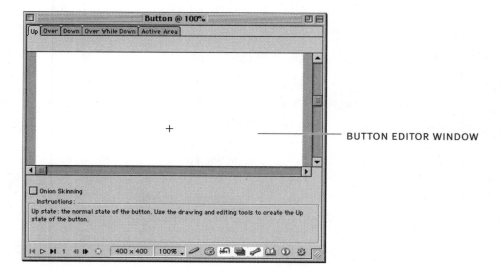

BUTTON EDITOR WINDOW

2) Select the Rounded Rectangle tool. Draw a rectangle within the Button Editor window for your button. Fill the button with any color.

The Rounded Rectangle creates rectangles with rounded corners. You can adjust the amount of roundness on the Object panel. Drag the Roundness slider to increase or decrease the roundness amount; the Roundness value can range from 0 to 100.

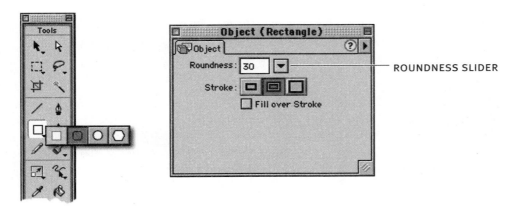

ROUNDNESS SLIDER

◎ POWER TIP *Hold down the left or right arrow keys (or the 1 and 2 keys) before you release the mouse button to change the roundness amount as you draw the rectangle.*

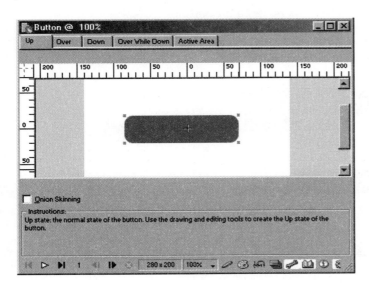

NOTE *You can also change the Roundness value on rectangles you draw with the Rectangle tool. A Roundness amount of 100 on a square results in a circle.*

3) Choose Bevel and Emboss > Inner Bevel from the Effect panel to add a beveled edge to the rectangle.

You can control several options on the bevel. Drag the Width slider to increase or decrease the edge width of the bevel. Drag the Contrast slider to change the contrast between the highlight and shadow areas of the bevel. Drag the Softness slider to control the blur effect on the edges of the bevel. Use the Angle pop-up menu to change the light source angle for the beveled edges. The Bevel Edge Shape pop-up menu offers several preset edge types for your bevel. Change the settings to your liking. Click outside the bevel settings window to close it.

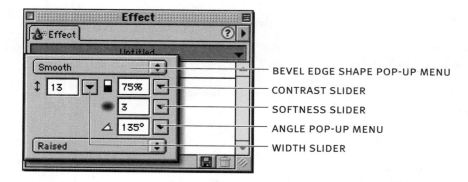

4) Use the Text tool to add the name *Home* to the button.

Place the text in the center of the button. Use center alignment and select a contrasting color for the text.

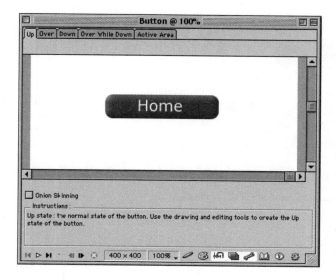

5) Select the rectangle with the Pointer tool. Choose Commands > Document > Center in Document. Select the text and choose the command again.

Your button and the text are aligned to the center of the Button Editor window.

6) Select the Over tab to create the rollover image. Click Copy Up Graphic to make a copy of the original button (the rectangle and the text) you just created.

The button you created in the Up window is copied and pasted in the exact location in the Over window. Normally, the rollover image is based on the original image, perhaps changing just the color of the text or shade of the button.

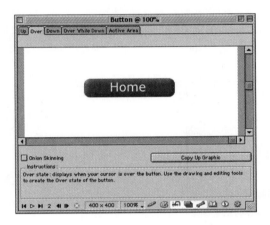

7) Select the rectangle and use the Effect panel to change the beveled edge to Inset. Double-click Inner Bevel in the Effect list to edit its settings. Click outside the settings window to close it.

The bevel effect provides four presets for changing the look of the beveled edge: Raised, Highlight, Inset, and Inverted. Raised is the default, leaving the bevel as originally styled. Highlight lightens the object. Inset reverses the lighting, making the button look as if it has been pushed. Inverted lightens the inset bevel.

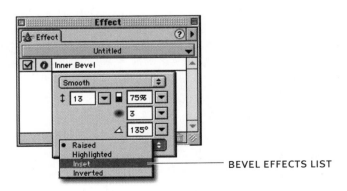

BEVEL EFFECTS LIST

217

8) Click the close box to exit the Button Editor.

When you exit the Button Editor, you are returned to the document window. The button is placed in the center of the canvas, but you can move it wherever you want. Your button is visible, and you see the slice (a green translucent overlay) and the red slice guide lines.

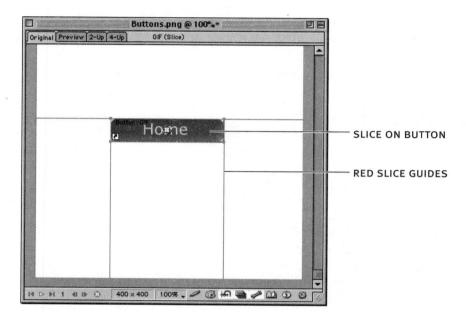

SLICE ON BUTTON

RED SLICE GUIDES

9) If the guides are not visible, choose View > Slice Guides to display them. If the slice is not visible, click Show Slices on the Tools panel to show it or Hide Slices to hide it again.

The slice guide lines are very helpful for placing other buttons on the page relative to this first one, but they can be distracting. You will find yourself showing them and then hiding them as you design your page. Hide them for the next task.

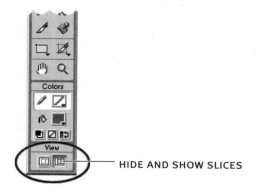

HIDE AND SHOW SLICES

10) Select the Preview tab in the document window to view your button.

Move the pointer over the button to see the rollover image. The button changes to the Over state and then returns to the Up state when you move off the button. Select the Original tab to return to the document window.

11) Select the button and use the Optimize panel to set the export format. For this exercise, select GIF, with WebSnap Adaptive (Windows) or Web Adaptive (Macintosh).

If you are concerned about the file size of your buttons, use the 2-Up or 4-Up preview tabs to set the optimization options as you did in Lesson 6.

USING THE LINK WIZARD

The button you've created works in the preview window, but it is not ready to export. You still need to add the links. After all, the purpose of a button is to link to another HTML page. You could do the linking in Dreamweaver, but you can do it in Fireworks as well. The Link wizard steps you through the process. You can access the Link wizard through the Object panel or within the Button Editor.

1) Double-click the Home button with the Pointer tool to open the Button Editor. Select the Active Area tab.

The Active Area displays the slice and the red guide lines.

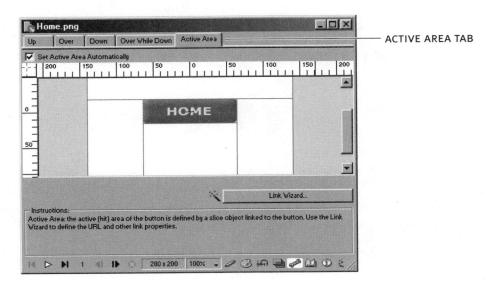

ACTIVE AREA TAB

2) Click the Link Wizard button. Pick the export format for the button from the pop-up menu or click Edit to open the Export Preview window.

The default export option is Export Defaults, which uses the settings on the Optimize panel.

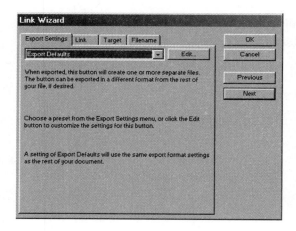

3) Click Next to set the link to the HTML file to branch to when the user clicks the button, or click the Link tab. For this example, type *home.htm* in the Link text box and *Home Button* in the Alt text box.

The Status Bar Text box sets the text displayed in the bottom left corner of a browser window. (This option may not be displayed correctly in all browsers.)

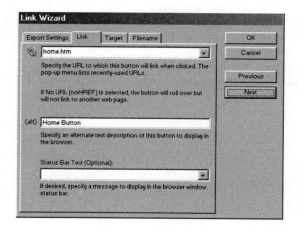

4) Click Next to set the target for your link, or click the Target tab.

The target is mainly used when designing Web pages using frames. Frames are a method of dividing your Web page into separate sections; each section is a separate HTML page. The Fireworks and Dreamweaver Help pages provide good examples of the use of frames. You can also use a target when you want your link to open in a new browser window. You can skip this option for this exercise.

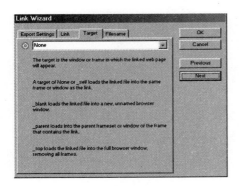

5) Click Next again to set the file name for your button, or click the Filename tab. Deselect the Auto-Name option and type *home* in the Name text box.

If you don't remove the Auto-Name option, Fireworks names your images based on the file name. That name could look something like Buttons_r4_c2_f2.gif, which is not very descriptive. Remember that you actually have two images for the button: the original image and the rollover image. It is much easier if your images have names that match the button function. Enter a short, descriptive name for your button. Don't use any spaces or special characters in the name.

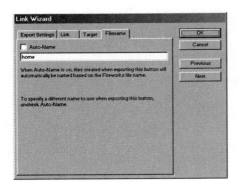

6) Click OK to close the Link wizard. You are returned to the Button Editor. Click the close box to exit the Button Editor.

ADDING A NEW BUTTON

The button with all the links and settings was added to the library. If you want to add another button, just drag the library entry onto your page.

1) Choose Window > Library.

The Button Editor added your button to the library as a symbol with the name Button. The next button you create is named Button 1, and so on. These names are not very descriptive, and you will want to change them to something more meaningful.

2) Double-click the button name in the Library list. Type *Home* in the Symbol Properties dialog box to change the name. Click OK.

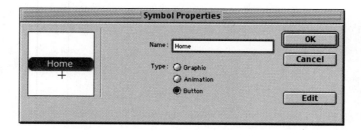

The Library now displays Home in the Name column of the library list.

3) With the Home button selected, choose the Options pop-up menu from the Library panel and choose Duplicate.

This adds a new button with the name Home 1 to the library.

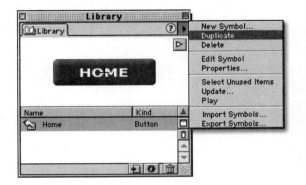 

4) Repeat step 2 and change the name of this new button to *About*.

5) Drag the About icon from the library onto the page and position it using the slice guides from the Home button.

This button has the same properties as the original button, including the text name on the button. You need to change the name on the button as well as the link information.

> **NOTE** *This is one way to copy a button. You can also make copies of the button on the canvas using any of the duplication methods you've learned: copy and paste, clone, duplicate, or Alt-drag (Windows) or Option-drag (Macintosh).*

6) With the About button selected, choose Window > Object. In the Button Text box on the Object panel, type *About* as the new title of the button.

You can change the text on a button using the Object panel. This is faster than opening the Button Editor, selecting the text, and changing the text in the Text Editor. If the button does not contain text, the Button Text field in the Object panel is empty and not editable.

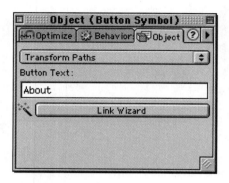

NOTE *Changing the text in the Object panel changes only the topmost text box in each state of the button. If you have multiple text boxes on a button, you will need to manually change the other text boxes in each state of the button.*

7) Press Enter to see your changes on the button.

The text is changed on all states of the button.

8) Click Link Wizard on the Object panel to change the Alt tag, the link, and the file name. For this example, change the Alt tag to *About button*, the file name to *About*, and the link to *about.htm*.

The Link wizard on the Object panel is the same wizard you used in the Button Editor. You can access it from either place.

EXPORTING AS HTML

You are now ready to export your buttons and create the HTML page that displays the buttons. Fireworks does all the work; you just have to set up the location where you want all your files saved.

1) Choose File > Export. Navigate to the Lesson08 folder. In the Save As Type (Windows) or Save As (Macintosh) box, select HTML and Images. From the HTML pop-up menu, select Export HTML File.

For this page, you want not only the images with the HTML code for the rollovers, you also want the page exported as HTML. You also want to make sure that you select the Lesson08 folder for exporting your files. That folder includes some HTML documents for testing the links on your buttons.

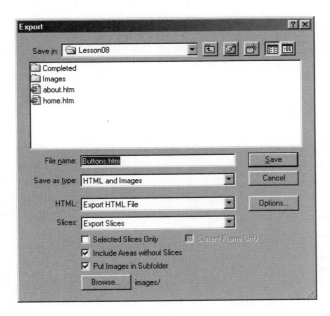

2) Select Export Slices from the Slices pop-up menu.

The slice (the translucent green area on top of each button) determines how Fireworks creates (cuts) the buttons. If you don't export the slices, the page is exported as one image. The slice also enables the JavaScript for rollovers—if slices are not exported, your rollovers will not work.

NOTE *Include Areas without Slices creates a graphic for areas without a slice. If you deselect this option, you create empty cells in the HTML table.*

3) Select Put Images in Subfolder.

Generally, you will want to separate your images from the HTML files. This is a file maintenance and organization issue only, but highly recommended. Fireworks defaults to a subfolder named Images. When you select Put Images in Subfolder, you'll see the default folder name—Images— next to the Browse button. If you want to store your images in a folder other than the Images folder, click the Browse button and locate the folder.

There is an Images folder already created in the Lesson08 folder for you to store your images. You don't need to click the Browse button for this exercise. If the folder did not exist, Fireworks would create one for you.

The files you export from Fireworks need to be saved in a folder (or in subfolder) that is defined (or will be defined) as a site in Dreamweaver. In Lesson 11 you will define the Lessons folder as the local site folder.

NOTE *Folder names and file names are capitalized throughout this book for readability. Some Web servers do not support capital letters for file names. When you are building your images and HTML pages, it is a good idea to use lowercase for all your file names. That way, you are assured the file names are supported on any server.*

4) Click Options to define the HTML options Fireworks uses when generating the HTML.

There are several options you need to set to define how Fireworks creates the HTML file. These options are defined in the HTML Setup dialog box. You can access this dialog box from the Export dialog box , as you just did, or you can choose File > HTML Setup.

On the General tab of the HTML Setup dialog box, you can choose the HTML style that Fireworks generates and the file extension.

5) For this exercise, with the General tab selected, choose Dreamweaver from the pop-up menu. Select htm (.htm) as the Extension. If you are on a Macintosh, choose Dreamweaver from the File Creator pop-up menu.

The File Creator option for the Macintosh enables you to double-click the file to open Dreamweaver from the Finder.

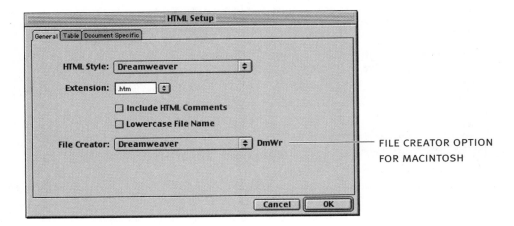

FILE CREATOR OPTION
FOR MACINTOSH

6) Select the Table tab.

The Table tab allows you to modify the spacing in the table that Fireworks creates. For this exercise, you will use all of the defaults.

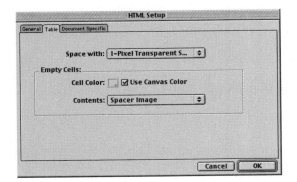

On the Document Specific tab, you can change the file naming scheme for the images in the rollovers. As you choose from each of the pop-up menus, an example of the resulting file name appears. For this example, you will use doc.name + Underscore + Frame #. Set the other options to None.

7) Select the Document Specific tab. Set the first row of Slices to doc.name, choose None for the rest, and set Frames to Underscore + Frame#.

The resulting file name appears as Buttons_f2.gif in the dialog box.

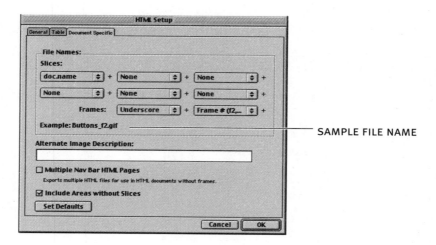

SAMPLE FILE NAME

NOTE *There are several options for naming your rollover file names. You could also choose Rollover from the Frames pop-up menu to add _over instead of the _f2 at the end of the file name.*

8) Click OK to close the HTML Setup dialog box and then click Save to export your slices and create the HTML page.

Fireworks exported your images using the Optimization settings on the Optimize panel and created an HTML file.

9) Open the HTML file in your browser to check the results.

The buttons and the links should work.

10) Save and close your file.

CHANGING GRAPHICS TO ROLLOVERS

The Button Editor is a tremendous time-saving tool and works great when you first create your buttons. You can even use it for graphics already drawn on the page. In this next exercise, you will add rollovers to the graphics on an existing page.

1) Open the Adventure.png file you created in Lesson 4.

If you no longer have this file, you can use the Adventure.png file in the Start folder within the Lesson08 folder. You will add rollovers to each of the graphics: Adventure Tours, Featured Destinations, and so on.

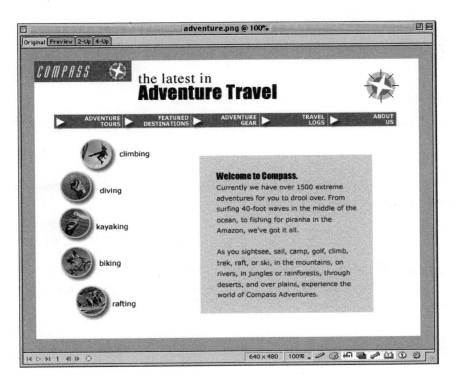

2) Select the elements and the text of the Adventure Tours object and group them if they are not grouped already. Choose Insert > Convert to Symbol. Type the name of the button in the Symbol Properties dialog box and choose Button. Click OK.

Once you've converted an object (or objects) to a button symbol, you can use the Button Editor as you did in the previous exercise.

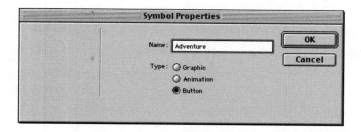

3) Double-click the button to open the Button Editor window.

The Up state of the button uses the existing object; you then need to create the look of the Over state of the button.

4) Select the Over tab and click Copy Up Graphic. Change the color of the rectangle to a darker blue and the triangle to a yellow orange.

Now each state of the button has a different look.

5) Repeat the steps using the Link wizard as you did in the previous exercise to add the Alt tag and change the file name of the button. Repeat these steps for the remaining buttons. Save your file.

Be sure to preview your buttons in Fireworks to verify that the rollovers work.

WHAT YOU HAVE LEARNED

In this lesson, you have:

- Created a rollover button using the Button Editor [pages 214–216]
- Added bevel effects to create realistic-looking buttons [pages 216–217]
- Used the Link wizard to set links for a button [pages 219–221]
- Exported a button and page as HTML [pages 225–228]
- Converted graphics to a rollover button [pages 229–230]

creating image maps and slices

LESSON 9

In this lesson, you will learn a variety of techniques to add interactivity to your pages. You will start by creating an image map where the user can click on multiple areas of an image to link to other pages in your site. You will further explore the concept of slicing an image, learning to add behaviors to the slice to swap images and add Pop-up Menus. Using the URL panel, you will quickly add links to your slices.

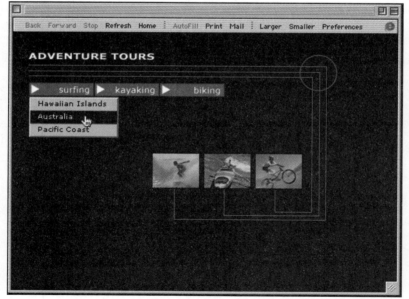

In this lesson you will learn to add pop-up menus to a Web page, create an image map, and add a disjointed rollover image.

WHAT YOU WILL LEARN

In this lesson, you will:

- Create an image map by drawing hotspots

- Create disjointed rollovers

- Slice an image into smaller pieces

- Use the URL panel and the URL library

- Add a Pop-up Menu

APPROXIMATE TIME

This lesson takes approximately 2 hours to complete.

LESSON FILES

Media Files:

Lesson09\Import_URLs\Links.htm

Starting Files:

Lesson09\Imagemaps\Worldmap.png

Lesson09\Disjointed\Travel.png

Lesson09\Slicing\Travel_log.png

Lesson09\Popups\Popup.png

Completed Projects:

Lesson09\Completed\Popup.png

Lesson09\ Completed\Travel.png

Lesson09\Completed\Worldmap.png

CREATING AN IMAGE MAP

By definition, all your exported graphics are rectangular. If you make a graphic a link, then the shape of the link is rectangular as well. You can make a portion of a graphic transparent, or make its background color the same color as the background color of the Web page, giving the illusion of a different shape, but you will still have a rectangle. If you want to make a link area a shape other than a rectangle, or if you want to create several links on one image, then you have to use an image map.

For example, suppose you have a map of the United States, and you want a link for each state. Most of the states have irregular shapes, and none are neatly ordered side by side. You need to distinguish the different shapes of each state and then assign a different link to each shape. This is what an image map does.

The link areas on an image map are referred to as hotspots. A hotspot area on an image map can be one of three shapes: a rectangle, a circle, or a polygon. The next exercise shows you how to create the hotspots on an image and then assign links to the hotspots.

Although it is easy to create image maps in an HTML editor such as Macromedia Dreamweaver, Macromedia Fireworks can accomplish the same task for you. The resulting HTML can then be pasted into your Web page or inserted into your Dreamweaver project.

1) Open the Worldmap.png file located in the Imagemaps folder within the Lesson09 folder.

For this exercise, you want your users to select the country that they want to visit. You will draw hotspot areas and then assign a link to each area.

2) Select the Rectangle Hotspot tool from the Tools panel and draw a rectangle around the Hawaiian Islands. A blue translucent rectangular area (the hotspot) appears.

The size of the hotspot rectangle determines where the user must click to select the link. If you are designing a site for small children, you want the hotspot area large enough for unsteady hands to select. In this exercise, you want to cover the text and the island area.

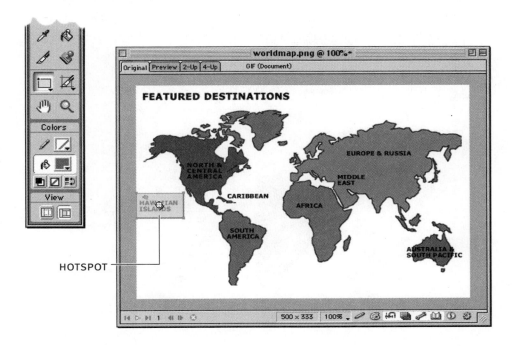

After you draw the rectangle, you may need to change its size or move it on the canvas. Make sure that you switch to the Pointer tool to make any changes to the hotspot.

NOTE *You'll notice a small white marker in the middle of your hotspot area. This marker (called the drag-and-drop behavior handle) is for adding behaviors to the hotspot. You'll use this later in the lesson.*

3) Click and hold the Hotspot tool to access the Circle Hotspot tool; then draw a circle around Australia.

The hotspot tools work like other vector tools. To draw from the center, hold down Alt (Windows) or Option (Macintosh) as you draw with the tool.

4) Use the Polygon Hotspot tool to draw a shape around North and Central America.

The Polygon Hotspot tool works differently than the other tools. Instead of clicking and holding to draw the shape, just click around the shape. Each time you click, a point on the hotspot is created. Continue to click until you have a hotspot that roughly outlines the area.

After the third point is added, the hotspot area begins to form. Continue to click around the shape. You can add as many points as you want; the more points, the closer the hotspot comes to defining the shape. A point to remember is that your users generally will click on or around the text description within the shape, so your hotspot area just needs to cover most of the area.

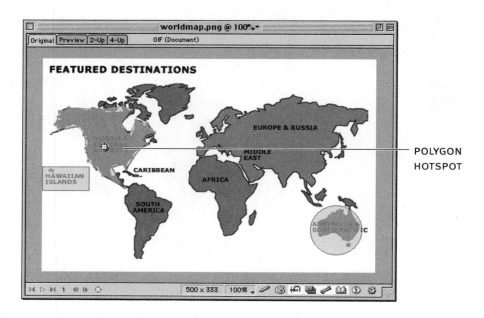

NOTE *When drawing your hotspots, make sure you don't overlap an existing hotspot. If you do, the topmost hotspot takes precedence.*

5) Select each hotspot with the Pointer tool. Open the Object panel by choosing Window > Object. Type *australia.htm* for Australia, *hawaii.htm* for the Hawaiian Islands, and *namerica.htm* for North America in the Link text box.

Once you have the hotspots on the image, you need to assign a link for each of them. In the Object panel, you assign the link, an Alt tag, and a target for the link. (The target generally applies to pages built with frames. You do not need to set it for this exercise.) You can also change the color of the hotspot using the color box on the panel.

The Alt tag displays text in the browser when the user rolls over the hotspot area. Adding some descriptive text helps users determine whether they want to link to that page. This feature may not be supported in earlier browsers, but it is a good idea to add Alt text to all of your links.

6) For this exercise, add the name of the area in the Alt text box for each of the hotspots. For example, type *North American Destinations* in the Alt text box for the North America link.

NOTE *You can change the shape of the hotspot using the Shape pop-up menu on the Object panel. If you change the shape, you will then need to resize or move the hotspot to cover the area.*

After you have assigned URLs and Alt text to all of the hotspots, you are ready to export the image map.

7) Choose Window > Optimize and choose the file format, palette, and any other needed options. For this exercise, choose the GIF file format and WebSnap Adaptive (Windows) or Web Adaptive (Macintosh) from the Optimize panel.

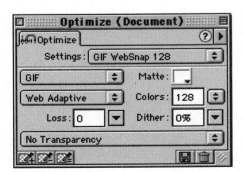

237

8) Choose File > Export. In the Export dialog box, type the file name if you want a different name from the one Fireworks assigns. Select HTML and Images in the Save As Type (Windows) or Save As (Macintosh) box. Make sure that the Slices option is set to None. Select Export HTML File from the HTML options. Click Save to save the HTML file and the image map graphic.

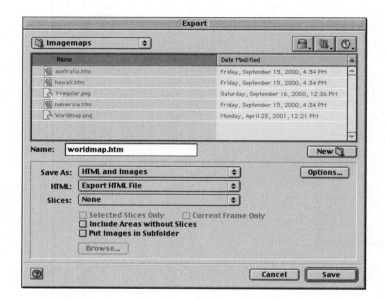

Make sure that you export your file in the Imagemaps folder within the Lesson09 folder. There are some HTML files in that folder for testing your links.

9) Open the HTML file and test it in your browser.

Move the pointer over each hotspot area. If you assigned an Alt tag to the slice, the descriptive text appears. Clicking a hotspot takes you to a test page.

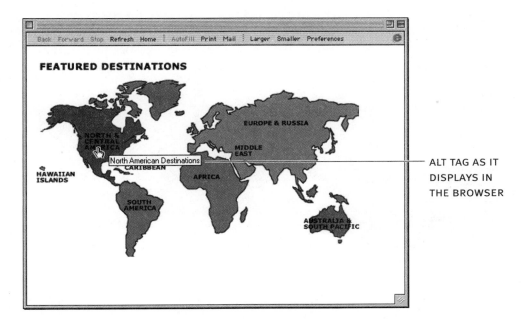

ALT TAG AS IT
DISPLAYS IN
THE BROWSER

TIP *If you are using Internet Explorer to test your page, you'll notice an outline (the same shape as the hotspot) around each hotspot area once you click the hotspot. This is the accessibility feature in Internet Explorer. Instead of clicking a link, you can press the Tab key to move to each hotspot area on the page. To select the link, press Enter (Windows) or Return (Macintosh). This feature works for all links on the page, not just your image map hotspots.*

10) You can close the browser and return to your Worldmap.png file in Fireworks.

You'll use this file for the next exercise.

WORKING WITH THE WEB LAYER

Hotspots and slices (covered later in this lesson) are stored on the Web Layer on the Layers panel. The Web Layer is the top layer by default and cannot be moved. As you work with your images, you may want to hide the hotspots or slices to edit the objects below. You can click Show/Hide Slices on the Tools panel or use the Layers panel. If you use the Tools panel, all hotspots, slices, and slice guides are hidden. If you use the Layers panel, you can hide individual slices or hotspots.

1) Choose Window > Layers to open the Layers panel.

The Layers panel displays the Web Layer as the top layer.

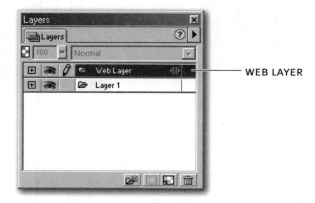

WEB LAYER

2) Click the plus (Windows) or triangle (Macintosh) to open the Web Layer.

The three hotspots for the image map are displayed as separate object stacks on the panel.

3) Click the Hide Layer icon (the eye) on one of the hotspot object stacks.

The hotspot on the canvas is hidden. Click the Hide Layer icon again to view the hotspot. You'll need to see all of the hotspots for the next exercise.

NOTE *If you hide the Web Layer in the Layers panel, hotspots will still be exported when you export as HTML.*

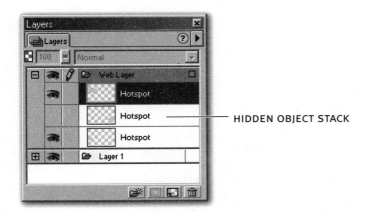

HIDDEN OBJECT STACK

NOTE *You can click the lock column (the column with the pencil) on the Web Layer to ensure that you don't delete or move the hotspots or slices. For this exercise, leave the Web Layer unlocked.*

USING THE URL PANEL

When creating a Web site, you may have several different buttons or image maps that all use the same link. So that you don't need to retype those links, Fireworks provides the URL panel, which you can use to save all of your URLs. The URLs are stored in a URL Library file stored within your Fireworks 4 application in the Configuration/URL folder. Besides just typing the URLs, you can import bookmark files or URLs from regular HTML files.

Each time you enter a URL for a button or hotspot, Fireworks remembers that URL and stores it in the URL History list. The next time you access either the URL panel or the Object panel, all URL history files are available for you to use again. When you quit Fireworks, the URL History list is erased. If you want to retain a URL for later use, you need to save it in the URL library.

1) Select the North America hotspot. Choose Window > URL to open the URL panel.

The link that you applied to the hotspot appears on the URL panel in the Link text box.

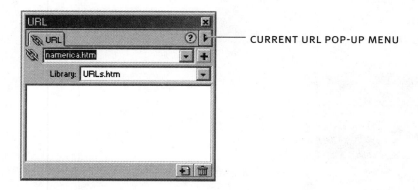

CURRENT URL POP-UP MENU

2) Click the Current URL pop-up menu on the URL panel.

The URL history list appears under the No URL item in the list. All the links that you created for the image map are listed.

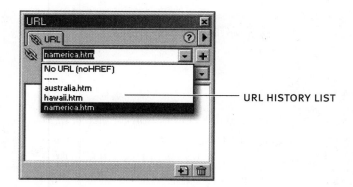

URL HISTORY LIST

NOTE *All links that you have created appear in this list. The URL History list is erased when you quit Fireworks. If you have not quit Fireworks, you may see your button links from Lesson 8 as well as the image map links.*

3) Draw a hotspot over South America. From the URL History list on the URL panel, choose namerica.htm. Press Enter (Windows) or Return (Macintosh) to apply the link to the hotspot.

Look at the Object panel. The link appears in the Link text box. Notice that there is a URL History pop-up menu on the Object panel as well as on the URL panel. You could have applied the URL link from the Object panel instead of the URL panel.

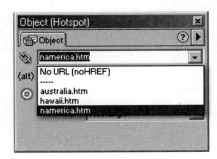

The URL History list is deleted when you quit Fireworks. If you are working on Web pages that use the same links, you will want to save those links in the URL library.

4) Select a hotspot on the page. On the URL panel click the plus (+) sign next to the link text box to add the current URL to the URL library.

The selected URL is added to the default library: URLs.htm. You'll see the library items listed on the panel.

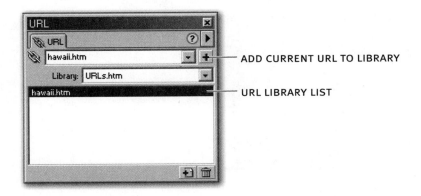

ADD CURRENT URL TO LIBRARY

URL LIBRARY LIST

If you want to add all of the links on the page to the library, you can choose to add them all at once, instead of one at a time.

5) Click the arrow at the top right of the URL panel to access the Options pop-up menu. Choose Add Used URLs to Library to save all of the URLs at once.

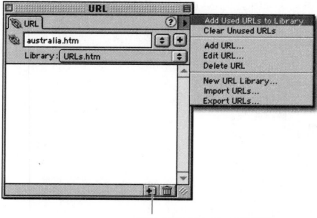

ADD NEW URL TO LIBRARY

All of the links either from your image map or from buttons on the page are added to the URL library and appear in the list.

You can also manually enter new URLs in the URL library.

6) Click Add New URL to Library on the URL panel and type *europe.htm* in the New URL dialog box. Click OK to close the window.

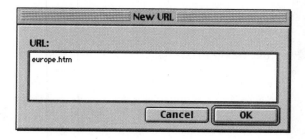

The URL is added to the library and also appears in the History list.

When you have a library of links, you can easily add them to any Web object on the Web layer. Just select a slice or hotspot and then click the Link pop-up menu on either the Object panel or the Link tab of the Link wizard to see a list of the history files and library files to choose from. The list order in the pop-up menu (separated by dotted lines) is No URL (to remove a link), the history files, and then the library files.

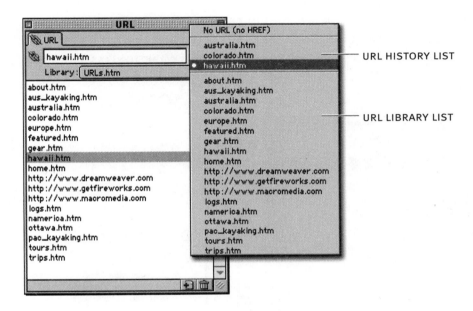

URL HISTORY LIST

URL LIBRARY LIST

CREATING IMAGE MAPS AND SLICES

IMPORTING AND EXPORTING URLS

If you are working with a team, you can make a list of the links within the site and give everyone on the team the URLs. Then there should be no mistakes in the spelling or paths of the links.

1) Click the arrow at the top right of the URL panel to access the Options pop-up menu and choose Import URLs. Select the HTML file you want to use. For this exercise, choose Links.htm from the Import_URLs folder within the Lesson09 folder.

The URLs from the file now appear on the URL panel.

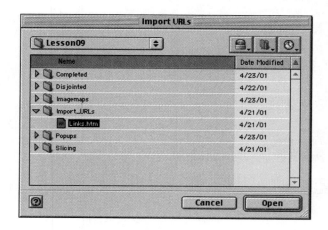

NOTE *The Links.htm file contains only links, although you could import any HTML file that contained the links you want to use. You could also import a bookmark file from your browser. You could use Dreamweaver to create an index page with all the links in your site, and then use the URL panel to import the links into Fireworks.*

⊙ POWER TIP *If you are using Internet Explorer on Windows, choose File > Import and Export from the browser menu bar. You can then use the Export wizard that appears to export from your Favorites list. If you are using Internet Explorer on a Macintosh, choose Favorites > Organize Favorites and then choose File > Export Favorites. Use the URL panel in Fireworks to import the links from your Favorites list. If you are using Netscape on Windows, choose Bookmarks > Edit Bookmarks and then choose File > Save As. If you are using Netscape on the Macintosh, the Bookmarks file is located in the Netscape folder within the Preferences folder. Look for the Bookmarks.html file.*

The imported URLs are added to your URL library list. You can then add more URLs as you build more pages. In the next step, you will export your library.

2) Click the arrow at the top right of the URL panel to access the Options pop-up menu and choose Export URLs. Type the file name and choose the destination for the exported file. Click Save.

Not only can you save URLs in a library, but you can also create multiple URL libraries. For example, you might want separate URL libraries for different Web projects.

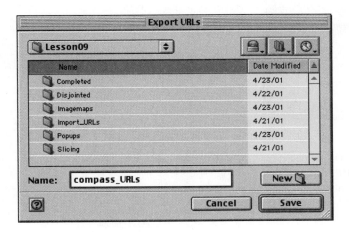

3) Click the arrow at the top right of the URL panel to access the Options pop-up menu and choose New URL Library. Type a name for the library and click OK.

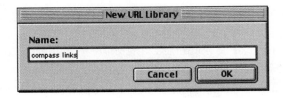

NOTE *Your URL library name is automatically appended with the .htm extension in the URL library list. Your library file is saved in your Fireworks 4 application folder within the Configurations/URL Libraries folder. Files saved in this location are the only ones that appear in the Library pop-up menu in the URL panel.*

To pick a URL library to use, choose the library from the Library pop-up menu on the URL panel. Only the items saved in that library list appear in the Link pop-up menu on the Object panel, the URL panel, or within the Link wizard.

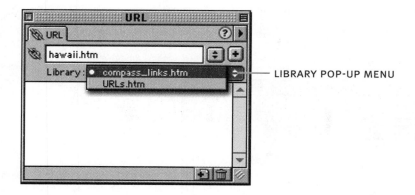

LIBRARY POP-UP MENU

4) Save and close the Worldmap.png file.

SLICING AN IMAGE

Slicing is a method of taking a large graphic, dividing it into smaller pieces, and then reassembling the pieces by using an HTML table. The sliced individual graphics can be used as rollovers. Performing this process manually can be tedious, but Fireworks makes it a breeze.

There are several advantages to slicing an image. For example, if you will be updating a section of a graphic often, slicing means you have to redo just that one piece of the graphic. In addition, each slice can be optimized differently for better overall results: for part of the image, JPEG may be the best choice for exporting; and for another part, GIF may be the best choice. Slicing takes a large image and carves it into smaller pieces. The pieces are then assembled in an HTML table.

In Fireworks, you use the Slice tool to draw an overlay where you want the slices to be located. When the file is exported, Fireworks divides the original image, creating as many smaller files as you requested.

If you create your images with Fireworks, you can use the built-in Button Editor and Link wizard to help you create your buttons and the Object panel to assign graphic links. If you receive an image from someone who doesn't have Fireworks, or if you have a huge graphic that you want to divide into smaller pieces, you can use the Slice tool and assign the links and optimization formats to each slice.

1) Open the file Travel_log.png in the Slicing folder within the Lesson09 folder.

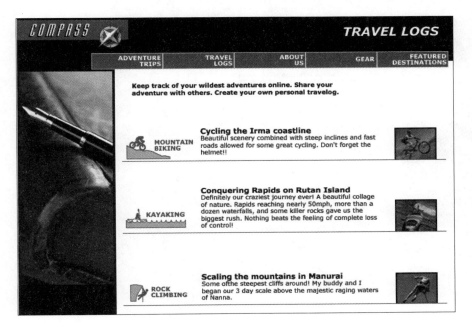

The file is one large graphic. For this exercise, you will use the Slice tool to "cut" the image into smaller pieces.

2) Use the Slice tool to draw slices over the pen image on the left, the three activity images on the right, and the five button areas across the top.

After you draw over each area, a green translucent shape—the slice—appears. The default green color is slightly different than the color for the hotspots you created earlier. You also see the red slice guides. Use the red slice guides to help you draw the other slices on the canvas. For example, once you draw the slice on the biking image, you can use the guides to draw the slice for the kayak and the climber.

TIP   *If Snap to Grid is on, you may have difficulty creating the slices on the buttons.*

The red slice guides define the the rows and columns in the table that Fireworks creates when you export your file to HTML. The more red lines, the more complex the table structure. Use the guide lines to make sure that your sliced items are aligned in columns. For example, if the slices on the images are different widths, you create extra columns in the table.

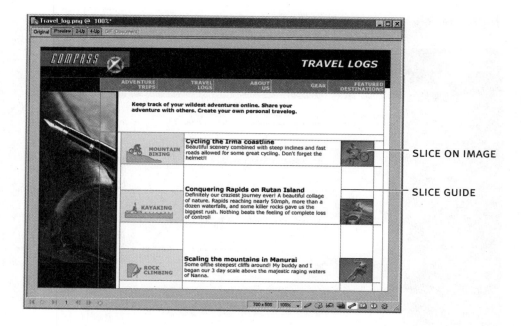

SLICE ON IMAGE

SLICE GUIDE

3) Select the slice on the Adventure Trips button. Then choose Window > Object if the Object panel is not already open. In the Link box, type *trips.htm*. Type *Adventure Trips* in the Alt text box. Remove the check mark for Auto-Name Slices and type *trips* in the Name text box.

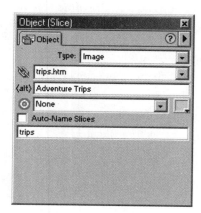

4) Repeat step 3 for all slices on the top buttons using *logs.htm*, *about.htm*, *gear.htm*, and *featured.htm*, respectively, for the links.

If you imported the Links.htm file in the last exercise, the links you need are already in your URL library list. You can select them from the Recent URLs pop-up menu on the Object panel.

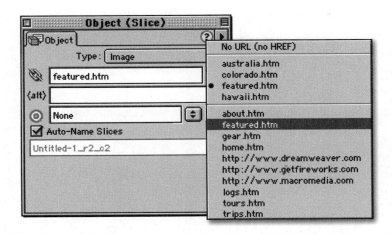

5) Save your file; then select File > Export to open the Export window. Choose Export Slices as the Slicing option and Export HTML File as the HTML option, and choose HTML and Images in the Save As Type (Windows) or Save As (Macintosh) box. Navigate to the Slicing folder within the Lesson09 folder. Click Save to export your slices and create the HTML page.

The export file name defaults to logs.htm. Use that name for your HTML file. The testing link pages use that name.

> **TIP** *If you select Put Images in Subfolder and do not have a subfolder defined, Fireworks creates the Images folder for you and places all of the exported images in that folder.*

6) Open the HTML document in your browser to see the results. You can save and close the Travel_log.png file.

CREATING DISJOINTED ROLLOVERS

In Lesson 8, you learned to use the Button Editor to create rollovers in which one image is swapped out for another image when the user moves over it. A disjointed rollover is an image that changes when the user moves the pointer over a completely different image.

To see this, you'll use a file that has been created for you. You will add graphics that appear when the user rolls over each of the buttons. Disjointed rollovers use frames to store the rollover images. For this example, you will add the frames and import the rollover images.

1) Open the Travel.png file in the Disjointed folder within the Lesson09 folder.

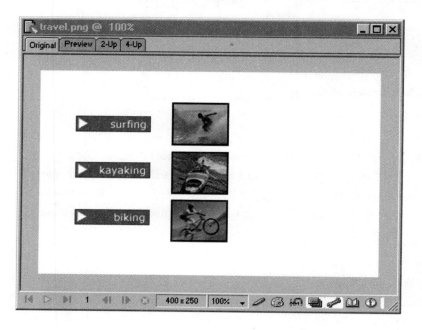

NOTE *You used frames in Lesson 7 to create animations. In this lesson, you will use frames to store images for the disjointed rollovers.*

2) Select the surfing image in Frame 1 and use the Info panel to check its size and placement on the page.

For this exercise, you want another image to replace the surfer image when the user moves over the surfing button. The new image needs to be in the exact same position and be the same size as the surfer image.

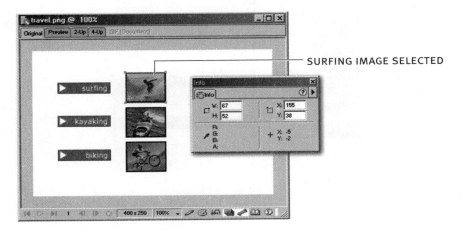

SURFING IMAGE SELECTED

3) Create a new frame in the Frames panel to place the rollover images. Draw a rectangle in Frame 2 using the size (W = width and H = height) and placement (X,Y) information from the surfing image. Color this rectangle the same color blue as the buttons and type *Surfing Adventures* within the rectangle.

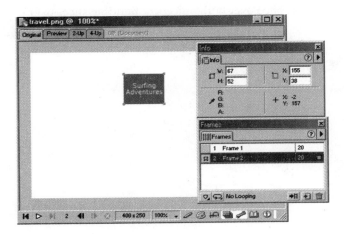

TIP *Be sure to press Enter (Windows) or Return (Macintosh) after typing values on the Info panel to change the size and placement of the rectangle.*

253

4) Repeat steps 2–3 for the kayaking and biking images, using *Kayaking Adventures* and *Biking Adventures* for the text.

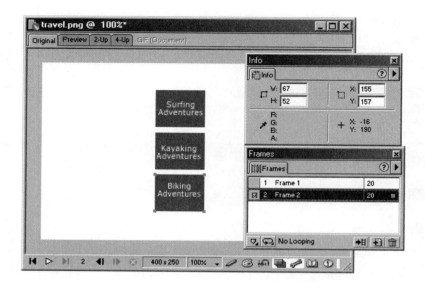

5) Select Frame 1 in the Frames panel. Select the surfing button and the surfer image. Choose Insert > Slice. Click Multiple in the alert box.

You could have drawn slices on each object with the Slice tool as you did earlier. The Insert Slice command creates a slice for you, the exact size of the selected object, which is much faster. Because you have two objects selected, an alert box appears asking whether you want one slice over both objects or multiple slices over each item. For this exercise, you want multiple slices.

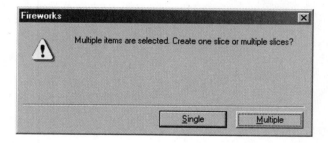

6) Repeat step 5 for the remaining buttons and images on the page in Frame 1.

The slice is where Fireworks stores all of the information for the button or rollover. When you export your file, Fireworks uses the information to generate the HTML or the JavaScript that makes the button or rollover work in the browser.

In the next step, you will create the interactivity for displaying the rectangles you created in Frame 2. In Fireworks (and Dreamweaver), you use behavior commands to add interactivity to your page.

7) Select the slice on the surfing button.

The center marker (the drag-and-drop behavior handle) contains the built-in behaviors for adding the interactivity to this button. If you are familiar with Dreamweaver, you'll recognize the icon that appears when you click the slice. In Fireworks, you use this handle to point to the slice over the image you want to swap out when the user rolls over the button.

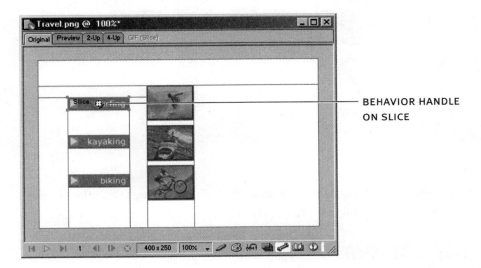

BEHAVIOR HANDLE
ON SLICE

8) Drag the behavior handle from the button to the slice on the image to create the disjointed rollover.

You'll see a blue line connecting the two slices, and the Swap Image dialog box will appear.

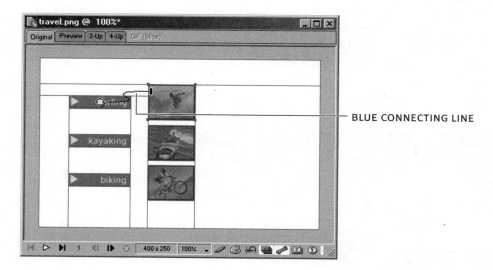

BLUE CONNECTING LINE

9) In the Swap Image dialog box, you choose the frame that stores the rollover image. For this exercise, the rectangle is drawn in Frame 2, so choose Frame 2. Click OK.

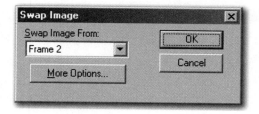

If you had one image under one slice that you wanted to change with each button, you could place the swap images in multiple frames. Then each button would point to different frames under the initial image.

10) Repeat steps 7 through 9 for each button slice.

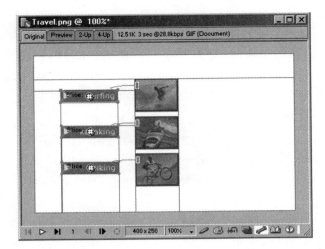

11) Click the Preview tab in the document window to see the rollovers in action.

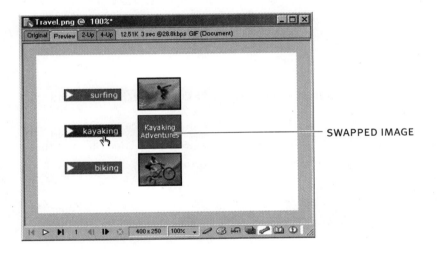

SWAPPED IMAGE

As you move the pointer over each button, the rectangle and text in Frame 2 replaces each image.

TIP *Click Hide Slices on the Tools panel to hide the slices when you are previewing the rollovers.*

257

USING THE BEHAVIORS PANEL

When the images are placed in the frames, you are ready to make the rollovers work. To do this, you need to add some JavaScript. Don't panic—Fireworks does all the hard work for you. Fireworks uses behaviors to add all of the JavaScript code to your pages. A behavior is simply a set of options that you can add to your rollovers. You define the images to use, and Fireworks does the rest. Behaviors in Fireworks work the same as they do in Dreamweaver.

Behaviors consist of two parts: an event and an action. The event is a user activity: for example, the user may move the pointer over a button. The action is the result that the event triggers. Behaviors in Fireworks can be assigned only to Web objects such as slices and hotspots.

Of course, the easiest way to create buttons is to use the Button Editor as you did in Lesson 8. In this exercise, you will be manually doing what the Button Editor does automatically for you.

NOTE *The Button Editor stores your rollover buttons in frames, but you do not see them on pages where you have not added frames to the Frames panel. If you have created frames on your page, as you did in this exercise, you will see the rollover images created by the Button Editor in the Frame 2.*

1) Select all the buttons in Frame 1 and choose Edit > Copy. Select Frame 2 and choose Edit > Paste.

To make sure that you copy the buttons and not the slices, click Hide Slices in the View area of the Tools panel before you select the buttons.

TIP *When you use Copy and Paste in Fireworks, the new pasted image is always placed in the exact same location as the original image.*

2) Change the color of the rectangles in Frame 2 to a darker blue.

These buttons will be the rollovers, so you need to change their appearance. The text and rectangles are grouped. You'll need to ungroup them or use the Subselection tool to select just the rectangle.

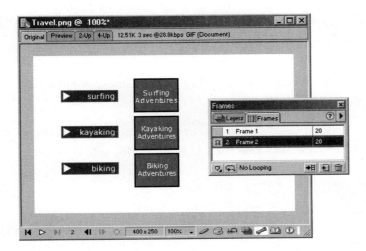

3) Click Show Slices in the View area of the Tools panel. In Frame 1, select the slice for the surfing button.

You'll see the blue line linking the slice on the button to the surfer image you added in the previous exercise.

4) Click the behavior handle. A pop-up menu appears where you can choose the behavior you want to add to this button. Choose Add Simple Rollover Behavior from the pop-up menu.

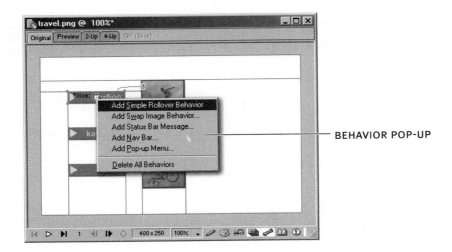

BEHAVIOR POP-UP

259

The Add Simple Rollover Behavior uses the image in Frame 2 for the rollover and adds the necessary JavaScript for the rollover.

5) Repeat step 4 for the remaining buttons and then check the results on the Preview tab of the document window.

When you roll over each button, the button changes to the rollover image, and the image displays the rectangle with the text description.

6) Click the Original tab. Select the slice on the surfing button. Choose Window > Behaviors to access the Behaviors panel.

You should see the Simple Rollover behavior that has now been attached to the button along with the Swap Image behavior you added previously for the disjointed rollover.

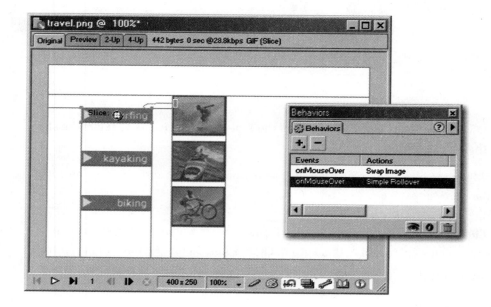

Fireworks adds the onMouseOver event to both the Swap Image and Simple Rollover behaviors. In this example, these events are what you want. If you wanted the Swap Image action to take place when the user clicks the button, for example, you could change the event by selecting Swap Image on the Behaviors panel and then clicking the arrow (that appears next to onMouseOver when selected) and choosing onClick from the pop-up menu.

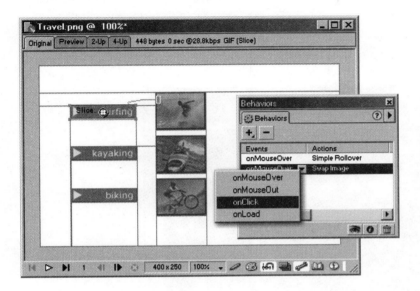

7) **Save and close the file.**

ADDING A POP-UP MENU

Pop-up Menus are currently very popular on Web pages. A Pop-up Menu on a Web page is a navigation tool that is hidden until the user rolls over a button or an image on the page. Because the menus are initially hidden, you can pack a lot of links into a small space. You can also include submenus to add even more navigational links to your page. Hand-coding the JavaScript needed to create Pop-up Menus is tedious, but Fireworks makes the process as easy as entering names and links in a dialog box.

1) Open the Popup.png file in the Popups folder within the Lesson09 folder.

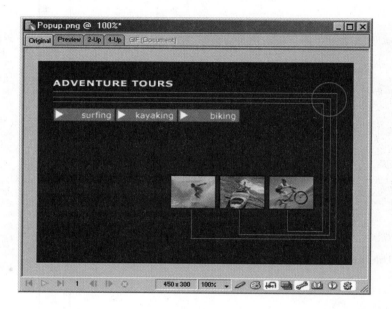

2) Select all of the buttons—surfing, kayaking, and biking—and then choose Insert > Slice. A dialog box appears asking if you want one slice or multiple slices. Choose Multiple to place a slice on each of the buttons.

Pop-up menus are added to slices using behaviors.

3) Select the slice on the surfing button and then choose Insert > Pop-Up Menu.

The Set Pop-Up Menu dialog box opens. Here you will enter the names and URLs for the pop-up menu on this button.

4) Type the text you want the user to see in the menu in the Text box. For this example, type *Hawaiian Islands*. Press the Tab key and enter the HTML page to link to if this item is chosen. Type *hawaii.htm* in the Link box. Click the plus sign next to Menu to enter the first menu item.

The menu name and the link URL appear in the list after you click the plus sign.

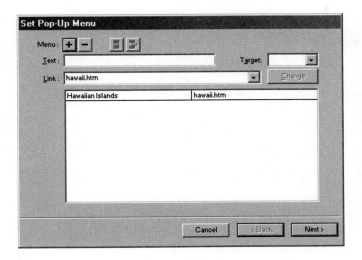

5) Type *Australia* in the Text box and *australia.htm* in the Link box. Click the plus sign to add this item. Repeat again, entering *Pacific Coast* and *pacific.htm*.

TIP *You must click the plus sign to add a new menu item to the list. If you want to make a change to one of the items in the list, select the menu item from the list, make the change, and then click Change. If you want to delete an item in the list, select the item and then click the minus sign.*

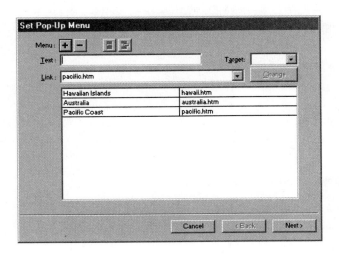

263

6) Click Next to customize the appearance of the Pop-up Menu. Choose a font, size, and color you like and then click Finish.

Choose the color of the text and the cell as it appears when initially displayed from the Up State options. Choose the color of the text and cell when the pointer is over the item from the Over State options. A preview of the Pop-up Menu is displayed in the dialog box.

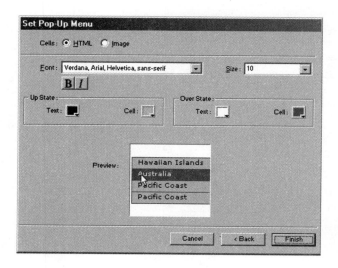

NOTE *If you click Image for the Cells option, you create a GIF image for background cells in the Pop-up Menu. If you select HTML for the Cells option, the Pop-up Menu is created with text. For this exercise, use the HTML option.*

You'll see a blue line and a series of three blue rectangles that represent the Pop-up Menu. When you move the pointer over a blue rectangle, the cursor changes to the pointing hand. When you see the hand cursor, you can drag the rectangle to place the Pop-up Menu where you want it to appear on the page.

7) Move the top blue rectangle to the bottom of the button.

TIP *Generally, you will want all your Pop-up Menus to appear in the same vertical position on the page. Once you place the first Pop-up Menu, drag a ruler guide from the top ruler to the top blue line.*

8) To preview the Pop-up Menu, choose File > Preview in Browser.

The Pop-up Menu does not appear in the Fireworks preview window. You must preview in the browser to see the Pop-up Menu. The links won't work until you export your file.

If you want to make a change to the items in your Pop-up Menu or add new items to the list, double-click within the blue rectangles of the Pop-up Menu. The Set Pop-Up Menu dialog box appears, where you can make your changes.

9) Select the slice on the kayaking button. Click the point-to marker on the slice and choose Add Pop-up Menu.

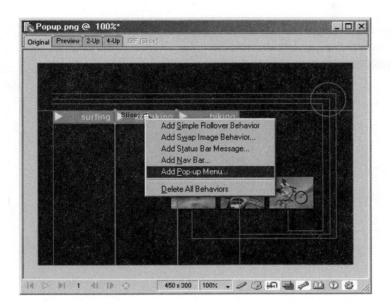

You will add a Pop-up Menu with a submenu to this slice.

10) Repeat from step 4, typing *River Kayaking* in the Text box. Click the plus sign. You do not need to enter a link for this item. Type *Colorado River* in the Text box and *colorado.htm* in the Link text box; then click the plus sign.

The first item, without the link, is the main category, and the next item, Colorado River, is the submenu item.

11) Select the submenu item in the list and then click Create menu.

The item in the list is indented. If you want to return the submenu item to a plain pop-up list, click Promote Menu.

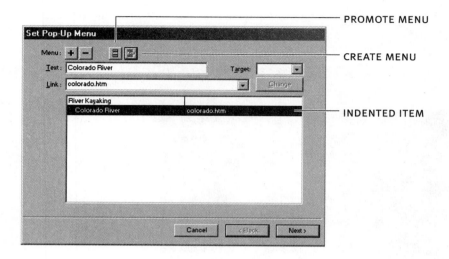

PROMOTE MENU

CREATE MENU

INDENTED ITEM

ON YOUR OWN

Finish the Pop-up Menu, adding *Ottawa River* with the link *ottawa.htm* as the second item in the submenu. Then add another category in the list: *Ocean Kayaking*. Add the submenu items *Australian Coast, aus_kayak.htm*, and *Pacific Coast, pac_kayak.htm*. Check your Pop-up Menus in the browser. Then export the file as an HTML file to test the links. Save the exported file in the Popup folder within the Lesson09 folder.

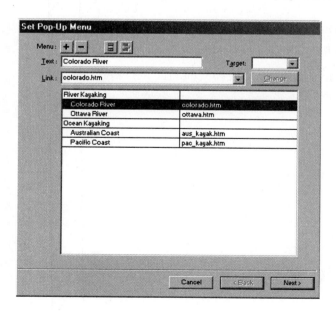

WHAT YOU HAVE LEARNED

In this lesson, you have:

- Added hotspots to a graphic to create an image map [pages 234–239]

- Used the URL panel to add links to hotspots [pages 241–245]

- Imported and exported URLs [pages 246–248]

- Sliced an image [pages 248–251]

- Added a disjointed rollover to a page [pages 252–257]

- Used the Behaviors panel to add a rollover [pages 258–261]

- Created Pop-up Menus [pages 262–266]

production techniques

LESSON 10

Macromedia Fireworks provides you with many ways to automate the process of creating images and making changes. You may need to change some text on multiple pages, or maybe you decide to change a color or the font used on your pages. The Find and Replace options can make those changes more quickly than you could make them manually. If you need to make similar changes to multiple files, you can easily define a script to execute those changes for you. Saving the script allows you to repeat the steps on other files or other sites.

You will change the text on multiple pages in this exercise and use batch processing to scale and export a group of images.

WHAT YOU WILL LEARN

In this lesson, you will:

- Learn to use Find and Replace in a document or multiple documents
- Learn the value of scripts and batch processing for repetitive tasks
- Use batch processing to convert or export files
- Create and run an export script

APPROXIMATE TIME

This lesson takes approximately 1 hour to complete.

LESSON FILES

Media Files:

Lesson10\Batch folder

Lesson10\Change folder

Lesson10\Scripts folder

Lesson10\Run folder

Starting Files:

None

Completed Projects:

None

USING FIND AND REPLACE

You've seen how useful Fireworks is for creating graphics and buttons for your Web page. Because text is editable in Fireworks, you can easily make a text change and update a button. What if the company name changes and all of the graphics for your site need changing? Making the changes manually could be quite a task. But with the Fireworks Find and Replace feature, you can easily make that change in an entire file or in all of the files in a folder. The Find and Replace feature works only in Fireworks PNG files and in files containing vector text imported from FreeHand or CorelDRAW. If text has been converted to a path, Find and Replace will not find that text.

Within Fireworks, you can find and replace text, fonts, colors, and URLs. The search can be within a selection, within a frame, within the document, within multiple files, or within all of the files in a folder.

For this exercise, you will work with four files that will be used on a Web site. The problem is that the company name was typed incorrectly in all four files. You'll use Find and Replace to change all four files.

1) Open the Bike.png file in the Change folder within the Lesson10 folder. The company name Compass Travel needs to be changed to Compass Tours.

Compass Travel appears on this page in two locations. One is the title in black text. Beneath the title is the drop-shadow text block with the text in gray. Both text blocks are grouped together. If you manually change the text, you first need to ungroup the text (or use the Subselection tool), change the text in the first text block, and then select the other text block and change its text. Using Find and Replace, you can change both text blocks on this page at the same time.

2) Choose Window > Find and Replace to open the panel. From the Search Selection pop-up menu, choose Search Document. Choose Find Text from the Attribute pop-up menu. Type *Compass Travel* in the Find box and *Compass Tours* in the Change To box.

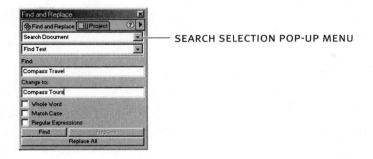

SEARCH SELECTION POP-UP MENU

You also have some options for limiting your search:

- Whole Word ensures that you get only text that is a word—not a portion of a word.

- Match Case limits the search to text that matches the case of the text you want to find.

- Regular Expressions enables you to perform more complex searches. For example, you can find words or numbers by using wildcards or find words that end in a particular string of characters.

For this exercise, do not select any of these options.

3) Click the top right arrow on the panel to access the Find and Replace Options menu. Choose Replace Options.

This menu contains two options. You can log each file that is altered (viewed on the Project panel), and you can set the Replace options. Note the check mark (Windows) or bullet (Macintosh) next to the option to see whether the option is turned on.

When finding and replacing among multiple files, select Replace Options from the Options menu to set the way multiple opened files are backed up after the file has been searched.

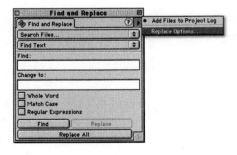

4) Check Save and Close Files to save and close all files in a multiple-file find and replace operation. Choose Incremental Backups from the Backup Original Files pop-up menu. Click OK.

Each file is saved and closed after the find and replace operation is performed. Only the original active documents remain open.

The options for backing up your files are as follows:

- Choose No Backups to have the changed files replace the original files.

- Choose Overwrite Existing Backups to create only one backup of each original file. If additional find and replace operations are performed, the previous original file always replaces the backup copy.

- Choose Incremental Backups to save every instance of a changed file. The original files are moved to an Original Files subfolder of their current folder, and an incremental number is added to the end of each file name. For example, for a file named Home.png, the first backup file is named Home-1.png, the second backup file is named Home-2.png, and so on.

5) Click Find to begin the search.

Fireworks finds the first occurrence of Compass Travel and highlights it on the canvas. When using Find and Replace, it is a good idea to find the first occurrence to verify that you have not inadvertently misspelled the word you are looking to replace.

Now replace Compass Travel with Compass Tours.

6) Click Replace All to make the change everywhere it appears in the file. A message appears telling you how many changes were made. Click OK.

272

The text is changed in both the title and the drop-shadow text block on the page.

The Bike.png file is changed, but you really wanted to make the change in all of the documents in your site, or in this exercise, in all of the files in a folder.

7) Close the Bike.png file without saving your changes.

In the following steps, you will make the same change to several files at once.

8) Choose Search Files in the Search Selection pop-up menu on the Find and Replace panel.

The Open dialog box appears. If you don't see the Open dialog box, choose Search Document and then choose Search Files again.

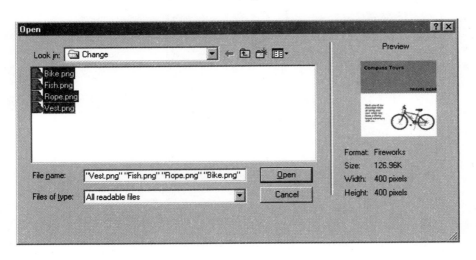

9) Hold Shift and click each file in the Change folder. Click Open.

You will not see any of the files once you click Open, but they are ready to be searched.

10) Click Replace All on the Find and Replace panel. Click OK when the find and replace operation is finished.

You will see each file briefly as it is opened, changed, saved, and then closed. The files are saved and closed because of the Replace option you selected in step 4. Your new files are saved in the Change folder. The original files are stored in a new folder named Original Files within the Change folder. This happened because you selected Incremental Backups in step 4.

There are other options you can use on the Find and Replace panel; for example, you can change the font or a color on the pages. You can experiment with these same files to see how these options work.

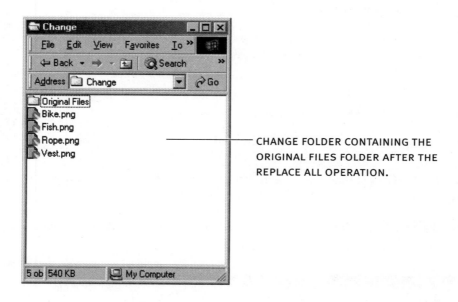

CHANGE FOLDER CONTAINING THE ORIGINAL FILES FOLDER AFTER THE REPLACE ALL OPERATION.

USING THE PROJECT LOG

The project log helps you track and control changes you've made in multiple files when using Find and Replace or when performing batch processing. Any documents changed during a find and replace operation are automatically recorded in the project log if you set the option. Click the Find and Replace panel Options pop-up menu and select Add Files to Project Log. This option is a toggle; if a check mark (Windows) or bullet (Macintosh) appears, the option is set.

You can use the project log to navigate through selected files, export selected files using their most recent export settings, or select files to be batch processed.

The project log records each changed document on a separate line and indicates which frame of the document contained the change, as well as the date and time of the change.

1) Choose Window > Project Log to display the Project panel.

You will see a list of the files you just changed in the previous exercise.

2) Click the right arrow at the top right of the panel to open the Options pop-up menu. Choose Clear All from the list. Click OK to close the warning dialog box.

This removes all of the entries from the project log. You want to clear the project log and then add new files to the log.

3) Choose Add Files to Log from the Project options pop-up menu and navigate to the Run folder within the Lesson10 folder. Select all of the files within this folder by holding Shift and clicking each of the file names. (In Windows, you may need to change the Files of Type option to All Readable Files.) Click Open to add all of the selected files to the project log.

After the files are in the project log, you can open them by double-clicking the file name on the Project panel or selecting the file and then clicking Open at the bottom of the panel. You'll use these files in the project log in a later exercise.

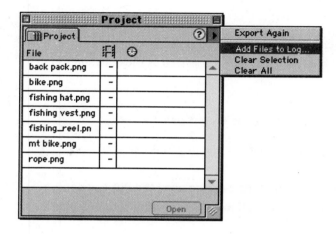

TIP *In the previous exercise, you opened a folder that contained files with the company name you wanted to change. You could have instead added those files to the project log and then selected Search Project Log from the Search pop-up menu on the Find and Replace panel. Fireworks would then search all of the files in the log and change the text.*

NOTE *The latest version of the project log is stored as an HTML file in the Configurations folder of your Fireworks application. Open the Project_Log.htm file in a browser to view or print the project log.*

PERFORMING BATCH PROCESSING

In large projects, you may have many images that you need to export in the same way. You can use batch processing to execute the same options on multiple files automatically. For example, perhaps you have a product catalog, and you want to display pictures for each of the items in the catalog. You've scanned in all of the images and have sized and color corrected the images. Now you want to optimize the files and export them in JPEG format. In addition, you want to create thumbnails of the images for the index page. This can all be done easily in Fireworks.

1) Choose File > Batch Process. The Batch (Windows) or Batch Process (Macintosh) dialog box opens. Locate and open the Batch folder within the Lesson10 folder.

This folder contains several PNG files that you will process with the Batch command.

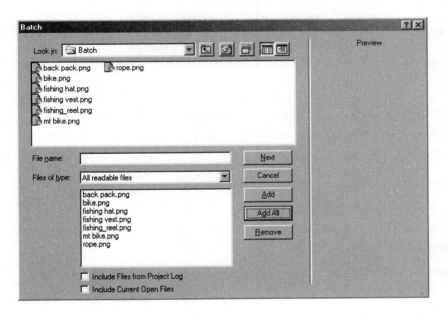

2) Click Add All to process all of the files in the folder. Click Next.

A second Batch (Windows) or Batch Process (Macintosh) dialog box appears.

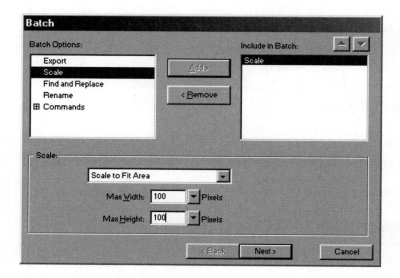

3) In the Batch Options column, choose Scale; then click Add. From the Scaling options pop-up menu, choose Scale to Fit Area and enter *100* in both the Max Width and Max Height boxes.

The options for scaling your images are as follows:

- Choose No Scaling to export the files unchanged.

- Choose Scale to Size and enter a width and height to scale images to an exact width and height.

- Choose Scale to Fit Area and enter Max Width and Max Height pixel values to proportionally scale images so that they each fit within a specified width and height.

- Choose Scale to Percentage and enter a percentage to proportionally scale the images.

NOTE   *The Fireworks 4.0.2 updater fixes a problem in the batch processing feature using the Scale to Size option if you set either the width or the height to Variable. Go to http://www.macromedia.com/support/fireworks/downloads.html to download the updater.*

4) In the Batch Options column, choose Export; then click Add. Choose GIF Adaptive 256 from the Export settings pop-up menu.

In the Export Options area, you can use one of the preset export options or use your own settings. Click Edit to open the Export Preview window if you want to customize the export settings.

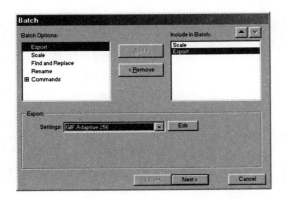

NOTE *You can continue to add other batch options to the list. You are building a batch function that executes the options in the order listed. The order is very important. For example, you will want to scale the images before you export them. If you add new options and want to change the order, select the option that you want to move and then use the up or down arrow to change its position in the list.*

5) Click Next. In the Saving Files area, select Same Location as Original File. Select either Overwrite Existing Backups or Incremental Backups.

If you want to change the location where the files are saved, select Custom Location and choose the new location. Either backup choice will work for this example. Overwrite saves only one copy of the backup files. Incremental keeps all copies, appending a number to the end of the file name each time you run the process.

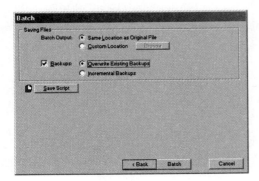

PRODUCTION TECHNIQUES

6) Click Batch to process all of your files. Click OK when the script is finished.

You'll see the files open briefly as the batch function executes. When the batch process is complete, a message appears telling you that the batch processing has finished normally.

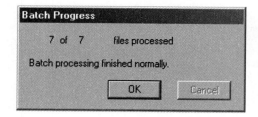

SAVING YOUR SCRIPTS

Batch processing is a real time saver when you have multiple files that you need to scale or export to the same format. If you know you are going to repeat the same steps for the batch process, you can even save your steps as a script that you can replay on another set of files. In the next exercise, you will repeat the steps you just completed in the preceding section. You will add a few more options and save the steps as a script to run again. The script can then be used to create thumbnails of your images.

In this exercise, you will repeat the previous steps, but you will add an option to create thumbnails of the images.

1) Choose File > Batch Process. Locate and open the Scripts folder within the Lesson10 folder. Click Add All and then click Next. Click Scale in the Batch Options list and then click Add. Choose Scale to Fit Area and enter *72* in both the Width and Height boxes. Click Export in the Batch Options list and then click Add. Choose GIF Adaptive 256 from the Settings pop-up menu.

These are the same steps you used previously, but the width and height of the scaled images are changed.

2) Click Rename in the Batch Options list and then click Add. Choose Add Suffix from the Rename pop-up menu and type _T in the box. This will add the _T suffix to the end of your file names. Click Next.

You could also have added a prefix to the file name. For this exercise, the smaller files are thumbnails, and the suffix helps you identify them as such.

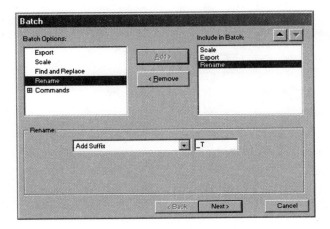

3) Click Save Script and type *Thumbnails.jsf* in the Save As (Windows) or Save (Macintosh) dialog box that appears. Click Save. Click Cancel to close the Batch dialog box.

Save the script file in the Scripts folder within the Lesson10 folder. Your script is saved for you to use again.

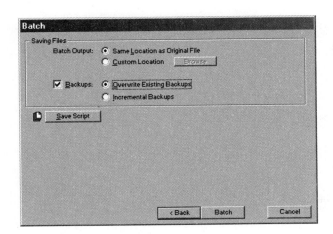

NOTE *If you click Batch in the Batch dialog box, you will execute the script you just created and would not need to perform the next step.*

PRODUCTION TECHNIQUES

4) Select File > Run Script.

Find the script you just created (Thumbnails.jsf) and open it. The Files to Process window appears.

5) In the Files to Process list, select Project Log (All Files) and then click OK. When the "Finished" message appears, click OK.

The project log contains the files in the Run folder. The script processes those files based on the options you selected.

WHAT YOU HAVE LEARNED

In this lesson, you have:

- Used Find and Replace to change text on multiple pages [pages 270–274]

- Used the project log to specify a selection of files for processing [pages 275–276]

- Used batch processing to scale and export a group of images [pages 277–279]

- Saved and run a batch script [pages 280–282]

integrating with dreamweaver

LESSON 11

Macromedia Dreamweaver is a robust visual Web page authoring tool, and Macromedia Fireworks is a powerful design and graphics editor. Used together, Fireworks and Dreamweaver are the dynamic duo of Web design tools. The two programs offer integration features to aid your workflow as you design and optimize your graphics, build your HTML pages, and place Web graphics on the page.

In the previous lessons, you created Web pages using Fireworks. In this lesson, you will use Dreamweaver to edit the pages created by Fireworks, return to Fireworks to make changes to the graphics, and then return to Dreamweaver to make other edits. The tight integration between the two applications makes these tasks as simple as clicking a button.

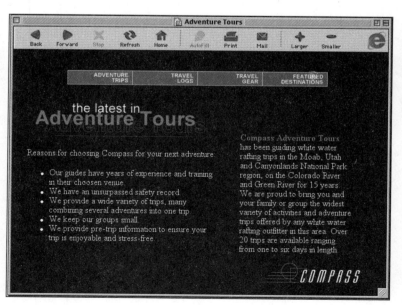

In this lesson you will build this Web page in Fireworks, and then add the text and buttons in Dreamweaver.

WHAT YOU WILL LEARN

In this lesson, you will:

- Create a site in Dreamweaver

- Use Fireworks images in Dreamweaver

- Edit Fireworks images from within Dreamweaver

- Optimize an image in Dreamweaver by using Fireworks

- Export from Fireworks as a Dreamweaver library

- Edit a library item in Dreamweaver

- Insert a library item in a Web page

- Create three-state navigation buttons

APPROXIMATE TIME

This lesson takes approximately 2 hours to complete.

LESSON FILES

Media Files:

Lesson11\featured.htm

Lesson11\gear.htm

Lesson11\logs.htm

Lesson11\trips.htm

Lesson11\Text\Start.txt

Lesson11\Text\survivor.txt

Starting Files:

Lesson11\Graphics\Survivor.png

Lesson11\Graphics\Tours.png

Lesson11\Navigation\nav_bar.png

Completed Projects:

Lesson11\Completed\buttons.png

Lesson11\Completed\survivor.png

FIREWORKS AND DREAMWEAVER

Generally, you will use Fireworks to create your Web graphics and Dreamweaver to build the Web pages. However, on pages with extensive graphics, you may prefer to use Fireworks as the design tool, exporting the HTML table structure as you did in the previous lessons. Rollovers created in Fireworks appear as native Dreamweaver behaviors when the resulting file is opened in Dreamweaver, ensuring a seamless workflow between the two applications. You can modify the Fireworks-generated table in Dreamweaver to add text or images. If a graphic needs updating, you can edit the image from within Dreamweaver. Dreamweaver launches Fireworks automatically so you can make the changes. Fireworks replaces only the HTML and image slice files needed to update the Dreamweaver file. Any changes you make in Dreamweaver are preserved.

When you launch Dreamweaver, you'll see some familiar interface features. Fireworks and Dreamweaver share a common Macromedia user interface that makes using both programs together even easier. The common interface reduces the learning curve and increases your productivity.

FIREWORKS MINI-LAUNCHER

DREAMWEAVER MINI-LAUNCHER

The Mini-launcher at the bottom right of the document window in both applications provides a quick way to access the most common panels. Icons and panels, where appropriate, have the same look and feel. For example, the Behaviors panels in Fireworks and Dreamweaver have the same icon and appearance.

FIREWORKS BEHAVIORS
PANEL (LEFT) AND
DREAMWEAVER BEHAVIORS
PANEL (RIGHT)

Customizable keyboard shortcuts enable designers to configure both products to fit in their personal design workflow. If you are accustomed to shortcuts from another graphics program—Macromedia FreeHand, for example—you can change Fireworks to use the same shortcuts. Again, the learning curve is reduced, giving you more time to design and produce your Web pages.

The communication between Fireworks and Dreamweaver occurs as comments in the HTML code and in Design Notes. Design Notes are like sticky notes attached to your HTML files. The information in the notes appears only within the Dreamweaver application—it is not in the HTML or placed on the server. If you are working with a team on a site, you can share information about the status of a file with Design Notes.

Fireworks saves the file name and path name of the original PNG source file in the Design Note when you have Design Notes enabled in Dreamweaver. When you save and export a Fireworks file within a Dreamweaver site, Fireworks creates a _Notes folder and Design Notes (files ending with .mno) describing the files. Save your Fireworks original graphics (the PNG files) in a folder within a Dreamweaver site to maximize the integration between the two applications.

CREATING A SITE IN DREAMWEAVER

Before beginning these lessons, you copied the Lessons folder from the enclosed CD to your hard drive. Each lesson then directed you to save your files within the Lessons folder. All the HTML files you created were saved in a folder within the Lessons folder. When you create you own Web site, you will create a folder on your hard drive where you will store of all your files. That folder will become your local site. This local site on your hard drive will mirror the actual pages on the Web server. The local site is where you do your initial development and testing. You will be able to view all of your files on your local hard drive, to test the links and preview the pages in your browser. Once the testing is complete, you upload all of the files to the Web server, and your site is up and ready to go.

1) In Dreamweaver, choose Site > Define Sites and then click New to define a new site.

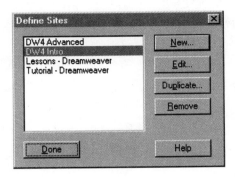

2) Type a name for the site in the Site Name text box. For example, type *Compass Travel* as the site name.

The name you enter is only for your reference. Make the name meaningful based on the content of the site. You can have multiple sites residing on your hard drive. For example, if you are creating Web pages for your company, school, church, or other organization, each needs a unique name. Store all of the files for each site within a separate folder on your hard drive.

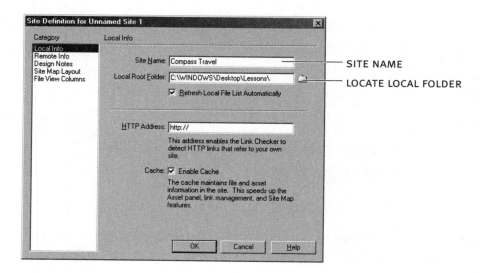

3) In the Site Definition dialog box, select Refresh Local File List Automatically and select Enable Cache.

Selecting the refresh option causes Dreamweaver to update the site list whenever you add a new file to the site folder. If you do not check this option, you will need to refresh the local files manually.

Enabling the cache speeds site management functions. When this option is selected, a local cache (an index of your files) is created, improving the speed of linking and site-management tasks. You will usually want to select this option; however, on very large sites, re-creating the cache can slow operations.

4) Click the folder to the right of the Local Root Folder text box and locate the Lessons folder.

- For Windows: Open the local folder and click Select.

- For Macintosh: Select the local folder and click Choose.

After you define the main folder, it becomes the root folder for your site. All of your files and subfolders are contained within that root folder. Dreamweaver uses the local root folder to locate all links specified as site-root-relative URLs. When you create your pages, the graphics and links are relative to that folder. When you are ready to publish your site, all you have to do is copy the root folder and all of its files to the remote server. The images and links should all work on the Web server (assuming that they work locally).

N O T E   *Design Notes and Fireworks PNG files do not need to be on the Web server.*

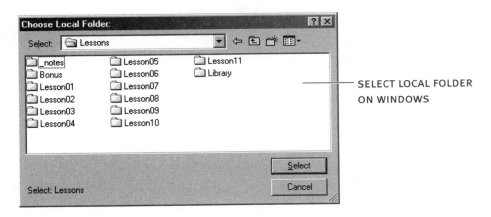

SELECT LOCAL FOLDER
ON WINDOWS

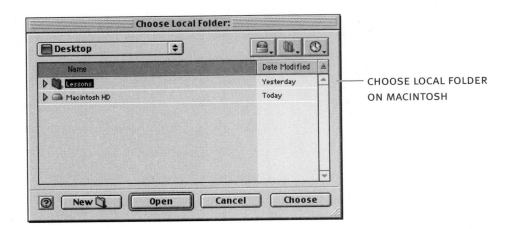

CHOOSE LOCAL FOLDER
ON MACINTOSH

5) Click Design Notes in the Category list and then choose Maintain Design Notes. Click OK and then click Done.

Design Notes are used for communication between Dreamweaver and Fireworks. If you are working with a team, you could select Upload Design Notes for Sharing. That option is not needed for this exercise.

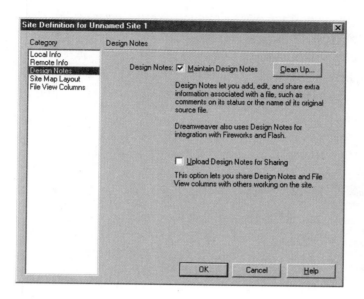

NOTE *You may see a message telling you that the site cache will be created. If you select Don't Show This Message Again, the message is skipped the next time you create a site. Click OK to close the message box and create the cache.*

The Site window displays your local folder in the right pane; the left pane displays the files on the remote server. For this exercise, you won't be using a remote site. You can close the remote pane by clicking the small triangle on the lower left side of the Site window. To view the remote pane again, click the triangle.

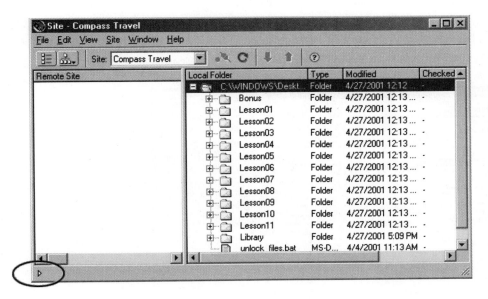

When you are working in Dreamweaver you will want to keep the Site window open, but on smaller monitors it does get in the way. Drag the size handle to make the window as small as possible and move it to the right side of your screen.

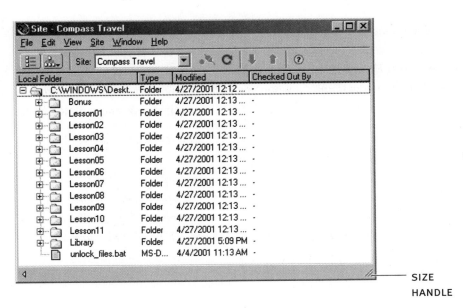

SIZE HANDLE

GETTING STARTED IN DREAMWEAVER

Once the site is created, you then need to set Dreamweaver preferences to designate Fireworks as the primary external image editor. This way, you can launch Fireworks to edit images while you are still in Dreamweaver.

1) In Dreamweaver, choose Edit > Preferences. In the Preferences dialog box, select File Types / Editors from the Category list.

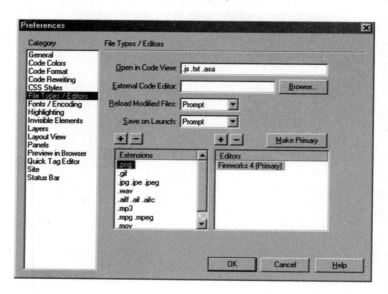

2) From the Extensions list, choose .png. If Fireworks 4 doesn't appear in the Editors list, click the plus (+) sign above the Editors list to find your Fireworks 4 application. Select Fireworks 4 from the Editors list. Then click Make Primary to make sure that Fireworks launches when you perform any edits. Repeat this process for .gif and .jpg in the Extensions list. Click OK to close the Preferences dialog box.

After you define the site and set the Dreamweaver preferences, you are ready to explore the integration between the two applications.

NOTE *If you are on a Macintosh using System 9.1, you need to update to Dreamweaver 4.01. Go to www.macromedia.com/support/dreamweaver/downloader/dw4_updater.html and download the updater. The updater fixes a problem viewing GIF images in Dreamweaver.*

3) In Dreamweaver, choose Window > Site Files.

The Site Window opens, or comes to the foreground if it was already open. You can also click Show Site (looks like an Org chart) in the Mini-launcher of the document window. The Mini-launcher is the fastest way to access many of the panels.

SHOW SITE ON THE MINI-LAUNCHER

You can customize the panels that appear in the Mini-launcher from the Preferences menu. Select Panels in the Preferences category list to add, delete, or change the order of appearance of the panels.

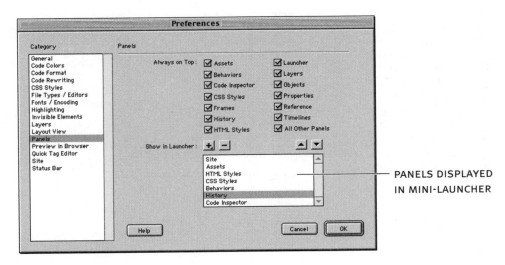

PANELS DISPLAYED
IN MINI-LAUNCHER

NOTE *Macintosh users: In this exercise, you will copy some text created on a Windows machine. You need to change your preferences to properly read the Windows formatting of the file. Choose Code Format from the Category list in the Preferences panel, and then select CR LF (Windows) from the Line Breaks pop-up menu.*

4) Click the plus sign (Windows) or the triangle (Macintosh) to the left of the Lesson11 folder in the Site window and then open the Graphics folder within the Lesson11 folder.

The folder opens, displaying any files or folders within that folder.

The Site window displays the file and folder structure of your site. You can add and delete files or folders, rename files and folders, and move files and folders. By doing all the file maintenance within the Site window, you are assured that your link information stays correct. Conversely, if you make file or folder changes within Windows Explorer (Windows) or the Finder (Macintosh), Dreamweaver doesn't recognize the changes and can't keep your links correct.

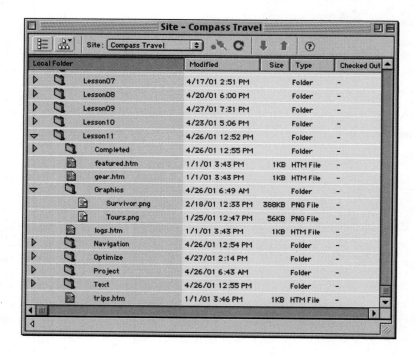

5) Right-click (Windows) or Control-click (Macintosh) the Tours.png file in the list. Select Open with Fireworks 4 from the context menu.

Because you set your preferences to use Fireworks 4 as the primary editor for PNG files, Fireworks 4 appears in the context menu. If you have not set your preferences, or if your preferences are set to another image editing application, this menu option does not appear.

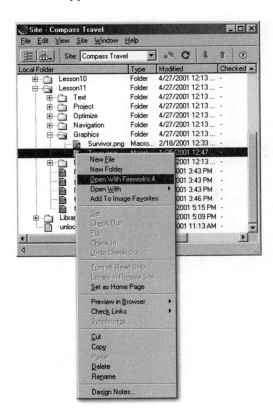

Dreamweaver launches Fireworks 4 (if it is not already open) and opens the Tours.png file. The Tours.png file contains a logo and some text.

TIP *Double-clicking the file in the Site window also opens the file in Fireworks if you set Fireworks as the primary editor.*

6) Now in Fireworks, select the Slice tool on the Tools panel and draw one slice over the top text block area.

When you draw the slice, leave room above the top text objects (see the following example). You will add some buttons above the text objects later in this lesson.

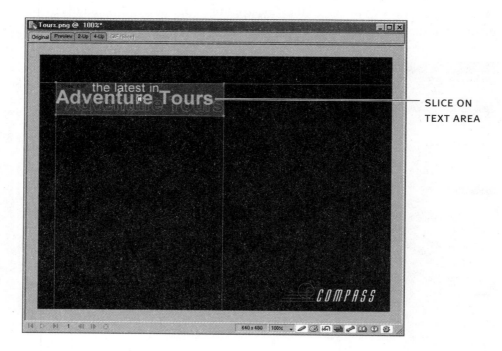

SLICE ON TEXT AREA

◎ POWER TIP *The quickest way to draw a slice on an object is to select the object and then choose Insert > Slice. The text at the top left of the page is actually four objects. Select all four objects, choose Insert > Slice, and then click Single to add one slice that covers all four objects.*

7) Select the slice over the Adventure Tours text area and name it on the Object panel. Deselect Auto-Name Slices and type *Ad_tours* in the text box at the bottom of the panel.

The name you enter in the Auto-Name Slices text box is the name of the graphic when you export the slice.

NOTE *The name Tours automatically appears in the text box because that is the name of the file.*

8) In the Alt text box, type *Adventure Tours*.

This adds text that appears when the user points to the image in the browser.

9) On the Optimize panel, select the image optimization you want for this slice. For this example, choose GIF and WebSnap Adaptive (Windows) or Web Adaptive (Macintosh).

Each slice on the page can be optimized to best fit the image. For example, you might have a photo on the page that you want to export as a JPEG file and text that you want to export as a GIF file.

10) Repeat steps 6 through 9 to create and name a slice over the logo. Name the slice *logo* and enter *Compass Logo* as the Alt text.

The red slice guide lines display the table cells that will be generated when you export the file to Dreamweaver. As you draw your slices, use the guides to help you, if possible, create less complex tables. The fewer slices you create in Fireworks, the fewer table cells are created in the exported HTML table. Download time increases when there are a lot of small slices in the table.

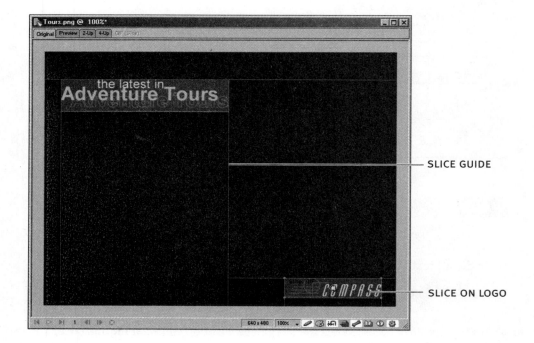

SLICE GUIDE

SLICE ON LOGO

11) Choose File > Export and open the Lesson11 folder. Set these options in the Export dialog box:

- Save as Type: HTML and Images

- HTML: Export HTML File

- Slices: Export Slices

- Selected Slices Only: Not selected

- Include Areas without Slices: Not selected

- Put Images in Subfolder: Selected

NOTE *Fireworks uses the same file name for the HTML file it creates. In this exercise, the name Tours.htm appears in the File name text box. This name is fine for this exercise.*

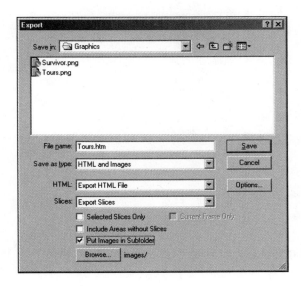

NOTE *When you select Put Images in Subfolder, you'll see "images/" displayed to the right of the Browse button to indicate the folder where Fireworks will store the images. If you want to designate a different folder, click Browse and locate the folder. If a folder named Images does not exist and you do not designate a different folder, Fireworks creates an Images folder for you.*

12) Click Options to open the HTML Setup dialog box and set the following options:

- On the General tab, select Dreamweaver as the HTML style. Leave the other options set to the defaults. On the Macintosh, choose Dreamweaver for File Creator. This assigns the Dreamweaver icon to the file so you can double-click to open the file from the Finder.

- On the Table tab, select the default of 1-Pixel Transparent Spacer, and for Empty Cells select Use Canvas Color and Set Contents to Spacer Image.

- On the Document Specific tab, choose the method for naming your image files.

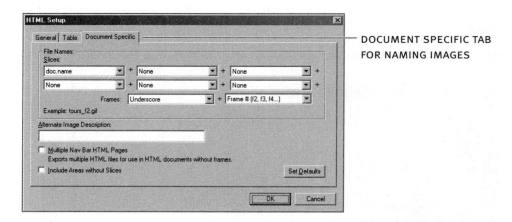

DOCUMENT SPECIFIC TAB
FOR NAMING IMAGES

POWER TIP *Click Set Defaults on the Document Specific tab to retain your file name settings for all your exported files.*

13) Click OK to close the HTML Setup dialog box. Then click Save to export your images and create an HTML page.

The images are stored in the Images folder, and the HTML file is placed in the Lesson11 folder.

14) Save the Tours.png file.

EDITING A FIREWORKS HTML FILE IN DREAMWEAVER

After you export your files, you can open the HTML page in Dreamweaver and add some text or change the table design. In the next exercise, you will open the HTML page created by Fireworks, add some text, and edit one of the images in Fireworks.

1) Switch to Dreamweaver and open the Tours.htm file Fireworks just created.

You should see the Tours.htm file in the Site window. Double-click the HTML file in the Site window to open it.

A table is displayed with the same cell structure as the red guide lines you saw in Fireworks. In the empty cells, a spacer image with the same color as the background (black in this exercise) is placed to preserve the table when the page is displayed in the browser.

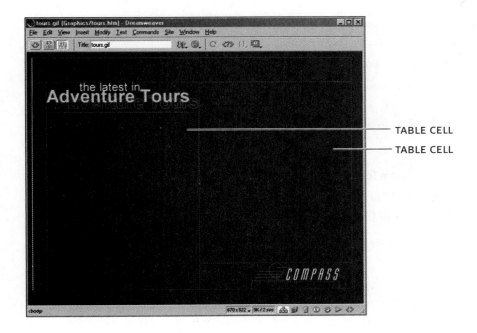

2) Open the Start.txt file in the Text folder within the Lesson11 folder.

Again, double-click the text file in the Site window to open it. Because it is a text file and not an HTML file, Dreamweaver opens the file in Code view.

3) Click View Options on the toolbar to turn on word wrapping if it is not already set. Copy the text in the first paragraph.

You can also display line numbers for the text, although that is not needed for this exercise.

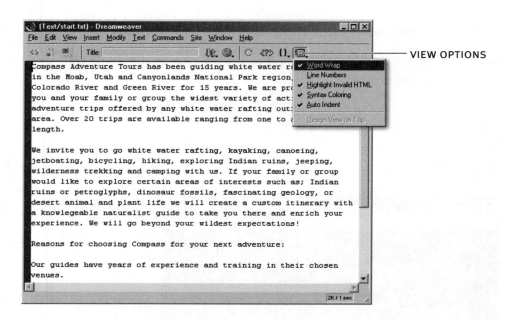

4) Switch back to the Tours.htm file (do not close the Code View window) and delete the spacer image in the cell above the compass logo. This gives you an empty cell for the text. Paste the text in this cell.

Because the page background is black, you will not be able to see the text until you change the color.

NOTE *Fireworks inserted the spacer image in the table to ensure that the table cells conform to the design you created in Fireworks. Deleting the image could mess up the table, especially if you insert more text than can fit into the cell or insert an image that is larger than the cell. In this exercise, the text you are inserting should fit within the cell.*

5) Choose Modify > Page Properties and change the color in the Text color box to white. Then click OK.

Color boxes in Dreamweaver look and work the same as in Fireworks.

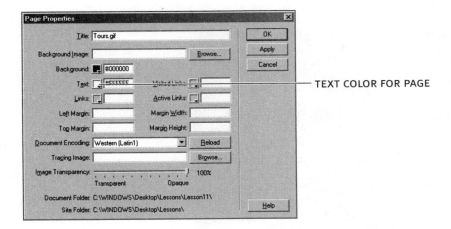

TEXT COLOR FOR PAGE

6) Place the insertion point within the text and click Text Indent in the Property inspector.

The text is indented within the table cell. Indenting the text indents on the left and right sides of the paragraph, adding the blockquote tag to the HTML.

The Property inspector displays information about the selected item on the page. In this step you selected text, and so you see text formatting options in the inspector. If you select an image, the inspector changes to display formatting options for images.

TEXT INDENT

MINIMIZE

NOTE *The Property inspector is initially placed at the bottom of your screen. You can move it or close it, but you will find that you use it often when creating your pages and will want to keep it open. In the lower right corner of the inspector is a triangle for minimizing and maximizing the inspector. To open the inspector if it is not visible, choose Window > Properties.*

7) Switch back to the Start.txt file in the Code View window and copy the six lines of text beginning with "Reasons for choosing Compass." In the Tours.htm file, delete the spacer image in the cell below Adventure Tours and paste the new text.

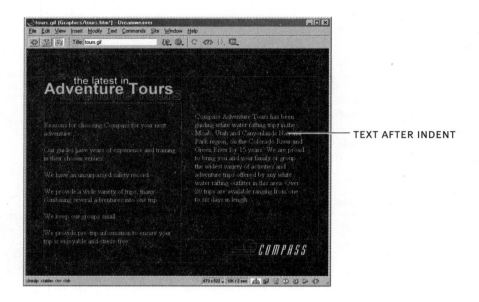

TEXT AFTER INDENT

8) Select the five sentences after the "Reasons" line and format them as a bulleted list.

Click Unordered List (it looks like a bullet list) in the Property inspector to format the lines as a bulleted list. If you want to remove the bullets, select all the lines and then click Unordered List again.

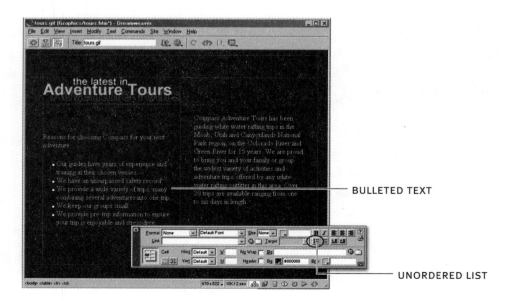

BULLETED TEXT

UNORDERED LIST

304

9) Save your page and view it in the browser.

Previewing your page works the same as it did in Fireworks. When you choose File > Preview in Browser, you should see a browser in the submenu. If not, select Edit Browser List and select a primary and a secondary browser.

10) Quit the browser and return to Dreamweaver.

Leave the Tours.htm file open in Dreamweaver. You will use it in the next exercise.

EDITING AN IMAGE FROM DREAMWEAVER

The Tours.htm page was created in Fireworks, exported, and then opened in Dreamweaver, where you added text. Next, you will change one of the graphics, accessing Fireworks from within Dreamweaver.

1) Select the Adventure Tours image.

The Property inspector identifies the selection as a Fireworks image and displays the name of the associated PNG file in the Src text box.

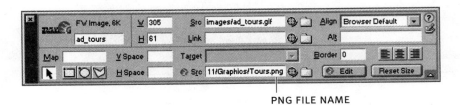

PNG FILE NAME

NOTE *The Fireworks PNG files must be saved within the Dreamweaver site for this integration between the two applications to work. In this exercise, the Tours.png file is in the Graphics folder in the Lesson11 folder which is within the site you defined at the beginning of this lesson. When you create your own site, it is a good idea to create a separate folder within your site for your original source files. That folder does not need to be uploaded to the remote Web server.*

2) Click Edit in the Property inspector.

The Tours.png file opens in Fireworks. The document window indicates that you are editing a file from Dreamweaver.

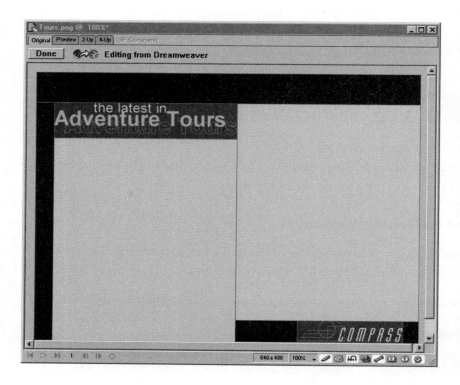

Here are other ways to edit the image:

* Right-click (Windows) or Control-click (Macintosh) the image and choose Edit with Fireworks 4 from the context menu.

* Hold down Ctrl (Windows) or Command (Macintosh) and double-click the image.

3) With the Pointer tool, select the slice below Adventure Tours.

You should see the text you pasted within this slice. The text contains the HTML tags for the unordered list you added in Dreamweaver. The slice above the compass logo also contains the text you added in this area in Dreamweaver.

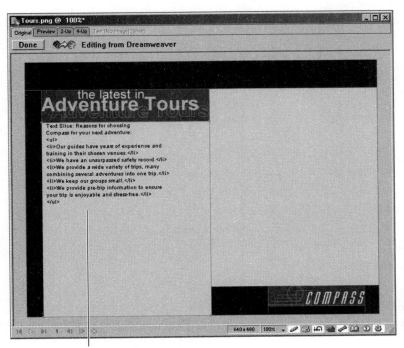

TEXT SLICE

4) Choose Window > Object to open the Object panel.

The panel displays Text as the type, and you see the text and its associated HTML that you added in Dreamweaver within the panel.

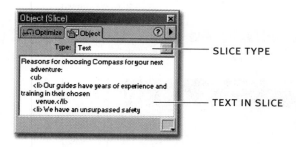

SLICE TYPE

TEXT IN SLICE

NOTE *A slice in Fireworks can be either an image slice (the default) or a text slice. To change an image slice to a text slice, select the slice and then choose Text from the Type pop-up menu on the Object panel. A text slice does not export a spacer image, eliminating the need to delete the spacer image as you did in Dreamweaver for this exercise. You can even type text on the Object panel on a text slice, and the text will be exported to the HTML page, but it is much easier to add the text in Dreamweaver.*

5) Click Hide Slices on the Tools panel to hide the slices. Use the Pointer tool to select the yellow Adventure Tours text and change the color to red. Click Done.

The PNG file is saved, and the current image is exported, using the same optimization settings you set originally for the slice. The GIF (or JPG) file used by Dreamweaver is also updated and reset within Dreamweaver. You are returned to the Dreamweaver file, with your text changes preserved within the page. If you view the page in the browser, you may need to refresh your browser to reset the cache to display the new image.

The Tours.htm page now has the edited Adventure Tours image, plus the text you added in Dreamweaver. When you edited the image and returned to Dreamweaver, the text and the table remained unchanged. As long as you don't make changes to the table structure in Dreamweaver, you can continue to edit the images in Fireworks as you did in the last exercise. If you make a change—for example, if you add a row to the table— and then edit an image, Fireworks removes the added row, returning the table to the original state.

6) Save the Tours.htm file.

You can leave this file open for the next exercise.

USING THE FIREWORKS BUTTON EDITOR

You decide to add some rollover buttons to your page. You could create the two images for the rollovers in Fireworks and use Dreamweaver to insert the images and add the Swap Image behavior to the buttons. Instead, you will create the rollovers in Fireworks, using the Button Editor as you learned in Lesson 8, and insert all of the HTML for the images and rollovers into your page.

The Fireworks Button Editor steps you through the button-creation process, automating many button-making tasks. The result is a button symbol that you can duplicate to create similar buttons, which you can use as navigation buttons on your pages. When you export buttons, Fireworks automatically generates the JavaScript necessary to display them in the browser. The generated JavaScript appears as Dreamweaver behaviors when you insert the HTML into a Web page and view it in Dreamweaver.

In the next exercise, you will create four navigation buttons with rollovers for your Web page.

1) Create a new page in Fireworks. Make the canvas size 600 x 200 and set the canvas color to black. Save your file as *buttons.png*. Choose Insert > New Button.

The Button Editor window opens. Here you can use all of the tools and commands as in the document window.

2) Draw a rectangle 114 x 27 pixels. Use the Info panel to set and verify the rectangle size. Color the rectangle blue and add a yellow 1-pixel soft-pencil stroke. Add the text *ADVENTURE TRIPS* to the rectangle.

Type the text on two lines to fit it within the rectangle. Color the text white and align it on the right.

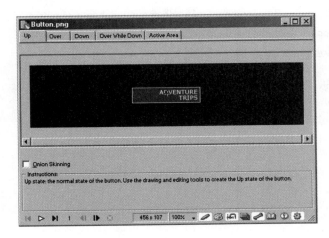

3) Click the Over tab and then click Copy Up Graphic.

A copy of the button is placed within the window.

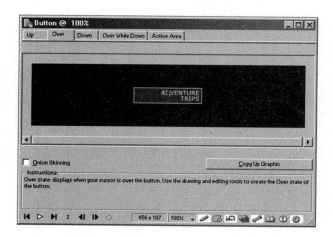

4) Change the color of the text to yellow. Click the Active Area tab and then click the Link wizard to add links to the button. On the Link tab, type *trips.htm* in the Link text box. Type *Adventure Trips* in the Alt text box. On the Filename tab, click Auto-Name to remove the check mark. Then type *trips* in the text box. Click OK to close the Link wizard and then close the Button Editor window.

You want three more similar buttons, placed to the right of the original button. What is the fastest way to add more buttons? You can copy and paste the button, duplicate the button, clone the button, or drag a copy of the button from the Library panel. After each of the methods, you would then need to move the new button and check the alignment. The fastest way to add duplicate buttons is to use the Repeat command.

5) Hold down Alt (Windows) or Option (Macintosh) and drag to the right to make a copy of the button. Add Shift as you drag to constrain the movement to a straight line. Position the new button so it touches the right edge of the first button. Choose Edit > Repeat Duplicate to make a new copy of the button.

The Repeat command lets you duplicate the last action. Because you actually performed two actions by using the copy-drag method, the Repeat command repeats the copy and the move of the button. If you moved your button after dragging it, the last action would be a move, and the Repeat command would duplicate only the move.

6) Double-click the second button to edit it in the Button Editor.

A message box opens, asking if you want to edit all of the buttons or the current one.

7) Select Current.

The first button you created is a button symbol; the copies of the button are instances. In this exercise, you want different text for each button, so you click Current. If you wanted to change all of the buttons in the same way, you would click All.

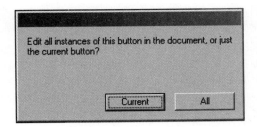

8) Change the text to *TRAVEL LOGS*. Click OK to close the Text Editor.

An alert box may open, asking if you want to change the text in the other button states.

9) Click Yes to close the alert box, if the alert box appears.

NOTE *There is a Don't Show Again check box within the alert box. If you previously checked this option, you will not see the alert message. To restore all alert boxes, choose Commands > Reset Warning Dialogs.*

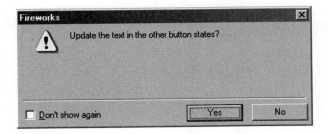

NOTE *If you change the text and the position of the text in the button in the Button Editor, the text in other states of the button is not repositioned—only the text changes.*

10) On the Active Area tab, use the Link wizard to change the link, Alt tag, and file name. Type *logs.htm* as the link and *Travel Logs* as the Alt text. Change the file name to *logs*. Close the Button Editor window.

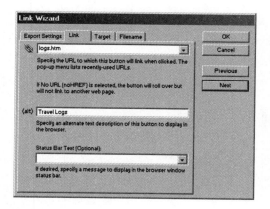

11) Repeat steps 6 through 10 for the other buttons, changing the text to *TRAVEL GEAR* and *FEATURED DESTINATIONS*. The links are *gear.htm* and *featured.htm*, and you should use *gear* and *featured* as the file names. Change the Alt text to match the text on each button.

If you export the entire canvas as an HTML file, the empty area is exported as spacer images in a table. For this exercise, you just want the buttons, so you need to trim the canvas before exporting.

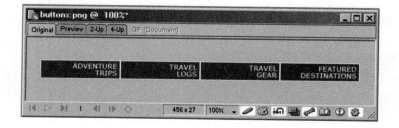

12) Choose Modify › Trim Canvas. Save the file.

After you have created the buttons, set all of the links and file names, and trimmed the canvas, you are ready to export to an HTML file.

13) Export the file and save the HTML in the Lesson11 folder. Save all of the images in the Subfolder (images subfolder). Select Export Slices from the Slices pop-up menu and click Options to open the HTML Setup dialog box. On the Document Specific tab, choose a method for naming your file. On the Table tab, choose Single Table, No Spacers from the Space With pop-up menu. Click OK and then click Save.

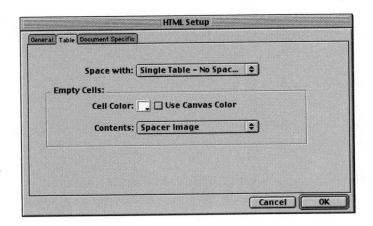

When you set the table to export as a single table with no spacers, Fireworks does not pad the table with a row of spacer images. In this exercise, you will insert the exported table into your Tours.htm page, so you don't want the extra spacer images.

You can close the buttons.png file for now. You will use the file again in a later exercise in this lesson.

NOTE *In this exercise you used two lines for the text on the buttons. You changed the text on the duplicate buttons you made with the Button Editor. For these buttons, this was the best method. If you have one line text on your buttons, it is faster the change the text on the Object panel. You can also change the links and the file name using the Link wizard on the Object panel.*

INSERTING FIREWORKS HTML INTO DREAMWEAVER

Now you have two HTML files: the Tours.htm file you have been editing and the HTML file for the buttons you just created. You want the elements in the two pages merged. The next step is to insert the buttons and their HTML into the existing Dreamweaver page.

1) Return to the Tours.htm page in Dreamweaver. Delete the spacer image in the top row.

The buttons are going to be inserted in this row.

NOTE *If you had drawn a slice over this area in Fireworks, you could have designated the slice as a text slice. Then the spacer image would not be exported and placed in this area.*

2) With the insertion point in the top row, choose Insert > Interactive Images > Fireworks HTML.

The Insert Fireworks HTML dialog box opens.

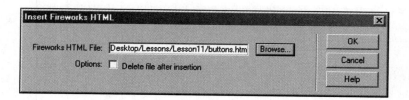

3) Click Browse, locate and select the buttons.htm file you just exported, click Open, and then click OK.

The four buttons and the rollover behaviors are inserted into the row.

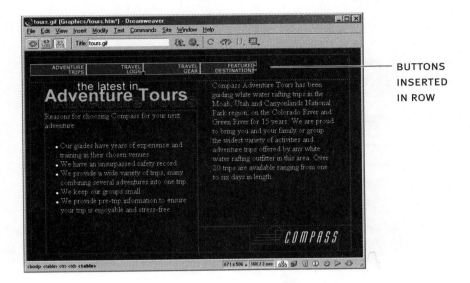

BUTTONS
INSERTED
IN ROW

The Property inspector identifies the inserted table as a Fireworks table.

4) Use the right arrow key to deselect the Fireworks table you just inserted. The insertion point is now in the cell. Center the buttons in the row by choosing Center in the Horz pop-up menu in the Property inspector.

CENTER CELL ALIGNMENT

5) Save the file and view it in the browser.

If you need to make a change to one of the buttons, select the button in Dreamweaver and click Edit in the Property inspector as you did for the Adventure Tours image. You can close the Tours.htm file.

OPTIMIZING IN FIREWORKS

Frequently Web designers inherit pages for their sites developed by outside sources or departments. Often the graphics on the page are too large, not only in visual size but also in file size. Because of the seamless integration between Fireworks and Dreamweaver, you can quickly and easily optimize graphics from within Dreamweaver.

1) In Dreamweaver, use the Site window to open the Optimize.htm file in the Optimize folder within the Lesson11 folder. Select the Climber image.

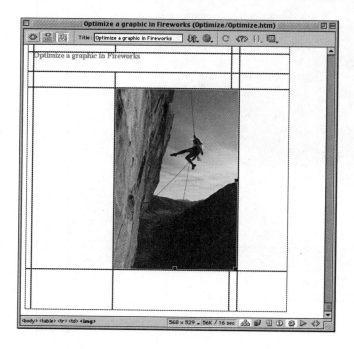

2) Choose Commands > Optimize Image in Fireworks. Click Yes in the Find Source dialog box and locate the climber.png file in the Optimize folder within the Lesson11 folder. Click Open.

If you did not have the original source file, you would click No, and you would then edit the GIF or JPEG file.

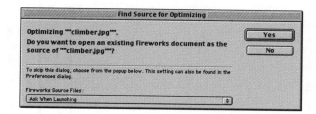

3) Make your optimization changes in the Fireworks Optimize window. For this exercise, select GIF file format and WebSnap Adaptive (Windows) or WebAdaptive (Macintosh).

The Optimize window can be divided into two or four panes, similar to the 2-Up or 4-Up Preview window in Fireworks. You can then select each pane and experiment with different export settings.

2 PANES 4 PANES

NOTE *If you re-optimize a JPEG image, you are essentially compressing a compressed image. On some images, you may see a severe degradation in quality. Make sure you preview your image before exporting.*

4) Click Update.

The image is exported again, and your Dreamweaver page is updated with the new file.

5) Save and close the Optimize.htm file.

USING SELECTIVE JPEG OPTIMIZATION

Selective JPEG compression allows the compression of different areas of an image at different levels. For example, at a commercial site, you want the photo of your product displayed at the highest level, but areas around the product may not be as important, so they can be compressed at a lower level. The end result is reduction in the overall size of the image, but the quality of the product image is retained.

To identify the areas you want to compress differently, use any of the Fireworks bitmap selection tools to create a marquee selection around the area of interest. You can then set that selection to a higher or lower compression level. The next exercise steps through this process.

1) Open the Rafting.htm file in the Optimize folder within the Lesson11 folder.

This page contains a large JPEG image.

2) Select the image and look at the Property inspector.

You'll see the file size, 176K , listed at the top left of the inspector. If you do not see the file size in the inspector, look in the Size column in the Site window. The file size needs to be reduced—it is too large for this Web page.

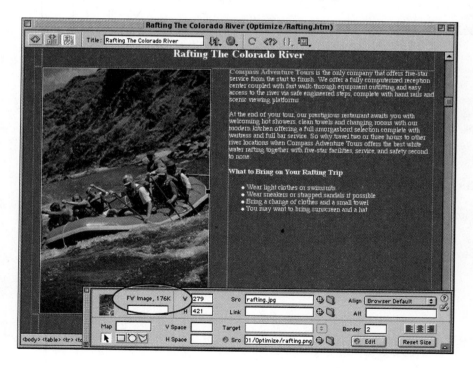

3) With the image selected, click Edit in the Property inspector. In the Find Source dialog box, click Yes and locate rafting.png in the Optimize folder—the original file.

Fireworks opens in bitmap mode, where you can edit the image.

4) Using the Lasso tool, draw a selection around the people and the raft.

You do not have to be precise in drawing the selection. The selection is the area you want to compress with the best quality. The other parts of the image are not as important and can be compressed at a lower quality.

SELECTION AROUND RAFT

5) Choose Modify > Selective JPEG > Save Selection as JPEG Mask.

A magenta overlay appears within the selection to indicate the area you want with
the best quality.

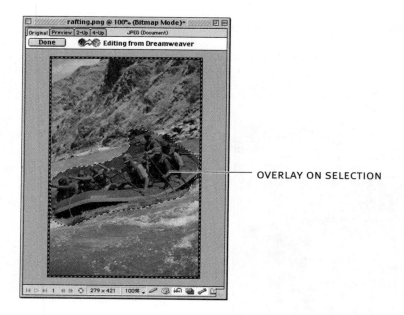

OVERLAY ON SELECTION

6) Click Edit Selective Quality Options on the Optimize panel.

The Selective JPEG Settings dialog box opens.

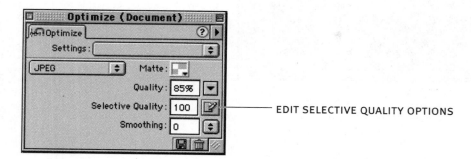

EDIT SELECTIVE QUALITY OPTIONS

7) In the Selective JPEG Settings dialog box, select Enable Selective Quality and type _100_ as the compression value in the text box.

Use a low value to compress the selection area more than the unselected part of the image. Use a high value to compress the selection area less than the unselected part of the image.

8) Choose an overlay color to highlight the selection. This color does not affect the image; it is for your visual reference. Click OK.

The other options are not needed for this image. Preserve Text Quality and Preserve Button Quality export text or buttons at a higher level regardless of the Selective Quality setting.

9) On the Optimize panel, change the Quality setting for the overall image. For this exercise, change the setting to _85_.

The Quality setting you choose changes the areas of the image that are not covered by the overlay.

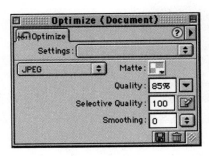

10) Click the Preview tab in the document window to see the results of the settings. Change the Quality setting to a lower number—65, for example—and look at the results of this setting.

Look carefully at the water below the raft. As the setting gets lower, you'll start seeing pixels forming. Also look at the file size as you change the settings. The original file size was 176K. You want to adjust the settings to decrease the file size but still leave an acceptable image.

11) When you are satisfied with the results, click Done.

The image is optimized and saved, and you are returned to Dreamweaver.

12) Save and close the file.

ON YOUR OWN

You can practice what you just learned with the following project.

• Open the Survivor.png file in Fireworks from the Graphics folder in Lesson11.

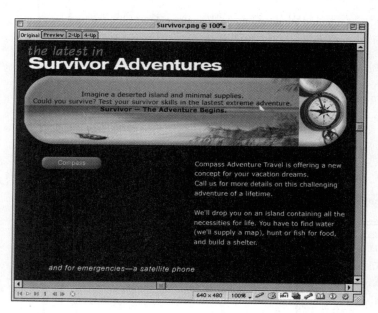

• Change the Compass button to a button symbol and add a rollover graphic. Make some change to the button—change the button color or the text color.

• Make four more buttons based on the Compass button, changing the text in each to Fishing Line, Map, Knife, and Tarp. Place these buttons below the current button.

• Create slices for the other images on the page. Remember that when you draw the slices, you are creating cells for the HTML table you will export.

- Export the page and save it in the Project folder within the Lesson11 folder. Create a new folder inside this folder for the images.

- Open the HTML page in Dreamweaver.

- Delete the white text description image and replace it with the text from the survivor.txt file in the Text folder within the Lesson11 folder.

- Select each of the buttons and edit them in Fireworks, changing the color of the buttons. Make sure you use the Dreamweaver Edit button to access Fireworks to edit the buttons.

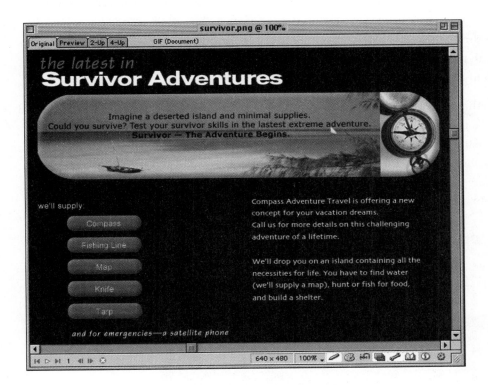

CREATING DREAMWEAVER LIBRARY ITEMS

One difficult task in maintaining a Web site is ensuring that buttons, copyright notices, and other cross-site elements remain consistent. Dreamweaver has a useful feature called Library Items that helps you maintain repeating elements in one location. When the element changes, you need to modify only the library item and then update the entire site.

If you create images in Fireworks that you want to include on several pages at your site, you can create the Dreamweaver Library item right in Fireworks as you export the image. The images can include image maps, rollovers, slices, and behaviors. All of the additional HTML is exported to the library file. If you know the name of the path to the files, you can also create the links in Fireworks, but adding the links from Dreamweaver might be easier.

In the next exercise, you will export some graphics to be used as a navigation bar and save them as a Dreamweaver library item. You will then edit the library item in Dreamweaver to add the links. When you create a library item, Dreamweaver creates a Library folder at the top level of your local root folder and stores each library item there. Because you are initially working in Fireworks, you will need to create the Library folder and save the library item in this folder.

1) Open the buttons.png file you created earlier. Choose File > Export.

If you no longer have the file, you can use the buttons.png file in the Completed folder within the Lesson11 folder.

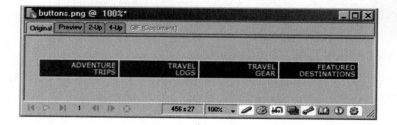

2) In the Export dialog box, create a new folder in the Lessons folder and name it *Library*.

If you don't have a folder named Library, Fireworks prompts you to create one after the next step.

3) Set the following options in the Export dialog box and then click Save.

- Choose Dreamweaver Library (.lbi) from the Save as Type pop-up menu.

- Change the file name to navigation.lbi.

- Choose Export Slices from the Slices pop-up menu.

- Choose Put Images in Subfolder. Fireworks will create an Images folder for you within the Library folder for the button images.

- Click Options if you want to change the HTML settings.

- Deselect Include Areas without Slices.

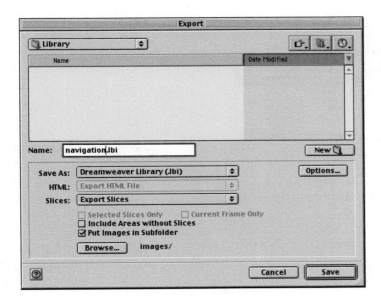

The files are exported, and the Dreamweaver library item is saved.

The next step is to return to Dreamweaver and insert the library item in a page. But before you do, you need to update the links in the library. The links you added in Fireworks link to pages within the same folder. Since the library file is in another folder, the links need to be updated with the new location.

4) Return to Dreamweaver and check the Site window.

The Library folder should be at the root level of the site. Inside the Library folder you should see the navigation.lbi file you just created.

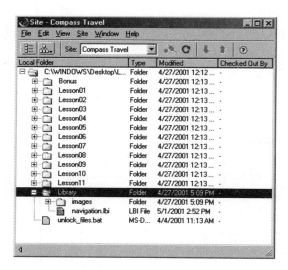

5) Choose Window > Assets to open the Assets panel.

The Assets panel is a convenient place where all of the elements used in your site, such as images, Macromedia Flash or Shockwave movies, templates, and libraries, are stored. When you create a site, Dreamweaver looks at all of the files within the site and builds the Assets panel. As you create more pages and add more images or movies, the Assets panel is updated.

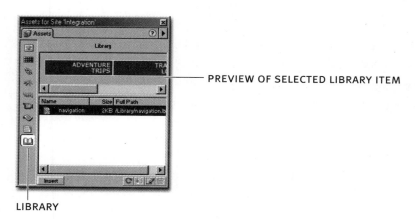

PREVIEW OF SELECTED LIBRARY ITEM

LIBRARY

In the left column of the Assets panel are category items you select to view the different areas of the panel.

6) Click Library on the Assets panel to access library items.

The name of your library item (navigation in this exercise) is listed, and a preview of the items in the library is displayed in the top portion of the panel. If you had multiple library items in your site, you would see all of them in the list.

7) Double-click the navigation library item to open it.

You can double-click the name of your library in the list, or you can double-click the preview of the library in the panel. A page opens displaying your buttons. Notice that the background color of the page is gray. The page color of the library item will not be used when you insert the item into your pages.

8) Select the first button: Adventure Trips. To change the link for this button, drag the point-to-file icon in the Property inspector to trips.htm in the Lesson11 folder in the Site window.

The point-to-file icon provides the quickest way to add or change links in your site. The icon, located to the right of the Link text box, looks like the drag-and-drop behavior handle you used in Fireworks when you created the disjointed rollovers in Lesson 10. Make sure to position your windows where you can see both the document window and the Site window. Open the Lesson11 folder in the Site window so you can see the HTML files. Drag the point-to-file icon from the Property inspector and drop it on the file to link to in the Site window. When you release the mouse button, the new link is updated in the Link text box.

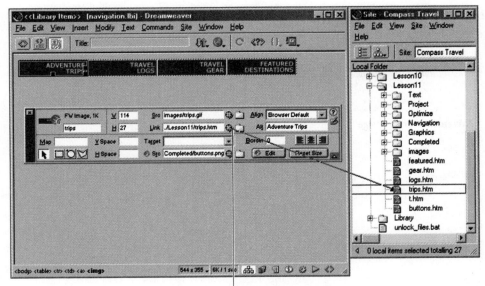

POINT-TO-FILE ICON

9) Repeat step 8 for the other buttons, linking to logs.htm, gear.htm, and featured.htm. Save the file.

When you save the library file, Dreamweaver may ask you if you want to update all documents that use the library. At this point, you have not created any pages that use the library, so you can click No. Once you insert the library items in your pages, you will want to click Yes so Dreamweaver can automatically update your files.

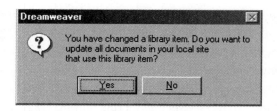

NOTE *If you have a large number of pages containing library items, you might want to wait for a more convenient time to update all of the pages with the changes. (Large sites could take some time to update.) You can update your pages later by choosing Modify > Library > Update Pages.*

After you update the links, you can insert the navigation bar on pages in your site. The links will work on all pages throughout your site. In the next steps, you will create several pages and insert the navigation bar from the library.

10) Open the trips.htm file in the Lesson11 folder.

In the Site window, double-click the file's icon to quickly open the file. The file is a generic page that you can use for testing your library and links.

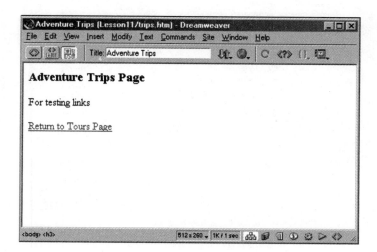

11) Place the insertion point before the Adventure Trips title and press Enter (Windows) or Return (Macintosh) to insert a new line. Move the insertion point to the new blank line at the top of the page.

You want to place the buttons from the library on this top line.

12) From the Assets panel, drag the navigation library item to the top line on the page.

You can drag the library item either from the list or from the preview pane of the Assets panel.

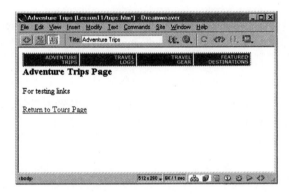

13) Save the page and test it in the browser.

The links should take you to the appropriate page. The Return To link on the page takes you to the Tours page you created earlier.

ON YOUR OWN

Add the navigation bar to each of the pages in the Lesson11 folder: featured.htm, gear.htm, and logs.htm. Save the files and test the links in the browser.

Libraries make it easy to add consistent content to your pages, but they display their real power when you need to make a change to one of the library items. Open the navigation library entry again and delete one of the images on the page. Save the library file. Dreamweaver asks you whether or not you want to update all of the pages that include the library. Click Update. A dialog box opens reporting all of the pages that were updated for you. Close the dialog box. Dreamweaver opened each file, made the change, saved the file, and then closed the file. If a file is open, Dreamweaver makes the change but does not save or close the file. You will need to do that. Now open one of the HTML pages. The page should reflect the change you made to the library item.

ADDING SITE NAVIGATION

You might have the most interesting content or the most appealing design for your site, but if your users can't find the information they need, your Web site has failed. Navigation is the science (or art) of getting people from one location to another. Web navigation should help users understand where they are and where they can go. Logical, easy-to-read buttons help, but when users click the buttons, they need verification that they went to the page they were seeking. For example, if a user clicks a button labeled "Updates," the resulting page should be labeled "Updates"—in the page title, as a heading, or as a graphic on the page.

If you have explored the Web, you might be familiar with navigation buttons that lead users to different areas of a site. These are popular means of adding graphical elements to the page that also serve a useful purpose. In their basic form, the graphics are one-state buttons that link to a page when the user clicks them. Rollovers are also very popular, especially because the Button Editor in Fireworks makes them so easy to create. Rollovers provide feedback to the user, changing when the user's pointer rolls over a button.

UNDERSTANDING NAVIGATION BARS

Although rollovers are graphically pleasing and surely provide a way for users to move from page to page, they don't provide a cohesive navigation system for your site. Navigation bars are a series of navigation buttons that work together to make navigating your site more intuitive. Navigation bars consist of related images that change based on the action of the user, providing feedback related to the action the user has taken. The first state of the button (Up) is the normal state—this is, the state of the button when the page first loads. The second state of the button (Over) appears when the user rolls over the button. The third state of the button (Down) appears when the user clicks the button. The fourth state of the button (Over While Down) appears when the user rolls over a button that has been clicked.

What distinguishes a navigation bar from a group of navigation buttons is the way they work together. If one of the buttons on the bar is in the down state and the user clicks another button, the clicked button changes to the down state and the other button returns to the up state. Much like the push buttons on an old-fashioned car radio, only one button on a bar can be depressed at a time. The inset button determines the selected radio station. Similarly, navigation bars provide feedback to the user—the current page is easily verified by the visual state of the button.

Dreamweaver includes an Insert Navigation Bar command that adds the JavaScript needed to display three- or four-state navigation buttons, but the buttons work only if you are building your pages by using frames. If you want to use the navigation buttons without frames, you have to change each button on each page. Fireworks guides you through the process of creating navigation bars and makes it easy to add the JavaScript needed to display the buttons without frames.

In the next exercise, you will add several three-state buttons to a page in Fireworks. Although you could add a fourth button state, it is not always necessary and doesn't always justify the extra download time. When you export the page, you will set an option to export not only the existing page but all of the pages using the navigation bar. Then you will open the HTML pages in Dreamweaver and make modifications. The hard work is done for you in the exported HTML.

1) In Fireworks, open the nav_bar.png file in the Navigation folder within the Lesson11 folder.

This file contains the first button (Featured Trips) for the navigation bar.

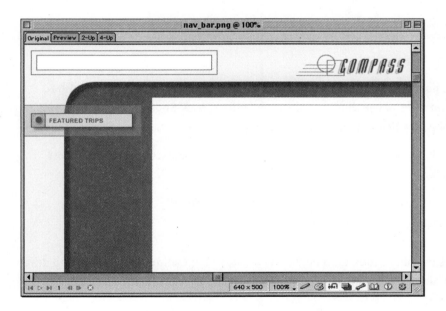

2) Double-click the button with the Pointer tool to open the Button Editor. Click the Over and Down tabs to see the design of each state of the button.

3) On the Down tab, choose Show Down State Upon Load. Click the Close box to exit the Button Editor.

This option displays the down state of the button when the page loads. Displaying the down state of the button when the page loads gives users a visual clue as to what page they are accessing.

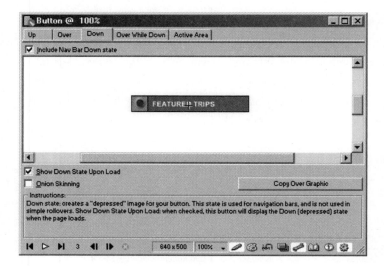

4) Drag a horizontal guide down and place it at the bottom edge of the Featured Trips button slice. If you don't see the green slices, click Show Slices on the Tools panel. Make sure Snap to Guides is selected (choose View > Guides > Snap to Guides).

The guide helps you place the second button. If you don't see the rulers, choose View > Rulers.

Now make a copy of the Featured Trips button by using the Alt (Windows) or Option (Macintosh) drag method.

5) Using the Pointer tool, hold down Alt (Windows) or Option (Macintosh) and drag the button down. Add Shift as you drag to constrain the movement vertically.

Because Snap to Guides is turned on, you'll feel the button "pop" as it reaches the guide. Stop dragging when you feel the pop.

6) Choose Edit > Repeat Duplicate to make another copy of the button. Repeat this command until you have a total of five buttons.

The Repeat Duplicate command repeats your most recent action. Because you used the Alt or Option drag method to make the first copy, both the copy and the move are considered one action.

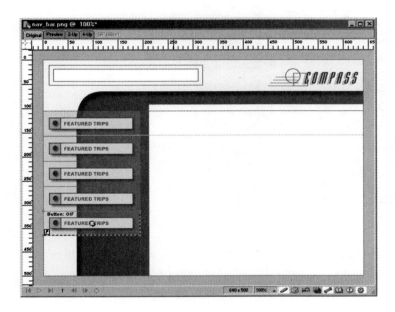

7) Select the first button. Choose Window > Object to open the Object panel. Click Link Wizard on the Object panel to open the Link wizard.

A message box opens, asking if you want to edit all instances of the button or just the current one.

8) In the message box, click Current.

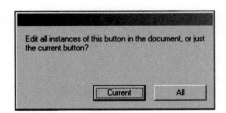

9) On the Link tab of the Link wizard, type *trips.htm* as the link and *Featured Trips* as the Alt text. On the Filename tab, deselect Auto-Name and type *trips* as the file name. Click OK.

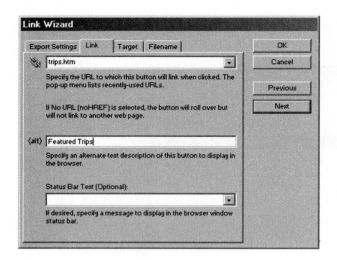

NOTE *The file name must exactly match the link name less the extension. For example, if the file name is trips, the link must be trips.htm. The extension must be .htm. Any other extension will not work, even if you set the HTML options to use another extension.*

10) Select the second button.

This button needs a different title, plus a file name, link, and Alt text.

11) Type *TRAVEL GEAR* in the Button text box on the Object panel to change the name on the button. Press Enter (Windows) or Return (Macintosh) to set the new name. When a message box opens asking if you want to edit all of buttons or the current button, click Current.

Changing the name of the button is much faster using the Object panel than editing the text in the Button Editor. All states of the button are changed.

12) Repeat step 9, entering *Travel Gear* as the Alt text, *gear* as the file name, and *gear.htm* as the link in the Link wizard. Change the remaining buttons to *TRAVEL LOGS*, *DESTINATIONS*, and *ABOUT US*. Use the button names as the Alt text, and use *logs*, *destinations*, and *about* as the file names, and *logs.htm*, *destinations.htm*, and *about.htm* as the links.

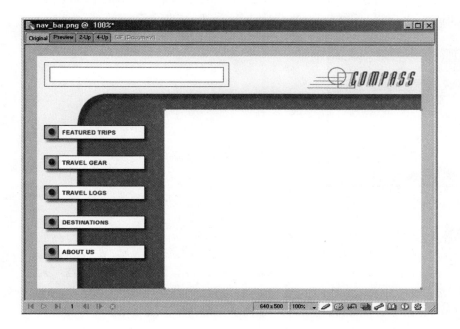

13) Select the compass logo and the white rectangles with the Pointer tool. Choose Insert > Slice. Click Multiple to create separate slices on each item. Select the logo slice, type *home.htm* in the Link text box of the Object panel, type *Compass Home* in the Alt text box of the Object panel, deselect Auto-Name Slices, and type *compass_logo* in the Name text box.

The slice on the white rectangle at the top is a placeholder for an image you will insert later. You do not need to name the slice.

14) Select the slice on the large white rectangle. On the Object panel, select Text in the Type pop-up menu for the last slice. In the blank area on the Options panel, type the following: (be sure to include the semicolon at the end). Click Hide Slices on the Tools panel to hide the slices. Then delete the large white box.

The characters ( ) are the ASCII code for a space character. When you export the file, Fireworks will insert the space character in the table cell.

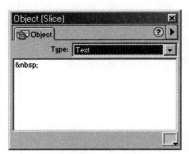

NOTE *Instead of deleting the white rectangle, you could also hide it in the Layers panel. Select the rectangle, and then open the background layer in the Layers panel. Click the eye icon to hide the object stack of the rectangle. Hidden objects in the layer are not exported. The white rectangle was drawn for you to show the placement for the text. When you design your own pages, you can just draw a slice (and change it to a text slice) where you want the text to be placed.*

15) Save your file and then click the Preview tab to view your page. Click each button to see the effect of the three-state buttons. Click the Original tab to return to editing the document.

As you click each button, that button changes to the down state, and the other buttons return to the up state.

NOTE *Part of the canvas may appear to be missing when you preview the buttons. After step 19, you should see the entire canvas when you preview the page.*

At this point, you have all the buttons you need for this exercise. But before you export, you need to change one setting to make Fireworks export not only the buttons but also the HTML for each of the buttons. Normally when you export, you get just one HTML page.

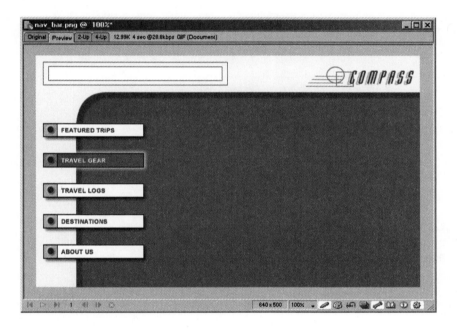

16) Choose File > HTML Setup.

The HTML Setup dialog box opens. This dialog box is the same as the one displayed when you click Options in the Export dialog box.

17) On the General tab, make sure the following options are set (these are the default settings, so you may not need to make any changes):

- HTML Style: Dreamweaver

- Extension: .htm

- File Creator: Dreamweaver (Macintosh only)

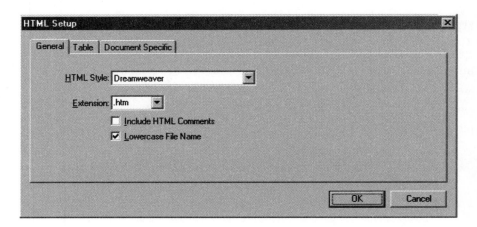

18) On the Table tab, set the following options:

- Space With: 1-Pixel Transparent Spacer

- Empty Cells: Use Canvas Color

- Contents: Spacer Image

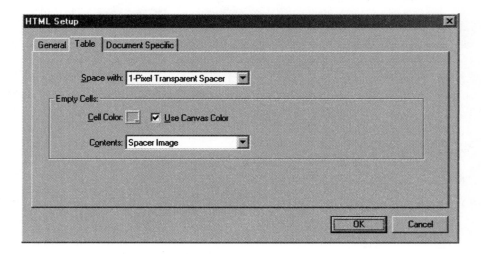

338

19) On the Document Specific tab, set the following options:

- Slices: doc.name + Underscore + Row/Column

- Frames: Underscore + Frame #(2,3,4)

- Multiple Nav Bar HTML pages: Selected

- Include Area without Slices: Selected

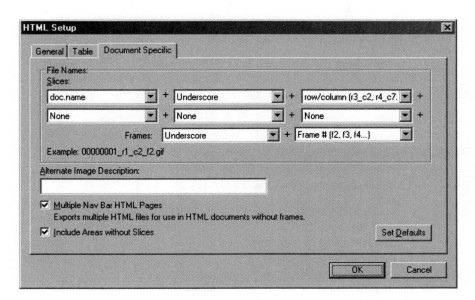

20) Click OK to close the HTML Setup dialog box.

NOTE *The naming scheme in the HTML Setup dialog box creates file names for the buttons such as trips.gif, trips_f2.gif, and trips_f3.gif. The _f2 and _f3 are the second and third states of the buttons. In this example, you need the entire canvas exported, not just the areas with slices. The naming scheme of doc.name + Underscore + Row Column defines the file name for graphical areas without a predetermined slice. For example, you might see a graphic named home_r3_c2.gif as one of the exported images.*

21) Choose File › Export and navigate to the Navigation folder within the Lesson11 folder. In the Export dialog box, set the following options:

- Name: home.htm

- Save as Type (Windows): HTML and Images
  or
  Save As (Macintosh): HTML and Images

- HTML: Export HTML file

- Slices: Export Slices

- Selected Slices Only: Not selected

- Include Areas without Slices: Selected

- Put Images in Subfolder: Selected

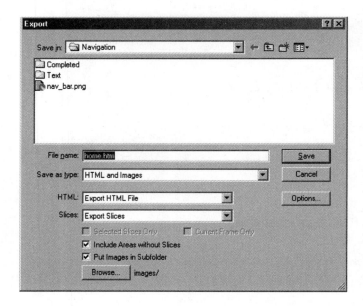

22) Click Save to export and save your files.

Fireworks creates the six HTML files needed for the navigation bar. The file names are the same as the ones you defined using the Link wizard. The images for the rollovers and the nonsliced areas are placed in the Images folder.

EXPORTING FRAMES FROM FIREWORKS

In the next exercise, you will create six titles for the HTML pages and insert them into the pages. Each title will be created in a separate frame in the document. Because the titles are all the same size, using frames to create the titles is faster, and you have only one file to edit if you want to make changes.

1) Switch back to Dreamweaver and open the home.htm file Fireworks just created. Select the top white rectangle and look at the Property inspector.

The white rectangle is a placeholder for another image with a width of 290 and height of 26 pixels. This new image will be a title for the page. All of the other HTML pages also need a title graphic that will fit in this same area.

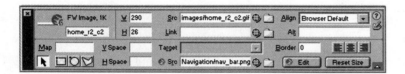

2) In Fireworks, create a new document 290 x 26 — the exact size that will fit in the rectangular area. Make the canvas color the same yellow color you used in the nav_bar.png file. Save the file as *titles.png* in the Navigation folder within the Lesson11 folder.

Make sure the nav_bar.png file is open before you create the new document. In the Canvas Color area of the New Document dialog box, click the Custom color box. Drag the eyedropper cursor over the yellow in the nav_bar.png file and click. The eyedropper picks up the yellow color for the canvas.

> **NOTE** *On Windows, you need to hold the mouse button down when you see the eyedropper cursor and drag to the other document to pick the color. On the Macintosh, you can move the eyedropper cursor to the other document and click the color you want to use. For this exercise, you can also pick the yellow color from the Dreamweaver document.*

3) Choose Window > Frames to open the Frames panel. On the Frames Option menu, select Add Frames and type *5* as the number of frames to add.

You now have six frames in the document: one frame for each of the HTML pages.

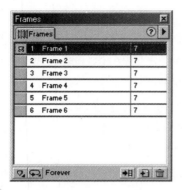

4) Select Frame 1 on the Frames panel, select the Text tool, and then click the canvas to open the Text Editor. Type *Compass Adventure Tours* as the title. Change the font and size to fit within the canvas size. For example, use Arial Black for the font and 20 for the point size. Use a dark gray for the color of the text. Click OK to close the Text Editor.

NOTE *In this exercise, this title contains the most characters. Formatting the longest title first ensures all of the text in the other titles will fit within the width of the canvas.*

5) Select the text with the Pointer tool and then choose Copy to Frames from the Frames Options pop-up menu. Select All Frames in the Copy to Frames dialog box.

The Copy to Frames option performs a copy-and-paste action for you in either all of the frames or selected frames. This ensures that the placement of the text is the same for all frames and is faster than manually pasting the text in each frame.

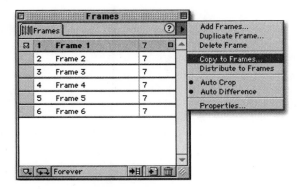

6) In Frame 2, double-click the text box and change the text to *Featured Trips*. Repeat this process for each frame, changing the text to *Travel Gear*, *Travel Logs*, *Travel Destinations*, and *About Us*. Choose Window > Optimize and check the optimization settings. For example, choose GIF and WebSnap Adaptive.

Each frame contains a different title, but when you export, the files will have names such as titles_f01.gif, titles_f02.gif, and so on. To distinguish each file, you can name the frames. The exported files use the frame names instead of the generic title names.

7) Double-click the frame names in the Frames panel one at a time to edit them. Type a name that identifies the title contained in that frame. For example, Frame 1 contains Compass Adventure Tours. You could type *compass_title* as the frame name.

> **N O T E** *Don't use the same names as you did for the buttons on the page. For example, the Travel Gear button is named gear. You don't want the same name for the title graphic. Use lower case for the frame names and no spaces. The frame names are used for the exported image file names.*

8) Save the file. Choose File > Export. Create a new folder within the Lesson11 folder and name it *title_images*; then open that folder. Change Save as Type (Windows) or Save As (Macintosh) to Frames to Files. Deselect Trim Images. Click Save.

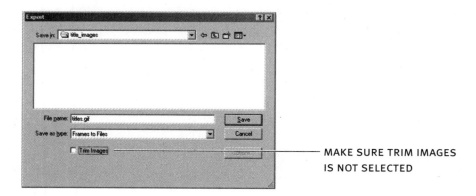

MAKE SURE TRIM IMAGES
IS NOT SELECTED

If the Trim Images option is set, your images will will not be exported at the proper size. You want all the images to be the exact size you specified as the canvas size.

> **N O T E** *Creating a separate folder for the title images makes it easier to find the images when you edit your HTML files in Dreamweaver.*

The final steps are inserting the title images and adding some text to the pages in Dreamweaver.

9) Open the home.htm file in Dreamweaver. Select the top white rectangle and delete it. Open the title_images folder in the Site window. Drag the compass_title.gif image to the empty cell.

The image is placed in the cell. Because you created the image the exact size of the cell, it should fit perfectly. The background color (yellow) of the title should match the yellow color in the frame.

N O T E *There are several ways you can insert images into your page in Dreamweaver. In this exercise, instead of deleting the top white rectangle, you could double-click it, and then select the title image from the Select Image Source dialog box that opens.*

10) Open welcome.txt in the Text folder in the Navigation folder within the Lesson11 folder. Select all the text and copy and paste it into the text area.

The text area is where the large white rectangle was on the page.

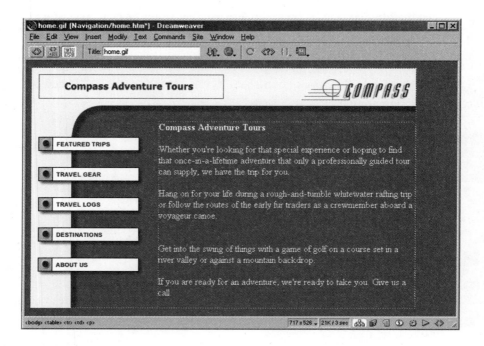

11) Save the file.

ON YOUR OWN

Add the other title graphics to the remaining pages. Make sure to change the HTML title for each page to the name you used in the title graphic. Save your pages and test the links in the browser. There are text files (in the Text folder) you can use for adding text to each of the pages.

EXTRA PROJECTS

To practice what you have learned in this book, there are two optional projects for you to do. The project files are located on the CD within the Xtras folder. In the first project, you will create a Web page with rollovers and disjointed rollovers on the pictures. The buttons at the top of the page are rollovers, and the first two buttons have pop-up menus attached. The second project covers navigation bars and editing your Fireworks files in Dreamweaver.

Project 1 (Using Fireworks)

All the files you need are located in the Project1 folder within the Xtras folder. Within that folder is a folder named Text, where you will find the text you need for the welcome message and the text for the area under the pictures, a Media folder containing the files you need to complete the project, and a Completed folder containing the completed files.

You can open the Final.gif file in the Media folder to see the colors of the buttons and background.

- Create a new document 640 x 480 pixels with a black canvas. Save your file as *Compass_home.png* in the Project1 folder. Your final document should look like the example shown here.

- Draw overlapping rectangles to create the brown background areas. Use the methods you've learned to create the cutout areas in the rectangles and the moon-shaped object. Be sure to use layers as you create your objects.

- Import the Compass_logo.png file you created in Lesson 3 and place it at the top left of the canvas. If you no longer have that file, you can use the file within the Media folder.

- Open the AdventureMap.png file in the Media folder and delete the white background using the bitmap editing tools. Place the edited image in your new file.

- Import the files biker.png, climber.png, fishing.png, kayak.png, rafting.png, and surfer.png in the Media folder for the photos.

- Make the top buttons—Adventure Trips, Travel Logs, About Us, Gear, and Featured Destinations—all rollovers, changing the color of the text on each rollover button.

- Add pop-up menus for the first two buttons. For Adventure Trips, use Australian Surfing, White Water Rafting, and Mountain Biking. Have the links for these pop-up menus go to surfing.htm, rafting.htm, and biking.htm. The Project1 folder contains some test HTML files with those names. For Travel Logs, use Scuba Adventures and Go Fast, Go Hard, and link those to diving.htm and biking.htm.

- Add a disjointed rollover for each of the pictures, making the text under the pictures change to new text as you roll over each picture.

- When you complete the page, export and save it as HTML. Check the HTML page in your browser.

Project 2 (Using Fireworks and Dreamweaver)

For this project, you will create a page in Fireworks with a tabbed navigation bar. Open home.htm in the Completed folder within the Project2 folder if you want to see an example of the page. Create the links and file names by using the Link wizard and set the option to export multiple pages. Export the pages, open them in Dreamweaver, and add the descriptive text and the side graphic. Each Web page has a different side graphic. The first page contains the image with Adventure Trips. The text on the other images changes, based on the page. For example, on the cycling page, the text on the image changes to Cycling Trips.

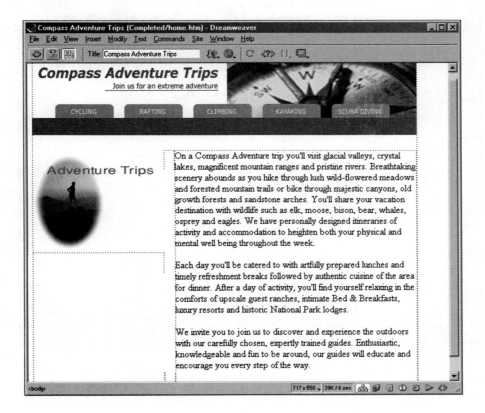

In Fireworks, create the Web page as shown here. Create the graphics in Fireworks, export them, and insert the text in Dreamweaver. The compass image is in the Media folder within the Project2 folder, and the text is in the Text folder. In Fireworks, create the Web page as shown here.

- Start by creating a new document in Fireworks, 640 x 500 pixels with a white canvas. Save the file as *home.png*.
- Create the tab buttons and insert the compass graphic and the title text. Draw slices for the descriptive text and the side graphic. Make the slice for the picture titles 219 x 17 pixels.

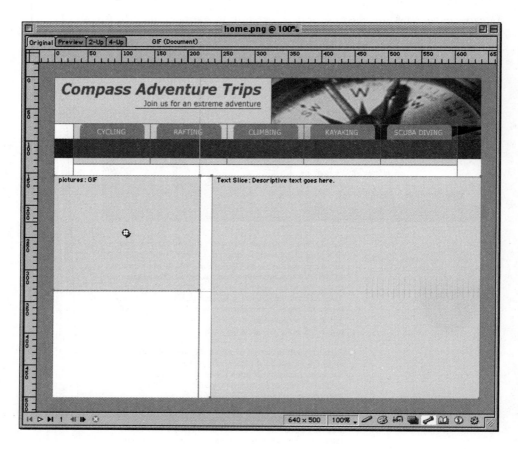

- To create the navigation tabs, use the Button Editor to create a three-state button. Draw a rectangle on top of a rounded-corner rectangle and make the two rectangles different colors. For the over state, make the tab a darker color. For the down state, make both rectangles the same color. This will make the tab button appear to move forward when it is clicked.

- The side graphic with text (Adventure Trips) is in the picture_title.png file in the Media folder. There are several frames, each with a different image. Export these frames to files. You'll insert these in Dreamweaver.
- After you export the pages, insert the text and the side images in Dreamweaver.

WHAT YOU HAVE LEARNED

In this lesson, you have:

- Created a site in Dreamweaver [pages 287–291]
- Exported files from Fireworks and edited them in Dreamweaver [pages 295–304]
- Edited a Fireworks image from Dreamweaver [pages 305–308]
- Created buttons in Fireworks, and then inserted the Fireworks HTML file in a Dreamweaver page [pages 309–315]
- Optimized a Dreamweaver image in Fireworks [pages 316–317]
- Used Selective JPEG compression on an image [pages 318–322]
- Exported Fireworks images as a Dreamweaver library item [pages 324–329]
- Created pages with a three-state navigation bar [pages 330–340]
- Used frames in Fireworks to create multiple title graphics [pages 341–346]

index

F

fading in objects, 204–205
Feather command, 30
Feather Selection dialog box, 29
feathering edges, 13
    of bitmap graphics, 29–30
    of vector masks, 151
file conversion options, 81
file formats
    bitmap graphics, 9
    exporting files, 152, 158
    vector graphics, 79
file size
    image export process and, 154–155, 157
    interlacing process and, 169
    loss compression and, 169–170
    optimization process and, 162
    smoothing and, 172
filename extensions
    adding to documents, 55
    for animated GIF files, 191
    for Dreamweaver Library items, 325
    for Fireworks file, 55, 153, 292
Files to Process window, 282
Fill Category pop-up list, 126
Fill color box, 72, 73, 104
    Options pop-up menu, 95, 105
Fill panel, 72
    Edge setting, 167–168
    Feather slider, 151
    Gradient Color controls, 127–128
    Texture pop-up list, 116
    fills
    colors applied to, 72–73, 95
    gradient, 127–128
    mask, 146, 151
    patterns applied to, 116–117
    setting before drawing, 62–63
    textures applied to, 116
    See also strokes

Find and Replace feature, 270–274
    changing multiple files with, 273–274
    initiating searches with, 272
    limiting searches in, 271
    Replace All option, 272–273, 274
    setting Replace options for, 272–273
Find and Replace panel, 271
Find Source for Optimizing dialog box, 316
Fireworks
    curriculum overview, 1–4
    Dreamweaver integrated with, 284–346
    extra projects using, 347–351
    filename extension for, 55, 153, 292
    system requirements for, 5
floating panels, 9
Font pop-up list, 88
formatting text, 88, 89, 90–92, 99
4-Up tab, 160–161, 169
frame delay, 184–185
Frame_animation.png file, 178, 204
frame-by-frame animations
    creating, 178–181
    exporting, 187–191
    previewing, 188–193
    See also animated GIF images
frames
    adding, 180, 342
    animation, 180, 182–183, 191
    exporting, 344–345
    naming, 343–344
    onion skinning, 182–183
    opening pages as, 81
    storing rollover images in, 252, 253, 256
    text, 342
    turning on and off, 191

357

INDEX

Rounded Rectangle tool, 215
Roundness slider, 215
Rubber Stamp tool, 22–24
   set point designation, 23
   Tool Options panel, 22, 24
   rulers, 58–60

S

saturation, 15, 16
Saturation slider, 16
Save As Type pop-up list, 170
Save Command dialog box, 67
Save dialog box, 55
Save Effect As dialog box, 110
Save Selection command, 31
saving
   actions as commands, 67–68
   animated GIF images, 181, 187, 191, 199
   effects, 110
   exported files, 157, 170
   library files, 328
   optimized files, 170, 173–174
   scripts, 280–282
   selections, 31, 320
   symbols, 209
Scale to Size option, 278
Scale tool, 97–98, 112
scaling
   images, 278
   imported files, 81
   objects, 79, 98
   setting options for, 278
   text, 90
Scaling options pop-up menu, 278
Scissors cursor, 104
scripts
   running, 282
   saving, 280–281

Scripts folder, 281
Search pop-up menu, 273
Search Selection pop-up menu, 271
searches. *See* Find and Replace
   feature
Select All command, 31
Select Behind tool, 48–50, 198
Select Image Source dialog box, 345
Select Inverse command, 30
Select Similar command, 30
selections
   adding, 19–20
   commands for modifying, 30–31
   constraining, 27
   copying, 21–22
   feathering the edges of, 29–30
   moving, 28
   optimizing images using, 319–320
   subtracting, 19–20
   text, 92
Selective JPEG Settings dialog box, 321
Selective Quality options, 320
Set Pop-Up Menu dialog box, 263–264,
   265
Shape pop-up menu, 75
shapes
   combining, 122–126
   cropping, 125
   filling, 124
   hotspot, 234, 237
   intersecting, 125
Share Across Frames option, 196
Show Grid option, 57
showing. See displaying
Simple Rollover behavior, 260